Women, Households, and the Economy

*The Douglass Series on Women's Lives
and the Meaning of Gender*

Women, Households, and the Economy

Edited by LOURDES BENERÍA and
CATHARINE R. STIMPSON

Rutgers University Press
New Brunswick and London

Library of Congress Cataloging-in-Publication Data

Women, households, and the economy.

(The Douglass series on women's lives and the meaning of gender)
Includes bibliographical references and index.
1. Sexual division of labor—United States—
Congresses. 2. Women—Employment—United States—
Congresses. 3. Women—United States—Economic
conditions—Congresses. I. Benería, Lourdes.
II. Stimpson, Catharine R., 1936– . III. Series.

HD6060.65.U5W65 1987   331.4'0973   87-4840
ISBN 0–8135–1263–8   ISBN 0–8135–1264–6 (pbk.)

British Cataloging-in-Publication information available

Contents

Acknowledgments

The editors wish to thank Marlie Wasserman for her editorial strength and counsel, and the scholars who commented on individual papers at the conference that gave rise to this volume. Their responses were shrewd and helpful, and we regret that we were finally unable to publish these remarks. Among the scholars whose written comments could not be included in this volume were Martha Ackelsberg, Eileen Applebaum, Joyce Beckett, Myrna Breitbart, Mariarosa Dalla Costa, Jane Humphries, and Laurie Nisonoff.

Preface

Catharine R. Stimpson

Since the 1960s, the United States has undergone at least two transformations: one in its economy, the other in gender roles. A series of deep, irrevocable changes have shaken men and women, the workforce and families, the job site and the home. Employed and unemployed, members of the public workforce and of the domestic workforce all sense that these transformations are going on. Yet, despite the study of work, and of women and work, the magnitude of these changes is still greater than our knowledge of them.

This volume adds to that knowledge, especially to our grasp of the connections among structural transformation, women, and family life; the relationships between contemporary capitalism and patriarchy; and the relationship between political economy and gender. For shifts in the economy and in gender roles necessarily influence each other in the public world, in the smaller world of the family, and in the self.

Women, Households, and the Economy began in the spring and summer of 1982. The Russell Sage Foundation awarded the Institute for Research on Women of Rutgers University an essential grant to bring together a group of scholars on a cutting edge of the thinking about women and the economy.[1] The group asked itself two questions: What do we really know about women and structural transformation? What should a major, original research conference to expand and enhance our understanding of this problem be like?

The group, fearful of confining itself to schematic analyses that seemed indifferent to people, did not want to print out bloodless representations of *femina economica* to supplement *homo economicus*. As we worked, we kept in mind complex images. Some were of single parents, uncertain of employment or benefits. Others were of women, of diverse races, creeds, or temperaments, whose husbands had lost their jobs. They had become the family providers. Still other images were of those husbands. Perhaps they were searching for work in order to keep on being the family provider. Perhaps their frustrations were choking them, to be released in violence against wives or in child abuse.

On 18 and 19 November 1983 the conference that the group designed took place at Rutgers University.[2] Generously underwriting it were the Department of Higher Education of the State of New Jersey, Rutgers University, and Douglass College. The program consisted of plenary sessions; workshops; films; and exchanges among researchers and students, foundation and government officials, policy makers and activists.[3] Several strong scholars from outside of the United States helped to compare the United States to other industrial democracies in order to see what features might be unique to the United States, what common to the industrial democracies.

This book now consists of edited papers from the conference. The volume is meant to speak to, and to seek, a broad audience: scholars, policy makers, and citizens who care about mapping and responding to social and economic change.

The Introduction and first part of the book offer major overviews of the vast changes the United States is experiencing in work, life, and gender. The second part, placing the past against the present, shows how the anguish of unemployment of women in the 1930s differs from that of today and outlines patterns of change: in regional economies; in ethnic families; in farm families; and in the growth of service industries in which women are finding novel, but problematic, job opportunities. The third set of papers focuses on three settings: the electronics industry; health workers (particularly part-time); and clerical workers. They dramatically exemplify the broad patterns the other papers have discerned. The fourth and final cluster of papers discusses an immense variety of institutional responses to change—in benefits, in welfare, in the individual states, or in unions.

The Institute for Research on Women is enormously grateful to the people who planned, funded, supported, gave papers and comments, and attended the conference that generated this volume. For the book seeks to show human beings—people of feeling, need, and will—during a period in which some of the bones of history are cracking and reforming themselves. If the book realizes even a part of this ambition, if it offers only an incomplete X–ray of time, we will be pleased.

Notes

1. The scholars were: Professor Lourdes Benería, Professor Barry Bluestone, Dr. Mariam Chamberlain, Professor Elizabeth Douvan, Dr. Heidi Hartmann, Professor Martha Howell, Professor Alice Kessler-Harris, Professor Michele Naples, Professor June Nash, Professor Paula Rayman, Dr. Karen Sacks, Professor Chiara Saraceno, Professor Rosemary Sarri, Dr. Ralph Smith, Professor Catharine Stimpson, Professor Louise Tilly, Dr. Kate Young, Professor Maxine Baca Zinn.

2. Catharine R. Stimpson and Lourdes Benería were the project directors of the conference; Gloria Cohn, the administrator. A National Advisory Committee consisted of: Professor Barry Bluestone, Dr. Mariam Chamberlain, Professor Bonnie Thornton Dill, Professor Elizabeth Douvan, Dr. Heidi Hartmann, Professor Alice Kessler-Harris, Professor June Nash, Professor Paula Rayman, Dr. Karen Sacks, Professor Helen I. Safa, Professor Chiara Saraceno, Professor Rosemary Sarri, Dr. Ralph Smith, Professor Louise Tilly, Dr. Kate Young, Professor Maxine Baca Zinn; a Rutgers Advisory Committee of: Professor Steven Director, Professor Charley Flint, Professor Briavel Holcomb, Professor Michele Naples, Professor George Sternlieb.

3. For a list of participants, write the Institute for Research on Women, Douglass College, Rutgers University, New Brunswick, New Jersey 08903.

Introduction

Lourdes Benería

The American economy is undergoing some far-reaching changes. The manufacturing sector that played a fundamental role in the post–World War II growth has been undergoing a profound crisis and millions of jobs have been lost or have been relocated abroad. This trend—initiated in the 1960s and intensified during the 1970s—has lead people to talk about the "deindustrialization of America." At the same time, new jobs have been created in the new high-tech industries and particularly in the services industries, which have absorbed an unprecedented inflow of new participants in the labor force. Technological change and industrial restructuring have resulted not only in changing employment patterns, but in redistributions of income and in other factors such as school attendance and family living arrangements. As the evidence depicting these profound changes mounts, we must ask where we are going and how change affects different sectors of the population.

These are the questions to which the essays in this volume mean to provide some answers. More specifically, the essays address the question of how the restructuring of the economy matters to women, to American households, to women's roles within them. Among the objectives set for the conference in which the papers were initially presented, two were the most basic. One was to emphasize the central role played by women in the changing economy, while presenting a global picture of how female participation in work and in families is taking new forms. The other was to bring together the work of researchers from different disciplines so that this global picture could best be evaluated. We also located change within the context of the international economy, even though the emphasis of research focused on that of the United States.

The essays in Part I deal with global economic changes in the United States during the post–World War II period. In doing so, they introduce the context within which the more specific essays that follow in Parts II and III provide further detail. Kuhn and Bluestone raise the issue of deindustrialization and the consequences of economic restructuring, which are characterized by crisis and by loss of jobs in manufacturing and by an unprecedented growth of the service economy. Although recognizing the ability of the United States' economy to generate new employment—twenty-three million new jobs have been created since 1970—they emphasize the proposition that these newly created jobs are not good substitutes for the jobs that have been lost. Hence the problem of "skidding," faced by workers "when they are forced down the earnings ladder after job displacement." That problem is connected with the tendency toward a dualistic economy based on a bimodal distribution of jobs between low wage/low skill categories on the one hand and high wage/high skill categories on the other. Although statistical evidence for the corresponding "missing middle" is limited, the authors summarize the debate and illustrate this tendency with cases of the department store and semiconductors industries, with a study of thirteen New England industries, and with data showing a greater inequality in the distribution of earnings across the economy. Their study of the department store industry shows that women are vastly overrepresented at the low end of the wage scale. Similar trends are reported in other industries. Thus, the authors argue that, in the semiconductor industry, "The virtual absence of middle-income jobs and the strong evidence of occupational segregation by sex give cause for serious concern about the ability of the semiconductor industry to do anything to advance the economic position of women." While the number of these jobs has increased considerably during the past fifteen years, they offer little potential for upward mobility. At the same time, the erosion of middle-income jobs for men, according to Kuhn and Bluestone, is pointing toward the disappearance of the "family wage" for all but high-income professionals. As a result, "women's labor force participation is increasingly important in maintaining family income." For single parent households, particularly if they are female-headed, employment in the low-wage sector does not guarantee escape from poverty.

Accompanying the postwar shifts in economic structure in the United States, there have been dramatic demographic changes in fertility rates, household composition, women's work, and women's labor force participation. These changes are underlined in the chapter by Heidi Hartmann. They include the delaying of marriage and childbearing by young women, the lowering of fertility rates or the fact that women are having fewer children over their lifetimes, and changes in living arrangements, such as women spending more time living alone or as heads of their own households. Divorce as well as marriage rates have been increasing, particularly since 1965, while the time spent in childcare over the life cycle has decreased. In fact, Hartmann reports, for most women childbearing has become increasingly compressed within a span of only a few years' duration. At the same time, a growing proportion of women are bearing children outside marriage—the proportion being higher among black women, despite some tendency toward convergence between black and white women. This has contributed to the significant increase in female headed households, particularly among teenagers, and in women's participation in the labor market.

One interpretation of these changes, Hartmann argues, is "to certify a family crisis and to bemoan the increased exploitation of women who must support households and children on their own or who bear the brunt of the speed-up for working-class families that occurs when both adults must work outside the home." However, she takes a more optimistic interpretation and tends to view these changes as largely positive for women on the basis of their increased autonomy from men, their greater economic independence, and even in respect to the number of hours they work. This is, of course, a controversial subject that needs to take into consideration the costs of this increased autonomy for women (see below). Class and race differences, still improperly evaluated, are likely to be very significant as far as such costs are concerned. In any case, Hartmann ventures to argue that post–World War II demographic changes indicate changes in the degree, extent, and forms of male domination—and she suggests that "patriarchy is weakening" and "that to the extent [that] there is a family crisis, it is by-and-large a healthy one, particularly for women." Many besides the New Right will disagree with this interpretation, as is indicated by current debates on the crisis of the black family. Yet Hartmann has raised an interesting question, which, in one form or another, permeates all the articles in this volume.

For Kessler-Harris and Sacks, one fundamental change brought about by the structural transformations of the last twenty-five years has been that families can no longer live on one wage. As they put it:

> . . . for most of the past, women were able to make up the differential between the male wage and the cost of survival through their own and community resources in ways that did not alter family relationships.

This, they argue, is no longer possible. The commoditization of domestic work and the shift of production out of the home has been parallelled by the increasing availability of wage work for women. For Kessler-Harris and Sacks, what might appear to be a neutral trade-off—the use of women's wages to purchase goods and services previously produced at home—has eroded men's power and authority within the home and expanded women's choices. As a result, the "imposed domesticity of the fifties" is disappearing. A series of struggles around home and work have emerged, while the locus of that struggle has shifted from the community to the workplace. In brief, the domestic code has become increasingly anachronistic. The significance of these changes takes us to the current polarization of views between those who defend the traditional family and those who see all family forms as legitimate.

Among the chapters included in this section, Sternlieb and Baker's takes the most optimistic view. Their emphasis is on the "remarkable" performance of the United States economy since 1940, which has been able to absorb an increasingly large number of workers, including women, into the workforce. The continuous increase in women's labor force participation rates has been parallelled by their heavy participation in the "growth industries." Sternlieb and Baker also point out that since 1982 women's unemployment rate is lower than men's and that women are now "less likely than men to be laid off or fired." They also note that the real problem is what they call the "non-elite, single wage earners" whose condition is documented in the chapter by Kuhn and Bluestone and in other chapters in this volume. However, their emphasis is on what they see as the successes rather than the failures in the United States economy.

The issue of women's employment and unemployment is dealt

with in greater detail by Milkman and by Kempers and Rayman in Part II. They provide a useful historical perspective to the analysis. Milkman's paper compares the impact of the economic downturn of the early 1980s with the Great Depression and finds both similarities and differences. In both cases, women took upon themselves an increased burden of family support. Women's unemployment rate was lower than men's because they concentrated in industries less affected by the economic crisis. In the same way, unemployment in the 1980s has meant an intensification of women's work in traditional husband-wife families. Economic hardships have also resulted in housing difficulties, with two generations often sharing a dwelling, and have produced a decline in divorce rates. Yet, in contrast to the 1930s, which registered a strong resistance to women's employment, women's participation in the labor force in the 1980s is viewed more as the rule than the exception. A large number of women no longer live in traditional husband-wife families. While for many female-headed households this change has been associated with the feminization of poverty, employed women without children enjoy relatively high incomes. What has been irrevocably altered, according to Milkman, is "the ideology of defining women's rights vis-à-vis paid work":

> With the rise of the two-income family, on the one hand, and the resurgence of feminism . . . on the other, it is no longer possible in the 1980s, as it was in the 1930s, to win popular support for an assault on women's right to employment opportunities.

Kempers and Rayman explore similar issues and compare the two periods; their focus is on the inadequacy of studies of unemployment in incorporating the unique experience of women—either as workers directly affected by the loss of a job or indirectly as wives and family members. They argue that most studies of unemployment during the Great Depression were inadequate either because women were not included as a separate category or because preconceived notions about women's roles precluded a full understanding of how unemployment affected them. Yet a basic difference between men and women is that while unemployment meant losses of activity for men, for women it meant "dramatic increases in both activity and responsibility." Recent studies of unemployment, they argue, try to document these differences and show that the unique experience of women is beginning to emerge.

The specificity of race and ethnicity within the context of structural transformation is the subject of Baca Zinn's paper. Focusing in particular on black and Chicano experiences, it begins with a historical overview of the significance of racial discrimination for the functioning of labor markets and family life. Baca Zinn locates women's roles within black and Chicano extended families as part of a strategy to meet basic family needs. Similarly, she argues that urban poverty and other problems such as those associated with female-headed households must be viewed as the results of the structural causes of poverty and she criticizes those who fail to understand this. She argues that these structural conditions leave black women disproportionately separated, divorced, and solely responsible for their children. Female-headed households are the result of these conditions rather than the cause of poverty among blacks.

A logical conclusion from this analysis is her warning against the generalization that women's increased economic independence and tendency to form their own households reflects a positive change for women. While this might reflect the experience of women with relatively high incomes, household arrangements in the case of minorities, she argues, "is caused in large part by the economic vulnerability of men rather than the economic well-being of women." Thus, the contrast between this view and Hartmann's, described above, raises a challenging question about how to evaluate the profound changes that have taken place in women's lives during the past twenty years.

In the agricultural sector, structural transformation in the United States has reached the stage at which traditional farm life is disappearing, giving way to business ventures and corporate farming. Elbert's paper takes up this subject, analyzing changes in women's roles throughout this process. Based on an oral history study of thirty-three farming families carried out at Cornell University, Elbert analyzes the extent to which the shift toward more capital-intensive farming has resulted in a variety of changes in the organization of production, the use of family labor, and the division of labor. She specifically argues that the choices made by farming families "occur within a context of gender hierarchy," while, "in the most threatened farm households, the struggle for survival may well entail a shift toward more egalitarian gender relations."

The traditional roles of farm women, with a constant interpenetration of home and farm duties, is being eroded by the shift toward more capitalist and business-like farming, which leaves little room for farm wives' and children's participation. In fact, women's exclusion from agricultural work and their corresponding "subordination to the husband's paternal authority and nurturance," is often viewed as a sign of family success. Yet, farm women's skills are being upgraded, while the amount of time that they spend on housework has decreased. They apply their skills and "free time" to tasks such as accounting, record keeping, and organizing/coordinating family labor. These new technical and managerial skills can be the root of greater gender equality. In fact, according to Elbert, the survival of farm families requires a reliance on more egalitarian gender relations, including the sharing of reproductive tasks. Thus she ends with an optimistic vision, were it not for the fact that it applies to a disappearing species in the North American landscape.

The first two papers in Part III present interesting analyses of specific sectors of the economy in which women are heavily represented, namely, office work and health services. Baran and Teegarden are concerned with the impact of office automation on women's work. Based on a case study in the insurance industry, they analyze the impact of the restructuring of the labor process that has resulted from office automation on the use of mental and manual labor, the changing nature of jobs, and the impetus toward team work, open offices, and multifunctional job categories. Thus, they argue, while the labor process has been centralized, rationalized, and computerized, occupational structures are undergoing profound changes. For the future, current trends indicate that further computerization will eliminate specific jobs, including professional functions. As a result, the workforce is likely to be reduced. At the same time, they argue, "increasingly occupational stratification will occur along class and race lines." Minority clerical workers "are in real danger of losing their jobs," while for the more skilled white clerical workers, the problem will be the lack of mobility from low-paid jobs. Only the middle-level positions filled by college-educated workers are likely to be filled by women in increasing numbers. This means that for office workers in the private sector, they project a gloomy picture.

Bennett and Alexander present an analysis of part-time work based on a study of part-time and full-time employed mothers in two metropolitan hospitals. They concentrate on testing the assumptions that part-time working mothers are likely to move in and out of jobs more quickly than other workers and that they are less committed to their work and more traditional in orientation toward women's social roles. They find no evidence for either of these assumptions, which are still being made by employers and used as the basis for discriminatory practices in the labor market. Because of the prevalence of women among part-time workers, the significance of this type of work goes beyond the health industry; Bennett and Alexander in fact call for similar studies that might allow their conclusions to be generalized.

Structural changes in the United States economy have had a clear world dimension. Although this dimension is not the focus of the essays in this volume, an illustration of the connections between changes in employment and the new international division of labor is given by O'Connor, who examines the employment of women in the specific case of the electronics industry.

The semiconductor and related industries, O'Connor argues, employ a large number of women, and particularly of minority and immigrant women, in low-paid, semi-skilled jobs. Many of the women are of Filipino, Indochinese, and Korean origin. This is in contrast to the employment of well-paid Asian and Asian/American males, of Japanese, Chinese, and Korean origin, who hold skilled technical jobs. Overall, female employment in these industries has increased over time, although offshore production has slowed down this growth and contributed to the deskilling of some operations and the downgrading of assemblers' skills (who are mostly women). In addition, the increasing use of automatic assembling has slowed down the employment of women.

O'Connor's chapter raises many questions about the use of gender in the workplace and its role in the process of the internationalization of production. These questions will require further investigation. In any case, his research reinforces what other authors have also pointed out, namely, the high degree of gender-based occupational segregation in the electronics industry and the use of women for short-term, low-paid employment in off-shore production.

The last two chapters in this collection address policy issues that concern women at the federal and state level. Sarri's study takes up federal policy changes affecting low-income working women since 1981. More concretely, this chapter presents an evaluation of the impact of the Omnibus Budget Reconciliation Act of 1981 (OBRA) on working women, single parents, and their children. It is based on data collected in six selected counties in Michigan with unemployment rates ranging from 9 percent to 20 percent. Her analysis of subjective and objective indicators leads her to argue that the post–OBRA period showed increased hardships for the families affected by these policies:

> These women . . . perceived that their economic and social situation had declined substantially since 1982, and many reported being in almost continual crisis. They felt themselves to be worse off than similar women in prior years in terms of their increased indebtness, problems of child care, and health.

This leads Sarri to criticize United States' income support policies and to point out that this country "stands apart from other industrialized countries" in its reluctance to help the poor. In addition, existing policies tend to be gender-biased in that they have a greater negative impact on women than on men. In particular, they have explicit and implicit requirements that tend to control the roles and behavior of women who are recipients of income support, and they have profound negative effects on children. Sarri therefore questions the nature and effectiveness of income support policies, even though she does not explore the further fundamental question of whether income support policies are in the last resort the most appropriate ones to deal with poverty and other welfare issues.

Wills, Beelar, Warren, and Friedman concentrate on state policies regarding women and their participation in the economy. This chapter explores various state initiatives targeted to three different clusters of women: working women, both privately and publicly employed and business owners; students and other women seeking employment and training; women economically dependent on either the private or public sector. Their assumption is that "economic issues are central to women's well-being" and they view state policies as an avenue to "integrating women into the economic mainstream." With this objective in mind, their analysis and concern ranges from policies dealing with state tax allowances for child care to pay equity in the private sector. The general steps for state action that they suggest emphasize, in the first place, the need to ensure that education and training programs ensure equal participation for men and women. Second, they recognize that "the demand side of the labor market represents the key constraint to opportunity," an important recognition to which we will return.

This collection, therefore, summarizes some of the major trends emerging from the restructuring of the United States economy during the past fifteen years: the important shift of employment toward the service sector, the parallel decrease in manufacturing employment, and the shift of investment to offshore production; the formation of low-wage and high-wage sectors in the economy, with its corresponding polarization in the distribution of income, and the structural transformation that the farming sector is undergoing. The collection also includes the analysis of more specific labor market issues, such as the impact of automation on office work and the consequences of cuts in public funds and changes in government programs. At the same time, the focus of this volume is on how these changes are affecting women's location within the economy. This includes the continuous and long-lasting increase in women's labor force participation, the corresponding increase in women's economic self-sufficiency and its effects on family formation, the sexual division of labor and domestic relations, the changing impact of unemployment on women, the impoverishment of female-headed households, and the specific problems of minority women and their families.

Unfortunately, comments made by discussants at the conference have not been included in this volume for lack of space. Nor have many important topics been covered. Beyond the information provided by each chapter, most of them raise further important theoretical and empirical questions. For example, a basic underlying theme that runs throughout the book is the extent to which, as women's economic location changes, and particularly as their labor force participation increases, gender roles are redefined at the workplace as well as the household level. Despite the many gains made toward women's greater economic self-reliance, educational attainment, and gender equality, examples of this redefinition of gender or gendering are numerous; they range from the concentration of women in low-wage sectors of the new industries to the gender-specific consequences of federal and state policies. Although it is important to celebrate the progress that has been made by many women during the past fifteen years, it is equally important to emphasize that the struggle for equality is far from over. For minority and working-class women, the road ahead is arduous. This is particularly the case for all those who have entered and remained below the frontier of poverty. In addition, we should be well aware of the limits and obstacles to this progress that are likely to affect all women. Although this is a subject beyond the scope of this introduction, I will conclude by calling attention, by way of illustration, to two such likely obstacles.

One is the difficulty of achieving equality in the labor market given the inherently hierarchical structure of the labor process under a class-differentiated and hierarchical organization of production. Given this hierarchy—increasingly more complex as large-scale production penetrates all sectors of the economy—criteria need to be developed for assigning workers to specific slots. Educational background, skills, and work experience are used, among other factors, as such criteria; to the extent that they are correlated with gender (and race and other such differentiating factors), the latter has an impact on the location of women workers within the labor hierarchy. In addition, even if progress is made in terms of equality and pay equity within a given job structure, structural transformation tells us of the possibility of a continuous redesigning of jobs and occupations. One of the reasons for the stubbornness of the wage gap is that while it is being narrowed in some occupations, the labor process is being restructured and new jobs are being created in such a way that a high proportion of women is being placed at the bottom of a constantly recreated labor hierarchy. Under such conditions, the concentration of women in low-paying jobs, with the complexity of results that this has for women in and outside of the work place, can constantly reappear, even if significant gains toward gender equality have been obtained elsewhere. This also implies that a more egalitarian structure of production, and particularly one that reflects the interests of those who work within it, would be more conducive to obtaining gender equality.

A second obstacle, related to the first, is the ideological resistance to equality and the backlash against women's gains that has surfaced in different ways in recent years. This resistance can appear in very subtle forms, as is illustrated by the current controversy over comparable worth. Opponents argue that the principle stands against the free functioning of market forces. Their argument is quite simple: women are paid less in female occupations because their supply, assumed to reflect women's own preferences, is concentrated in a few (female) occupations—in such a way that the relationship between supply and demand generates a tendency toward a relatively low average wage. That is, the problem is one of women's preferences, as expressed through market forces.

There are several problems with this argument. First, it amounts to a blaming-the-victim argument, since women are viewed as making free choices as free individuals.[1] It does not take into consideration the fact that women's supply is heavily influenced by their own perception of demand. That is, women will tend not to supply themselves for jobs and occupations that tend to be "destined" or "viewed" as male, therefore making it difficult for them to be employed or promoted. It is at the firm level that the decision whether some specific jobs and occupations are to be filled by men or women is made. This implies that the problem has its roots on the demand and not on the supply side. In addition, the argument does not explain why women would choose these women-related jobs rather than those that offer more favorable conditions. Second, the argument rests on the belief that wages are clearly set by market forces. Yet, in an economy that has moved very far from the pure competitive model, price and wage rigidity is a built-in reality, influenced by economic factors as well as by what Lester Thurow has called the "sociology of wage determination." As currently illustrated by the labor market for nurses and managers in the United States, significant shortages of nurses have not resulted in relatively higher wages for them; on the contrary, the unprecedented high levels of pay for executives have taken place at a time when students are crowding business schools, therefore increasing the supply of managers.[2] It is ironic that those who use the market forces argument against comparable worth do not acknowledge the obstacles to a free-competitive wage formation. Third, the argument ignores the whole process of gender construction, the extent to which both supply and demand are influenced by a set of preconceived notions and attitudes about the sexual division of labor and women's roles both in the market place and in the household. Rather than dealing with the artificiality of gender construction, it is taken as a given—which amounts to a rationalization of existing conditions.

All of this indicates that much remains to be done to eradicate gender differences. The essays in this volume make clear that the profound structural transformations of the United States economy have altered women's relationship to it in ways that seem irreversible. However, while some changes can be viewed as positive, many problems remain. We hope that their identification is part of this volume's contribution.

Notes

1. For an illustration of this type of argument, see the reasoning given by Rosalind Rosenberg in March 1985 on behalf of Sears and Roebuck & Co. in its defense against the EEOC's court case about discrimination (or possible violation of Title VII of the 1964 Civil Rights Act). An economist's illustration of this argument can be found in Mark Killingsworth, "The Economics of Comparable Worth: Analytical, Empirical, and Policy Questions," in *New Directions for Comparable Worth,* ed. Heidi Hartmann (Washington, D.C.: National Academy of Sciences, 1984), 86–115.

2. See "Executive Pay: How the Boss Did in '85," *Business Week,* 5 May 1985.

PART 1

Women, the Family, and the New Division of Labor

Economic Restructuring and the Female Labor Market: The Impact of Industrial Change on Women

Sarah Kuhn and Barry Bluestone

After several years of growth following a decade of the most profound economic stagnation since the Great Depression, a vigorous debate is under way about the nature and extent of the present recovery and its social implications. On one side are those who are unabashed celebrants of the recovery. Pointing to a gross national product that has been expanding since the beginning of 1983, an official unemployment rate down more than three points since the end of 1982, and a rebound of sales and profits in the manufacturing and construction sectors, the optimists believe that the economy has finally turned the corner. Ten years of wrenching economic and social adjustments are credited with having set the stage for a new era of prosperity.

To others, the trends do not appear as promising. Continued erosion in the international competitiveness of basic industry; interindustry, interregional, and international capital mobility followed by plant closings; and the transformation of America into a "service economy" allegedly made up of low-wage dead-end jobs are all believed to be creating a society characterized by chronic underemployment, growing inequality, and insecurity. Even with a burst of aggregate growth, it is argued, the present trajectory of the economy will not provide a sufficient number of jobs of "good quality" to meet existing or future needs. A growing structural mismatch between the newly created jobs and the existing set of job skills, combined with a labor market dominated by low-paying jobs, will presumably dislodge an entire class of workers and their families from the middle class.

Economic transformation and social restructuring, of course, are not new. Historically, every economic era from feudalism and mercantilism in the twelfth to seventeenth centuries to the stages of competitive and monopoly capitalism in the nineteenth and twentieth centuries has both created and been influenced by shifts in social class relations and in gender and family roles. As the world's economies now move toward more highly integrated global markets and undergo accelerated technological change, one may examine the continuing metamorphosis of gender, family, and class relations. Whether the emerging relations are more equitable and life-enhancing or inequitable and socially debilitating depends on the nature of these social and economic developments.

This chapter explores basic trends in the labor market, particularly as they affect women and their families. To do this, we shall first examine developments in the manufacturing sector and the growth in the service economy. Next we will argue that increasing inequality may be emerging in the nation's wage structure and discuss some of the evidence to support this hypothesis. Finally we discuss the implications for women and families of the changes we have described.

THE "DEINDUSTRIALIZATION OF AMERICA": FACT OR FICTION?

In a controversial 1983 *Brookings Review* article, the chairman of the Council of Economic Advisors to President Carter, Charles Schultze, castigated those who support industrial policies as a means of reviving the American economy (1983). Calling industrial policy an inappropriate solution to a nonexistent problem, Schultze suggests that standard macroeconomic policy is sufficient to move the United States back toward full employment and stable economic growth.

In a similar vein, Leon Taub of Chase Econometrics rejects the notion that the economy has undergone any fundamental transformation. In a briefing paper prepared for his clients, Taub writes:

> Rather than de-industrializing, the United States is merely specializing in the output of some types of manufactured goods, while other nations are doing likewise in other types of manufactured goods. This type of specialization, which is a logical consequence of increased world communication, travel, and interdependence, not to mention world political agreements such as GATT, simply means that the production possibility frontier of the world is expanding, and that world real incomes can be increased. (1983)

The evidence for these sanguine assessments is ostensibly found in a number of aggregate indicators for manufacturing employment. Robert Z. Lawrence of the Brookings Institute notes, for example, that the aggregate level of manufacturing employment in the United States remained almost constant over the most widely acknowledged period of structural change, 1973–1980 (1982). Manufacturing establishments employed 20 million workers in the United States in 1973 and 20.4 million in 1980.

Reinforcing the claim that deindustrialization is of trivial consequence, Mark Bendick of the Urban Institute has argued that few of the millions who have lost their jobs in basic manufacturing sectors have ended up "dislocated." Using the March 1980 *Current Population Survey*, Bendick calculates that fewer than 90,000 workers displaced from declining manufacturing industries had not found jobs within twenty-six weeks of being laid off (1982). He concludes that "economic dislocation—the changing industrial or occupational patterns of employment—does not seem to be at the heart of the unemployment problems of either the nation as a whole or of most individual workers." Summed up, the Brookings and Urban Institute positions suggest that the alleged decline of the manufacturing sector is either altogether illusory, or at most of little social importance.

What are we to make of this? Admittedly, none of the aggregate trends reported by Lawrence or Bendick are in dispute. Manufacturing employment taken as a whole has indeed remained fairly stable and displaced workers eventually do find new jobs. But such evidence, we believe, is largely irrelevant to the issue at hand. The aggregate trends in employment and the fact that unemployed work-

5

Table 1.1.   **Changes in Total Employment and Number of Production Workers in the United States, by Industry, 1960–80**

Industry	Total employment		Production workers		Production worker average wage
	1960–73	1973–80	1960–73	1973–80	1980
Total manufacturing	16.7%	0.13%	17.9%	−4.7%	$7.27
Durable goods	25.7	2.0	23.2	−3.8	7.75
Nondurable goods	12.6	−2.4	9.9	−5.9	6.55
Primary metals	6.3	−9.7	5.6	−13.5	9.77
Machinery (except electrical)	41.2	19.9	35.3	14.9	8.00
Electrical distribution equipment	14.8	−11.2	29.2	−16.0	6.96
Electrical industrial apparatus	32.3	−0.5	40.8	−3.8	6.91
Household appliances	27.3	−17.9	31.3	−18.1	6.95
Radio/TV receivers	42.6	−27.2	46.5	−30.9	6.42
Electronic components and accessories	75.9	25.6	60.4	17.7	6.05
Motor vehicles	34.9	−20.3	57.6	−25.3	9.85
Aircrafts and parts	−15.8	24.6	−23.1	24.6	9.28
Instruments and related products	33.1	27.6	27.9	22.4	6.80
Textile mill products	9.2	−15.4	6.1	−16.2	5.07
Apparel and other products	16.6	−12.8	13.8	−10.5	4.56
Chemicals and allied products	25.3	6.3	19.7	2.1	8.30
Tires and tubes	25.1	−12.6	25.1	−16.4	9.74
Footwear	−24.6	−22.0	−26.8	−23.2	4.42
Department stores	87.1	5.8	86.6	7.6	4.95
Eating and drinking establishments	84.6	51.2	—	48.7	3.69
Finance, insurance, real estate	53.9	26.6	45.5	24.3	5.79
Services	74.3	37.8	—	35.8	5.85
Total employment	41.7	16.9			

Source: U.S. Department of Labor, Bureau of Labor Statistics, *Employment and earnings statistics for the United States, 1909–1980* (Washington, D.C.: GPO, 1981).

ers eventually find new jobs of some kind does not prove or disprove anything about the experiences of individuals and households in the "restructured" economy. With respect to human welfare, the basic issue in any economy is not only the level of employment or unemployment per se, but the quality of the jobs that exist, the living standards that those jobs permit, and the distribution of income that the economy generates. Thus it is critical to understand the transformation of specific industries and regions and to explore the changes in the occupational and earnings histories of individual workers and their families. More detailed and disaggregated data are needed for this purpose.

The employment performance of key sectors of the economy is displayed in Table 1.1. While a flat trend (as opposed to a sharp drop) in employment is confirmed by the small (+0.13 percent) change in the number of total manufacturing jobs between 1973 and 1980, production employment shrank by 5 percent (693,000) and employment in certain sectors including radio and TV receiver manufacture, motor vehicles, footwear, household appliances, and textile mill products fell sharply. Together the ten sectors in Table 1.1 experiencing employment losses accounted for 790,000 fewer jobs in 1980 than in 1973. By 1982, another 601,000 jobs had been lost in these ten industries alone.

The sharp improvement in the overall economy in 1983 and 1984 did little to improve matters in a large number of these and other manufacturing industries. In twenty-nine (of seventy-four major) manufacturing sectors, including the entire set of machine tool industries, glass, and tires, employment continued to decline right through the economic boom. In 1978 these twenty-nine industries provided jobs for six million workers, nearly a third of the total manufacturing labor force. Another twenty-eight industries with seven million jobs experienced "incomplete recoveries" with 1984 employment significantly below 1978 levels. These two sets of industries— which account for nearly 75 percent of manufacturing employment—have lost nearly 1.9 million jobs since the 1983–85 recovery began.[1] Most of this loss is now considered permanent.

Other manufacturing sectors, of course, were growing during this period. The so-called "high-tech" industries expanded rapidly during the 1980s to fill part of the aggregate employment vacuum left by the older mill-based and smokestack industries. But the total number of production jobs in these sectors comprises only a small portion of overall manufacturing employment. As of 1980, the four most important high-technology industries (Office & Computing Machinery, Communications Equipment, Electronic Components, and Instruments & Related Products) accounted altogether for only 1.2 million production jobs. This was equal to less than 9 percent of all manufacturing production jobs in the nation. Over time, the number of manufacturing positions in these high-technology sectors may expand, but given the removal of many of these jobs to overseas locations, the growth is expected to be modest. At best, the number of new jobs generated in the expanding manufacturing sector will hardly exceed the expected losses in the older production industries.

Even then, the newly created jobs may not be a very good substitute for the jobs that are lost. The average manufacturing wage in 1984 was $9.17 an hour. Of the four important high-tech industries, all but the communications sector provided wages below the all-manufacturing average. The typical production worker in the electronic components industry earned $7.81 an hour in 1984, providing a weekly salary only 68 percent as high as that of the average non-supervisory employee in the primary metals industry. Hence, it is necessary to create 146 electronic components jobs to compensate for the wage bill loss of 100 steelworkers.

Data collected in a special supplement to the January 1984 *Current Population Survey* conducted by the U.S. Bureau of Labor Statistics can be used to measure the overall incidence of "skidding," the problem faced by workers when they are forced down the earnings ladder after job displacement. According to the BLS, 11.5 million workers lost their jobs to plant closings, plant relocations, or the abolishment of a position or a production shift sometime between January 1979 and 1984. Of these, 5.1 million had three or more years of seniority on the jobs they lost. Nearly half of these workers (2.5 million) were in the manufacturing sector. Women had a slightly higher probability of being displaced from the manufacturing sector than did men. Nearly 13.5 percent of women employed in this sector between 1979 and 1984 lost their jobs to total or partial plant closings. The comparable statistic for men was 13.0 percent.

Wage loss due to displacement is substantial. Twenty-five percent

8

of the 5.1 million displaced workers were still looking for work when surveyed in January 1984. Fourteen percent had dropped out of the labor force altogether and 7 percent were now in part-time jobs instead of the full-time jobs they had had before. Of the remaining workers—those who found new full-time positions—45 percent were earning less in the new job than in the one they had lost. Thus, only 1.5 million (30 percent) of the 5.1 million displaced workers were earning as much or more after industrial restructuring as before.

FROM MANUFACTURING TO SERVICES:
SOME GENDER IMPLICATIONS

Despite the crisis in the manufacturing sector, overall employment has been expanding at a record pace as a result of the burgeoning service economy. Job growth in the service-producing industries (transportation and public utilities; wholesale and retail trade; finance, insurance, and real estate; government; and business and personal services) has dwarfed any increase in the goods-producing industries (mining, construction, and manufacturing of durables and nondurables). Indeed, since 1970 over 94 percent of aggregate nonagricultural employment growth has occurred in the service sector, while the goods-producing sectors have been responsible for a net growth of only 1.3 million jobs out of the more than 23 million created. Consequently, employment in the service-producing industries has grown from 58 percent of all domestic employment in 1948 to 74 percent in 1984.[2] Actually, the number of workers now engaged in service occupations accounts for an even higher percentage of U.S. employment than these figures suggest, since many services are performed by employees in the manufacturing industries.

At first glance, the shift from manufacturing to services bodes well for U.S. women. Three-fifths of the 23 million new jobs created in the economy since 1970 went to women, reflecting both the increase in women's labor force participation and the disproportionate increase in service industries and in occupations where significant numbers of women are employed.

The critical importance of the service sector to women's employ-

9

Table 1.2. Twenty Occupations with Largest Absolute Growth in Employment, 1978–1990

Occupations	Total empl. 1981 (1000s)	Percent female 1981	Median full-time weekly earnings for women 1981	Ratio female to male wage × 100	More than 80% female	Less than 20% female	Above median earnings for all women	Below 125% of poverty level[b]
Janitors and sextons	993	14.6	188	83.6		X		X
Nurses' aides and orderlies	832	84.3	167	82.2	X			X
Salesclerks	1,032	60.3	154	67.4				X
Cashiers	712	85.1	166	92.0	X			X
Waiters/Waitresses	532	85.1	144	72.0	X			X
General office clerks (misc.)	997	81.5	222	68.3	X			
Professional nurses (RNs)	924	95.8	331	—	X		X	
Food preparation and service, fast food restaurants	107	85.0	140	—				X
Secretaries	3,199	99.3	229[a]	—	X		X[a]	
Truckdrivers	1,560	2.1	[a]	—		X		
Kitchen helpers (food service n.e.c.)	239	68.2	160	90.0	X		X	
Elementary schoolteachers	1,244	82.2	311	82.2	X		X	
Typists	801	96.4	211	—	X			
Accountants and auditors	960	39.7	308	71.2			X[a]	
Helpers, trades	704	1.5	[a]	—		X	X	
Blue-collar worker supervisors	1,772	10.5	262	64.2		X	X	
Bookkeepers, hand	1,290	90.6	222	69.4	X		X	
Licensed practical nurses	263	97.3	227	—	X		X	
Guards and doorkeepers	500	12.8	214	90.7		X	X	
Automotive mechanics	813	0.7	(2)	—				
All full-time workers, all occupations	72,491	39.5	224	64.7			X	(2)

Sources: Occupations from Max L. Carey, "Occupational Employment Growth Through 1990" in Economic projections to 1990, U.S. Department of Labor, Bureau of Labor Statistics, Bulletin 2121. Statistics from Nancy F. Rytina, Earnings of men and women: A look at specific occupations, Monthly Labor Review 105 (April 1982).

Note: Occupations are listed in declining order of total new jobs projected 1976–1990.

[a] Earnings are not given for women when base population is smaller than 50,000.

[b] The 1981 poverty threshold is $7,323 for a three-person family which includes two children under eighteen. This figure is divided by fifty weeks to yield a weekly poverty level of approximately $183.

ment is confirmed by Labor Department data. In a Bureau of Labor Statistics ranking of fifty-two industries, eight of the ten industries with the highest percentage of women in their labor forces were in the service sector. These eight industries alone were responsible for the jobs of more than 28 percent of all employed women in the economy. The ten industries with the smallest percentage of women were all in manufacturing (see Table 1.4). Furthermore, of the twenty occupations projected to provide the most new jobs during the 1980s, eleven—all services—had workforces that were more than 80 percent female in 1981 (see Table 1.2). Hence, the transformation of the economy seems to benefit women by expanding employment opportunities in the occupations and industries where women are most often found, while the erosion in manufacturing seems to be concentrated (in absolute numbers) among men.

INEQUALITY AND ECONOMIC PROSPECTS

Given the explosion in the number of service sector jobs—particularly those that have gone to women—how can the current economic transformation possibly be labeled a problem? The answer lies in the fact that the majority of these newly created jobs are poor substitutes for the ones that are disappearing. The changing structure of the national job distribution is responsible, we believe, for creating a mismatch between the skills and income needs of displaced workers and new labor market entrants on the one hand, and the skill requirements and wage levels of the new jobs on the other. To better understand the mismatch, consider the internal job structures of the growing and declining sectors.

The smokestack industries (e.g., auto, steel, tires, household appliances, and petrochemicals) came to be characterized during the period 1930–1980 by a labor market structure that contained a relatively small high-wage segment at one end of the job spectrum, a small low-wage set of jobs at the other, and a large semi-skilled and skilled blue-collar and white-collar "middle." In the automobile industry, for example, there is a small group of highly remunerated managers and skilled designers and engineers. At the other end of

11

the auto labor market, some of the smaller shops that supply General Motors, Ford, and Chrysler with parts and components offer low wages that approach the government mandated minimum and provide few employee benefits. But the vast majority of workers in the industry are employed in fabrication and assembly jobs or in manufacturing support positions that pay annual wages in the $15,000–$25,000 range. The nature of the production process combined with the demands of the trade union movement helped create such a "unimodal" distribution of jobs.

The industries that are expanding today may have a very different employment distribution. Within high-technology manufacturing, in business services, and in personal services and retail trade, the distribution of jobs may be characterized by a "dual" market structure, with a well-paid bureaucracy at the top and a large pool of part-time, poorly paid workers at the bottom. In dual market industries, there are few jobs analogous to the middle-wage blue-collar work of the smokestack sector. Across industries, a similar erosion of middle-income jobs may be taking place as the fastest growth is registered among the highest and lowest paying industries. While such changes would not necessarily indicate a shift toward a dual distribution of jobs in the overall economy, they are fully consistent with growing inequality in the American labor market.

THE EVIDENCE FOR INCREASING INEQUALITY

Statistical evidence of growing inequality—or its more extreme manifestation, an economy with a "missing middle"—is presently quite limited. Indeed, recent work by Robert Z. Lawrence of the Brookings Institution and Neal H. Rosenthal of the BLS suggest that little or nothing of this sort is occurring (Lawrence, 1984; Rosenthal, 1985). Using unpublished BLS data on usual weekly earnings of employed full-time wage and salary workers, Lawrence finds that there was some erosion in the proportion of workers receiving middle-class earnings, but the decline was limited, and it was overwhelmingly related to the changing age and gender structure of the labor force. Overall, the proportion of workers earning $250–499

12

per week ("middle-class earnings") fell from 50 to 46 percent between 1969 and 1983. Almost all the decline can, however, be attributed to the crowding of the baby-boom generation (those under
age thirty in 1983) into lower-wage occupations. Males above age
thirty-five actually moved from the low and middle earnings categories into the high end of the distribution, while females above age
twenty-four showed significant movement out of low-wage jobs into
the middle of the wage distribution. The shift in employment from
manufacturing into services, according to Lawrence, is responsible
for a trivial portion of what middle-earnings decline did occur. Contrary to common perception, the proportion of full-time workers
earning middle-class incomes in the goods-producing sectors is identical to the proportion in the rest of the economy.

Rosenthal comes to very much the same conclusion about the alleged "missing middle," using occupational data. Arraying the 416
detailed occupations in the Current Population Surveys for 1973 and
1982 into three equal groups ordered by earnings, he finds that the
proportion of full-time earners in the "middle third" declined by an
almost imperceptible amount. Including part-time workers in his
analysis did not alter this finding (1985:10).

Lawrence's and Rosenthal's work might have put an end to the
missing middle debate if it were not for serious flaws in both pieces
of work. Lawrence's research failed to account for part-time employment, which almost assuredly would increase the number of workers in the lower-class earnings segment. Moreover, as Birnbaum and
Tilly have demonstrated, Lawrence's results are highly sensitive to
the earnings ranges he used and the years over which he ran the
analysis. Changing the end year and the middle-earnings range
leads to results that suggest a larger impact of deindustrialization
on the earnings distribution (Birnbaum and Tilly, 1985). Rosenthal's
error is more fundamental. In segmenting by occupation, the widths
of the upper, middle, and lower wage ranges are allowed to change
over time rather than remain fixed proportionately. In this particular case, the wage range for the middle category more than doubles
between 1973 and 1982, allowing a broader range of wages to constitute the "middle." Accordingly, it comes as no surprise that a large
number of workers fall into the middle in the later year.

The correct procedure to assess changes in the distribution of earnings would consist of analyzing microdata on individuals not grouped by industry or occupation. Grouping eliminates the effects of any intraindustry and intraoccupational shifts in the distribution of earnings that may substantially contribute to greater inequality or emerging dualism. Unfortunately, this analysis has not been carried out, with the exception of the research conducted by Henle and Ryscavage, which we will briefly review later in this section.

Until additional statistical studies are pursued along this line, we do not believe that the missing middle—or at least the growing inequality—hypothesis should be dismissed out of hand. This is particularly true because of the sizable amount of anecdotal evidence that points to substantial restructuring in key sectors of the economy. The department store industry, described below, offers perhaps the most graphic example of this pattern. In this industry, new management practices, changing consumption patterns, and the use of advanced technology have combined to dramatically restructure employment and earnings patterns.

While traditional department stores benefited from the postwar consumer boom that peaked in the late 1960s and early 1970s, an even bigger winner was the discount segment in this industry. Discount stores were able to undersell traditional retail establishments by reducing the level of service offered to customers, substituting advertising for skilled sales help, and by using automated equipment operated by low-wage sales clerks to create assembly-line conditions at the checkout counter.

The consequence of this transformation was an enormous swelling in the ranks of low-wage, high-turnover, part-time jobs, and a simultaneous increase in high-level corporate activity. While the typical department store clerk earned less per year in current dollars in 1975 than in 1957, the size of the managerial hierarchy nearly doubled during this period, expanding the ranks of highly paid corporate staff (Bluestone et al., 1981:103). As a result, the distribution of earnings in the industry became increasingly unequal, with women and young workers confined to low-wage sales positions, and prime-age male workers dominating the upper-tier, high-paying managerial slots.

By 1970, more than half of the department store industry's labor

14

force was made up of workers under 25 years of age, up from only 30 percent twelve years earlier (Bluestone et al., 1981:95–96). Turn-over among employees, high since at least the late 1950s, grew to staggering proportions. In some years, half of the industry's labor force left the industry, according to an analysis of the Social Security Administration's Longitudinal Employer-Employee Data file (LEED) (Bluestone et al., 1981:85).[3] In New England, as many as 100,000 employees exited the industry in 1969, making it necessary for employers to hire over 92,000 workers in order to keep the net employment decline to 8,100! Turnover of this magnitude can only be consistent with the presence of relatively unskilled jobs requiring little firm-specific training and offering few returns to job tenure.

Perhaps the most striking feature of the pronounced dualism that arose in the department store industry is the extent to which the industry's good jobs and bad jobs are divided along gender lines. While there are men—mostly young men under twenty-five—in the low-wage jobs that the industry provides in such great numbers, the vast majority of low-wage employees are women. The high-wage jobs in the industry go almost exclusively to men. A third of all women in the industry earned less than $3,000 in 1975, and almost two-thirds made less than $5,000. In that same year, only 28 percent of all men in the industry made less than $5,000. At the high end of the scale, one-fifth of all men earned more than $15,000 in 1975, while only three women in a thousand earned this much (Bluestone et al., 1981: 105). Overall, men employed year round averaged $6,800 per year in 1975, while women earned only $2,800. Some of the difference between men's and women's pay is a consequence of the fact that women are much more likely to work part-time than men; the remainder of the difference is accounted for by discrepancies in employment position and in hourly wages between the two groups.

The pronounced difference between men's and women's earnings in the department store sector in 1975 is shown in the top graph in Figure 1.1. Women are vastly overrepresented at the low end of the wage scale, with few women earning five-figure salaries. Men, by contrast, have a bimodal wage distribution, with the largest group of men in the $12–20,000 range and another cluster in the $3–6,000 range. The recent situation contrasts sharply with the distributions

15

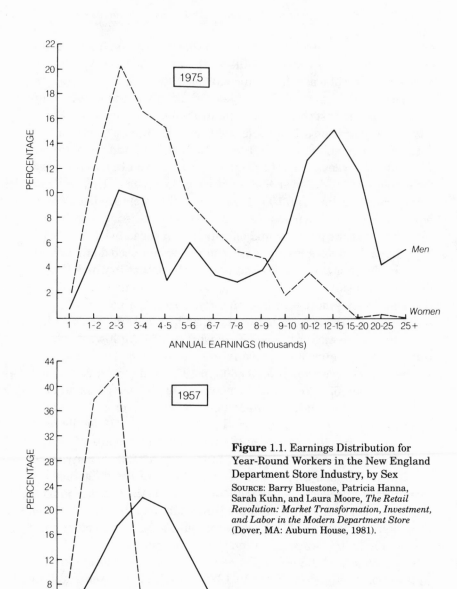

Figure 1.1. Earnings Distribution for
Year-Round Workers in the New England
Department Store Industry, by Sex
SOURCE: Barry Bluestone, Patricia Hanna,
Sarah Kuhn, and Laura Moore, *The Retail
Revolution: Market Transformation, Investment,
and Labor in the Modern Department Store*
(Dover, MA: Auburn House, 1981).

for 1957, when men's incomes, although higher, were more nearly equal to those of women, and both distributions, as well as their combined distribution, were clearly unimodal.

The department store industry, then, provides an example of a transformation that has restructured the employment characteristics of an entire sector of the economy in a short period of time. Employers' responses to intense competition, made possible by the availability of a labor force willing to work part-time for near-minimum wages, led to a transformation characterized by pronounced and increasing inequality in the distribution of wages, an inequality in which the major predictor of income level is gender.

A similar pattern of dualism may exist in parts of the high-technology sector, particularly in semiconductor manufacturing. In semiconductors, some circumstantial evidence supports the assertion that the earnings distributions of men and women might resemble the highly unequal distributions found in the retail sector. Hazardous, low-wage production jobs are overwhelmingly filled by female workers. A Bureau of Labor Statistics survey of the industry found that in 1977 the lowest-paid occupation in the industry, that of crystal coater, paid an average of $3.38 per hour and was 90 percent female. Pipe fitters, who were all men, earned $7.94 an hour, the highest average wage in the plant. The highest-paid engineering technicians were also all men (Applebaum, 1983:9). This may indicate that women as a rule are confined to the lowest-paying jobs in the industry, while men hold the more lucrative positions.

The other piece of evidence that supports the hypothesis that the semiconductor industry resembles the department store industry in its distribution of wages by gender is that, like the department store industry, there are relatively few middle-level jobs in the sector. The vast majority of jobs are either low-paying or high-paying. Eileen Appelbaum reports that, "A wage below $6 an hour placed a U.S. worker in the bottom third of the [national] income distribution in 1977, while a wage above $9.50 placed that person in the top third. On that criterion, 28 percent of the jobs in this industry were good jobs at the top of the distribution, 9.2 percent were in the middle, while 62.8 percent were low paying jobs" (1983:10). The virtual absence of middle-income jobs and the strong evidence of occupational segregation by sex give cause for serious concern about the ability of

17

Table 1.3. **Level and Distribution of Nominal Annual Earnings of Four-Quarter Workers: 1957–1975**

Industry and sex	1957–1958[a]		1975[a]	
	median	gini[b]	median	gini
All covered employment	$3,640	.332	$8,270	.381
Manufacturing				
Women's outerwear				
all	2,170	.325	5,135	.352
women	2,065	.196	4,970	.202
men	5,175	.404	9,920	.474
Paper mills				
all	4,425	.187	11,430	.188
women	3,260	.119	8,210	.165
men	4,610	.176	11,690	.176
Commercial printing				
all	4,135	.315	9,830	.279
women	2,880	.221	6,225	.236
men	4,969	.297	10,820	.254
Shoes				
all	2,720	.286	5,600	.315
women	2,380	.184	4,910	.179
men	3,540	.311	7,140	.384
Metalworking machinery				
all	4,980	.270	11,290	.294
women	3,190	.164	7,270	.235
men	5,590	.258	11,790	.280
Office machines & computers				
all	4,010	.184	10,840	.287
women	3,360	.138	8,310	.196
men	4,380	.173	13,280	.270
Electronic components				
all	3,740	.293	7,040	.328
women	2,860	.175	5,760	.179
men	5,195	.245	11,375	.301
Aircraft engines				
all	5,000	.197	13,150	.217
women	3,810	.081	9,740	.104
men	5,250	.191	13,850	.208
Nonmanufacturing				
Dept. stores				
all	2,305	.386	4,616	.443
women	2,036	.294	3,968	.325
men	3,892	.380	9,716	.432
Supermarkets				
all	2,860	.367	4,680	.430

18

Table 1.3. *(continued)*

Industry and sex	1957–1958[a]		1975[a]	
	median	gini[b]	median	gini
women	1,960	.270	3,700	.319
men	3,630	.352	6,975	.422
Commercial banks				
all	3,080	.296	7,375	.302
women	2,755	.133	6,395	.206
men	4,185	.327	11,710	.301
Hotels, motels				
all	1,880	.364	4,010	.398
women	1,450	.344	3,200	.344
men	2,380	.315	5,140	.401
Hospitals				
all	2,365	.323	7,440	.310
women	2,255	.271	7,205	.252
men	3,130	.400	9,070	.401

SOURCE: Computations by Alan Matthews, Social Welfare Research Institute, Boston College, using Social Security Administration's *Longitudinal Employer-Employee Data File,* containing a 1 percent sample of the social security records of all covered employees who ever worked inside New England between 1957 and 1975. Table includes only wages and salaries actually earned in New England. From Bennett Harrison, "Rationalization, Restructuring, and the Decline of Older Regions," Harvard–MIT Joint Center for Urban Studies, 1981.
[a]Because some of the first year (1957) data in our file were defective, we used 1957 if possible, otherwise 1958 as the first year in the series.
[b]The gini index, a measure of distribution commonly used by social scientists, is constructed so that increases in its value signify growing inequality, while decreases indicate a more equal distribution. The range in gini values is bounded by 0 and 1. When the index is 0, there is perfect equality—each individual receives an equal amount of resources. When the index equals 1, there is "perfect inequality" where one individual receives everything and all others get nothing.

the semiconductor industry to do anything to advance the economic position of women.

There is some evidence that other industries have undergone changes that, if not as dramatic and pronounced as those in the department store industry and in semiconductors, at least tend to increase inequality among all workers employed in the industry. Bennett Harrison, working with Alan Matthews of the Social Welfare Research Institute at Boston College, used the LEED file to study New England employees in selected industries (1982:75–78). The

19

gini coefficients generated for each of thirteen industries point to increasing inequality among wage workers in all industries except commercial printing and hospitals, in which inequality declined, and paper mills, in which it remained essentially unchanged between 1957–58 and 1975 (see Table 1.3). In ten of the thirteen industries, the inequality among all workers of both sexes was greater than the inequality among men alone or among women alone. While these figures support the idea that inequality is increasing, it is not possible to know precisely from the evidence shown here whether the changes within industries are as pronounced as those in the department store industry.

Turning away from the question of whether individual industries are becoming more unequal in their wage distributions, we can also examine the evidence for the assertion that there is greater inequality across the economy as a whole. Using unpublished BLS data, Bluestone, Harrison, and Gorham have calculated that 45 percent of all private-sector jobs in 1969 were in industries with an annual average wage of $13,600 or less (in 1980 dollars). However, this same set of lower-wage industries accounted for two-thirds (67 percent) of all new jobs generated between 1969 and 1982 (Bluestone, Harrison, and Gorham, 1984). Furthermore, data from the *Current Population Surveys* for 1958 through 1977 point to greater earnings inequality across the entire occupational spectrum, especially for men. Henle and Ryscavage have calculated gini coefficients for all wage and salary earners (including part-time employees) and for year-round full-time workers (1980). Among men, the gini index for the former group increased by 14 percent from .327 to .374 between 1958 and 1977, while the index for year-round full-time male wage earners increased by 13 percent from .254 to .287. For women the results are more ambiguous, with no clear trend toward greater or lesser earnings inequality over this time span being manifested. Nevertheless, the overall level of inequality is greater for women than men because of a greater variance in hours of work. Across industries, the highest gini coefficients for both sexes are generally found in precisely the fastest growing sectors—retail trade and business services. This may point to greater future inequality in the women's earnings distribution as these industries expand and low gini index industries stagnate or shrink.

This tendency toward inequality suggests a rather disturbing forecast. The good news is that unemployment rates may eventually decline as a consequence of the rapidly expanding trade and service sector. The bad news is that underemployment, not unemployment, may become our most acute economic problem. Even a national 4 percent unemployment rate would not be inconsistent with exaggerated underemployment, economic inequality, and social insecurity.

THE IMPLICATIONS FOR WOMEN AND FAMILIES

What are the implications for women and their families of the significant changes we have described? While the number of jobs for women is clearly increasing, the effect on women of overall changes in the structure of the economy depends not only on the number of women's jobs available, but also on the quality of those jobs, and—for women who have access to a husband's or male partner's income—on the employment opportunities open to men. Furthermore, the economy affects different women in different ways, so that the impact of these changes varies for women depending, for example, on their marital status, number of dependents, race, and class.

In the current climate of economic turbulence, there are what appear to be some good omens for women. The greatest cause for optimism lies in the sheer number of jobs being created in occupations and industries that are currently majority female. Although significant job growth is projected for occupations where women are a vast majority of the workforce, it is important to remember that there is nothing immutable about the sex-typing of a particular occupation. A century ago most secretaries were men, and the proportion of men is now increasing in some female-dominated occupations (e.g., "flight attendant"). Employment prospects for both women and men are affected by both the extent and the rigidity of occupational sex-typing. The growth in "women's" jobs, combined with both structural and cyclical unemployment among male workers, has brought about some convergence in male and female unemployment rates. In every year between 1948 and 1981 the official unemployment rate

21

for women aged 20 and over exceeded that of men. It was 41 percent higher in the 1960s and averaged 35 percent higher in the 1970s.[4] In 1982 and 1983, with the plummeting of employment in male-dominated manufacturing, the jobless rate differential was finally reversed. In 1984, however, the unemployment rate for adult women (6.8 percent) once again exceeded that of men (6.6 percent).

Also on the positive side, there have been recent signs that the earnings gap between men and women at the level of the overall economy has narrowed. Having hovered between 57 and 60 percent for at least two decades, the ratio of women's to men's median annual earnings has recently climbed to 62 percent (Pear, 1983:B15). While this may to some extent be a function of women's success in breaking down barriers to entry into higher-wage occupations, we suspect that the change has chiefly been caused by the pronounced effects of the recession and of industrial dislocation on men's wages. The suddenness of the change suggests that it is the product of such dislocation, not necessarily of upward mobility among women.

The good fortune of women in the economy, it appears, is therefore good largely because the recent fortunes of men have been so bad. If the narrowing of the wage gap is indeed the result of male "skidding" rather than of women's progress, increased equality is accompanied by a decreased standard of living for those women who depend on men's incomes.

This would almost certainly be the implication of research based on the LEED file undertaken by Louis Jacobson and his associates (Jacobson, 1978; 1979). Tracing male workers who were displaced permanently from basic manufacturing industries, Jacobson finds dramatic declines in earnings. Two years after losing his auto industry job, the average autoworker is found to be earning 43 percent less than if he had been able to maintain his job. Even six years after layoff, the ex-autoworker has still not caught up to where he would have been if the layoff had not occurred. His annual earnings are still 16 percent lower. For ex-steelworkers, the loss is 47 percent after two years, 13 percent after six. Some workers in the second tier of manufacturing also lose as a result of permanent displacement. The average earnings shortfall for those laid off from the men's clothing industry—a much lower-wage industry than auto or steel—is 21 percent after two years and 9 percent after six. Obviously, the family

22

suffers a depressed standard of living when the male earner in the family is forced to settle for a lower wage after working in a basic manufacturing industry.

Looking at the increased employment of women in the economy, there is no basis for great optimism. A proliferation of jobs available to women does not constitute an economic windfall—particularly for women maintaining families by themselves—if the jobs are generally low-wage with little potential for upward mobility. For women who already work the "double day" of wage work and home work, it is a higher hourly wage, not the ability to choose among marginal jobs, or increased hours of work at a low wage, that is needed.

Of the twenty occupations that will produce the most jobs between now and 1990, seventeen have enough women in them to enable the Bureau of Labor Statistics to report median weekly earnings for women. Eleven of those seventeen have wages below the average weekly wages for all women in the economy (recall Table 1).

Most of these growing occupations are not only low-paying but highly sex-segregated: eleven are more than 80 percent female and six are more than 80 percent male. While the fact that a majority of the largest job-producing occupations are overwhelmingly female means lots of jobs for women, such pronounced sex segregation generally signifies low pay in the female occupational ghetto. Table 1 reveals that within industries, there is a strong inverse relationship between the percentage of women in an industry and the wage level of that industry. More low-wage jobs, while they may be a hedge against unemployment for women, guarantee underemployment for many.

There is one group of women for whom the expansion of service-sector employment has provided some clear benefits. Immediately after World War II, black women's earnings were about half those of white women. By 1981, black women's wages had risen to 92–95 percent of those of white women.[5] This significant rise in the earnings of black women is largely due to the fact that black women workers are today no longer confined chiefly to domestic service jobs, but have moved into a wider range of occupations (Albelda, 1983). Approaching parity with white women does not exactly guarantee financial security, but for black women it nevertheless represents substantial improvement. Offsetting the benefits of this gain, how-

23

Table 1.4. Employment and Average Hourly Earnings by Industry, Ranked by Proportion of Women Workers from Highest to Lowest, July 1982

Industry	All employees (in thousands)	Women workers (in thousands)	Percentage of women workers	Average hourly earnings[a]	Rank of proportion of women workers	Rank of average hourly earnings
Apparel and other textile products	1,095.9	897.9	81.9	$5.18	1	50
Health services	5,820.8	4,732.9	81.3	7.01	2	36
Banking	1,667.8	1,180.6	70.8	5.80	3	46
Apparel and accessory stores	948.9	664.1	70.0	4.85	4	51
Credit agencies other than banks	587.7	409.7	69.7	5.99	5	43
Legal services	583.6	404.7	69.3	8.75	6	21
General merchandise stores	2,193.8	1,447.9	66.0	5.40	7	47
Insurance carriers	1,230.5	745.9	60.6	7.70	8	30
Leather and leather products	195.7	117.8	60.2	5.31	9	49
Eating and drinking places	4,883.2	2,746.9	56.3	4.06	10	52
Miscellaneous retail	1,950.1	1,058.6	54.3	5.36	11	48
Textile mill products	727.0	349.0	48.0	5.81	12	45
Miscellaneous manufacturing industries	378.4	171.4	45.3	6.40	13	38
Communication	1,397.8	627.8	44.9	10.01	14	14
Food stores	2,463.2	1,072.7	43.5	7.25	15	34
Business services	3,304.1	1,436.7	43.5	7.03	16	35
Electric and electronic equipment	2,004.7	852.3	42.5	8.18	17	25
Instruments and related products	708.3	299.8	42.3	8.30	18	23
Amusement and recreation services	976.3	402.1	41.2	5.87	19	44
Motion pictures	227.6	92.5	40.6	8.22	20	24
Printing and publishing	1,262.4	511.2	40.5	8.72	21	22
Tobacco manufacturing	60.8	22.0	36.2	10.32	22	11
Rubber and miscellaneous plastics products	689.8	240.5	34.9	7.67	23	31
Furniture and home furnishings stores	586.5	200.3	34.2	6.20	24	41

Industry					
Miscellaneous services	1,069.0	363.0	34.0	10.22	25	13
Furniture and fixtures	429.1	129.1	30.1	6.33	26	39
Food and kindred products	1,672.9	492.0	29.4	7.87	27	29
Wholesale trade—nondurable goods	2,188.0	625.0	28.6	8.17	28	26
Chemicals and allied products	1,075.0	280.7	26.1	10.01	29	15
Building materials and garden supplies	598.6	155.0	25.9	6.02	30	42
Local and interurban passenger transit	230.0	57.4	25.0	7.43	31	33
Wholesale trade—durable goods	3,126.0	766.0	24.5	7.99	32	28
Paper and allied products	659.4	149.1	22.6	9.40	33	16
Machinery, except electrical	2,262.3	476.0	21.0	9.31	34	17
Fabricated metal products	1,426.9	299.8	21.0	8.85	35	20
Electric, gas, and sanitary services	881.3	174.7	19.8	10.70	36	8
Miscellaneous repair services	296.3	58.7	19.8	8.00	37	27
Stone, clay, and glass products	598.1	114.1	19.4	8.93	38	19
Automotive dealers and service stations	1,659.6	319.8	19.3	6.28	39	40
Auto repair, services, and garages	582.0	100.6	17.3	6.68	40	37
Transportation equipment	1,738.6	285.5	16.4	11.26	41	7
Oil and gas extraction	710.6	112.7	15.9	10.43	42	9
Petroleum and coal products	209.3	32.0	15.3	12.40	43	2
Lumber and wood products	630.8	91.3	14.5	7.63	44	32
Trucking and warehousing	1,209.6	153.8	12.7	10.26	45	12
General building contractors	1,039.5	122.1	11.7	10.41	46	10
Primary metal industries	909.1	105.8	11.6	11.38	47	6
Metal mining	64.8	6.3	9.7	12.24	48	3
Special trade contractors	2,195.4	199.0	9.1	12.08	49	4
Nonmetallic minerals, except fuels	118.1	9.5	8.0	8.94	50	18
Heavy construction contracting	913.6	66.2	7.2	11.47	51	5
Bituminous coal and lignite mining	229.5	11.7	5.1	13.05	52	1

Source: U.S. Department of Labor, Bureau of Labor Statistics, *The female-male earnings gap: A review of employment and earnings issues*, Report 673, September 1982, p. 7.

[a] Average hourly earnings are for all production and nonsupervisory workers.

Table 1.5.   Families in Poverty, by Race and Female Householder (in thousands)

	All Races			White			Black		
	Total	no. in poverty	% in poverty	Total	no. in poverty	% in poverty	Total	no. in poverty	% in poverty
All families with children under 18 years	32,587	5,191	15.9	27,223	3,362	12.4	4,455	1,652	37.1
Families with female householder, no husband	6,488	2,877	44.3	4,237	1,564	36.9	2,118	1,261	59.5
Female-headed households/All families	19.9%	55.4%		15.5%	46.5%		47.5%	76.3%	

SOURCE: U.S. Department of Commerce, Bureau of the Census, *Current population reports Characteristics of the population below the poverty level: 1981,* Table 18, p. 73.

ever, are the serious financial strains caused by changes in family structure, the erosion of community services, and the fact that even incomes approaching those of white women are inadequate to the needs of many families. Families maintained by black women alone comprise nearly 48 percent of all black families. For white families, the analogous figure is but less than 16 percent (see Table 1.5).

Changes in the structure of employment, when combined with ongoing changes in the family and in community services, help to define the economic context for women. The transformation of the family has a dynamic of its own that is beyond the scope of this paper, but family arrangements are to some extent influenced by, and in turn influence, the employment opportunities and decisions of family members. Marital status and number of dependents are among the factors affecting the income needs of women, while both the race and the class of a working woman will in part determine her prospects within the present structure of available jobs.

Married women are affected by both the changes in their own employment prospects and by changes in the employment status and earnings of their husbands. The erosion of middle-income jobs for men, particularly in the high-wage blue collar area but also in lower and middle management in the hardest-hit industries, is pointing toward the demise of the "family wage" for all but high-income professionals. While many male workers (particularly black workers) have never had access to a job paying wages that could support a family, some unionized manufacturing jobs had allowed even blue-collar families to achieve a significant level of material comfort without requiring paid labor on the part of the wife. Today, however, the wife who is not in the paid labor force, although by no means extinct, is a member of a shrinking population. Similarly, the aspirations of a blue-collar family that could once have ascended to a middle-class standard of living on the basis of incomes from two manufacturing jobs are now threatened.

Because of the inability of family incomes to keep pace with rising costs—recall that median family incomes fell 11 percent between 1973 and 1983 (U.S. Department of Commerce, 1983:9)—women's labor force participation is increasingly important in maintaining family income. Whether through the failure of wages to keep abreast of inflation, or through unemployment, or through the "skidding" characteristic of many displaced male workers in high-wage industries, a significant part of the increased labor force participation of married women is propelled by sheer economic need. While women also have other motivations for seeking paid employment, in 1981 a married couple (intact) family had a 3.2 percent chance of being in poverty if both the husband and the wife worked, and a 10 percent chance if the husband alone was the breadwinner (Terry, 1983:15).

Married women with husbands who live in the same household, however, are only 55 percent of the female population over age fifteen. In 1981, approximately one in five families was maintained by a woman (recall Table 1.5). The ratio of divorced persons who have not remarried to married persons more than doubled between 1970 and 1981 (U.S. Department of Commerce, 1981a:1), and one out of five children under eighteen lived in one-parent families in the latter year compared with one in eight in the former (U.S. Department

27

of Commerce, 1981a:2). By 1984, more than one-quarter of all families with children under eighteen were headed by a single parent (U.S. Department of Commerce, 1984:1). The economic prospects of women earners are thus becoming increasingly important to family welfare in the United States. While married couple families have more latitude in which to adjust their labor force participation to meet prevailing economic circumstances, female heads of households have less flexibility and as these figures show they are an increasingly important part of the population.

As a result of poor earnings prospects, the growth in female-headed families, and the shortage of affordable day care, an increasing proportion of the impoverished are found in families headed by women—the so-called "feminization of poverty." In 1960, only 21 percent of all poor persons lived in female-headed families; by 1981 the proportion was 44 percent (U.S. Department of Commerce, 1981b:7–8). Of the total number of families in poverty, female-headed families comprised more than half, although they are only 20 percent of all families (U.S. Department of Commerce, 1981b:2; 1983:60). For black female-headed families the poverty figure rises to 60 percent, while even for white female-headed families it is 37 percent.

Because of the job opportunities available to many women, employment itself does not always allow a family to escape poverty. Of all female-headed families with related children under eighteen, 27 percent were still in poverty in 1981, despite the fact that the mother worked an average of thirty-one weeks during the year. Even full-time, full-year work is not sufficient for some to escape poverty. One in twelve female-headed families where the mother worked full-time throughout the entire year remained impoverished in 1981 (U.S. Department of Commerce, 1981b:106).

These statistics reflect the fact that the wage a woman earns is often not a "family wage." Six of the twenty fastest growing occupations paid a weekly wage in 1981 that was below 125 percent of the poverty level for a family that consists of a single parent and two children under age eighteen. As a result, nearly half of the largest job-producing occupations that are majority-female have a wage that is scarcely adequate to support even a small family (recall Table 1.2).

CONCLUSION

The world economy is undergoing a substantial restructuring, which in the United States has led to the "deindustrialization" of certain key economic sectors and the displacement of thousands of workers, particularly men of moderate income. At the same time, the expansion of the service sector has brought a proliferation of relatively low-wage jobs in occupations and industries that employ disproportionate numbers of women. The changing structure of employment is such that one can expect to see in the future not only more jobs for women and proportionately fewer jobs for men, but also an emerging inequality, if not dualism, in the distribution of earned income within the United States. With growth in the upper-level professional and managerial tier and legions of new marginal, low-wage part-time slots at the lower end of the scale, it is the "middle" of the distribution—the jobs that pay a modest family wage—that is being most rapidly eroded by changes in the economic structure.

The shrinking of the middle suggests that in the future even fewer families will have access to a comfortable family standard of living. Class barriers to financial security are likely to be reinforced. Workers who, because of gender, race, and other factors, have rarely managed to leave lower-tier employment will find their ranks swelled with downwardly mobile families and individuals. Remedies such as affirmative action, important as they are, cannot address problems in the overall job structure of the economy. For large numbers of women trapped in low-wage dead-end employment, the middle-level jobs that could allow them to advance simply will not exist.

The increase in families maintained by a woman, combined with the shrinking earnings of displaced male workers, means that men's wages are declining in importance as a source of women's income. Among married couple families (still the majority of all families), those where wives worked earned 20 percent more in 1960 than those where wives did not work. By 1980, the differential had risen to 29 percent, reflecting the increasing importance of women's wages in families (U.S. Department of Commerce, 1982–1983:434). The percentage of women who have no access to male incomes is growing rapidly, and families maintained by women alone are far more likely to be in poverty than other families, particularly if the female householder is black. Many women have always needed to work, but the importance of female wage income for the population as a whole has never been greater. The possibility that, in the restructured domestic economy, a proliferation of female-typed jobs could disguise serious underemployment among women is thus not just a problem for women but a problem for all of us.

Notes

THIS CHAPTER was prepared for the Conference on "Women and Structural Transformation: The Crisis of Work and Family Life" sponsored by the Institute for Research on Women at Rutgers University, 18–19 November 1983. It was extensively rewritten for inclusion in this volume of readings. We would like to thank Teresa Amott, Bennett Harrison, Heidi Hartmann, and Lucy Gorham for their assistance in developing some of the ideas in this paper.

1. These statistics are based on Bureau of Labor Statistics *Employment and Earnings* data through 1984 and rely on Bureau of Economic Analysis industrial categories for the selection of the seventy-four industries under investigation. These seventy-four manufacturing industries employed 83 percent of all U.S. manufacturing workers in 1984.

2. Calculated from U.S. Bureau of Labor Statistics, *Employment and Earnings Statistics for the United States, 1909–1967* (Washington, D.C.: Government Printing Office, 1968) and U.S. Bureau of Labor Statistics, *Employment and Earnings* (Washington D.C.: Government Printing Office, March 1985) p. 39.

3. The national one percent Longitudinal Employer-Employee Data File (LEED) contains approximately 1.5 million records, each comprising the complete Social Security covered work history for an individual for the period 1957–1975. The large size of the data set and the rich longitudinal employment data make this file useful for tracing tenure and job turnover, earnings trajectories for groups of workers, and for generating industry earnings profiles for various years. Unfortunately, this file is not available for the period following 1975.

4. These statistics are calculated from data found in the Council of Economic Advisers, *Economic Report of the President, 1983* (Washington, D.C.: Government Printing Office, 1983) Table B–31, p. 199.

5. See, for example, U.S. Department of Labor, Women's Bureau, "Twenty Facts on Women Workers," no date (although some of the data given are for 1981).

Reference List

Albelda, Randy Pearl. 1983. Black and white women workers in the post–World War II period. Ph.D. dissertation, University of Massachusetts-Amherst.

Appelbaum, Eileen, 1983. The future of work: Expectations and realities. Department of Economics, Temple University. Photocopy.

Bendick, Marc, Jr. 1982. The role of public programs and private markets in reemploying workers dislocated by economic change. *The Urban Institute* (November).

Birnbaum, Birny, and Chris Tilly. 1985. The declining middle: Baby boom or structural bust? Department of Urban Studies and Planning, M.I.T. Typescript.

Bluestone, Barry, Patricia Hanna, Sarah Kuhn, and Laura Moore. 1981. *The retail revolution: Market transformation, investment, and labor in the modern department store.* Boston: Auburn House.

Bluestone, Barry, Bennett Harrison, and Lucy Gorham. 1984. Storm clouds on the horizon: Labor market crisis and industrial policy. Brookline, Mass.: Economic Education Project.

Harrison, Bennett. 1982. Rationalization, restructuring, and industrial reorganization in older regions: The economic transformation of New England since World War II. Joint Center for Urban Studies, M.I.T.–Harvard Universities, Working Paper No. 72 (February).

Henle, Peter, and Paul Ryscavage. 1980. The distribution of earned income among men and women, 1958–77. *Monthly Labor Review* 103 (April).

Jacobson, Louis S. 1978. Earnings losses of workers displaced from manufacturing industries. In *The impact of international trade and investment on unemployment,* ed. William G. Dewald. Washington, D.C.: GPO.

Jacobson, Louis S. 1979. Earnings loss due to displacement. The Public Research Institute of the Center for Naval Analyses, Working Paper CRC–385 (April).

Lawrence, Robert Z. 1982. Deindustrialization and U.S. international competitiveness: Domestic and international forces in U.S. industrial performance, 1970–1980. *The Brookings Institution* Mimeo. (19 October).

Lawrence, Robert Z. 1984. Sectoral shifts and the size of the middle class. *The Brookings Review* 3 (Fall).

Pear, Robert. 1983. Earnings gap is narrowing slightly for women. *New York Times* (3 October).

Rosenthal, Neal H. 1985. The shrinking middle class: Myth or reality? *Monthly Labor Review,* 108 (March).

Schultze, Charles L. 1983. Industrial policy: A dissent. *The Brookings Review* 2 (Fall):3–12.

Taub, Leon, 1983. The deindustrialization of the United States? *Chase Econometrics* (Fall) Newsletter to Clients.

Terry, Sylvia Lazos. 1983. Work experience, earnings, and family income in 1981. *Monthly Labor Review* 106 (April).

U.S. Department of Commerce. Bureau of the Census. 1981a. Marital status and living arrangements: March 1981. *Current population reports: Population characteristics,* Series P–20, No. 372. Washington, D.C.: GPO.

U.S. Department of Commerce. Bureau of the Census. 1981b. Characteristics of the population below the poverty level: 1981. *Current population reports: Consumer income,* Series P–60, No. 138. Washington, D.C.: GPO.

U.S. Department of Commerce. Bureau of the Census. 1982–1983. *Statistical abstract of the United States, 1982–1983.* Washington, D.C.: GPO.

U.S. Department of Commerce. Bureau of the Census. 1983. Money income of households, families, and persons in the United States: 1983. *Current population reports: Consumer income,* Series P–60, No. 146. Washington, D.C.: GPO.

U.S. Department of Commerce. Bureau of the Census. 1984. Household and family characteristics: March 1984. *Current population reports: Population characteristics,* Series P–20, No. 398. Washington, D.C.: GPO.

2

Changes in Women's Economic and Family Roles in Post–World War II United States

Heidi I. Hartmann

In this essay I describe some of the changes that have occurred in the living arrangements of women and men since World War II. Together with changes in women's labor force participation and in their economic activity generally, these recent changes suggest fundamental alterations in gender relations. These changes have been dramatic and hold the potential for further, perhaps more sweeping, changes in the relations between women and men.

A great deal can be said about the effect on women of changes in the economic structure. The current structural transformation of the economy, sometimes viewed as a set of long-term trends in motion since World War II and sometimes viewed as a short-term economic crisis of recent origin, can be held responsible for the feminization of poverty, the high divorce rate, the increased labor force participation of women, and a host of other changes affecting how we live our intimate lives.

While many decry these changes, particularly for their supposed negative impact on women, children, and families, I argue that on the whole the economic changes of the past several decades have been positive for women. Women in advanced industrialized countries today have more access to economic resources independently of men than ever before in human history. They have more control over the conditions of their lives, and probably have a higher standard of living relative to men than at any time previously. Of course, I do not deny that the recent economic downturns (in 1980 and 1982),

33

coupled with cutbacks in social welfare programs, have affected women negatively. I argue only that they have not erased the progress of the past thirty to forty years. Confining my analysis to the United States, I will attempt to show how this general progress has occurred and demonstrate the potential for further, positive changes in women's status, as gender relations continue to evolve and to affect economic change as well.

RECENT ECONOMIC CHANGES

In order to describe the economic context for gender relations since World War II, let me digress for a moment to summarize some of the economic changes that have occurred during this period. In my view, the current economic situation has its roots in long-term economic and political changes within the United States as well as changes in the position of the United States relative to other countries in the postwar period. The current retrenchment of social welfare spending in the Reagan administration is at least partly a reflection of a U.S. economy that has been experiencing difficulty for some time. Most obvious among the long-term changes have been the decline in U.S. military hegemony since WW II; the deterioration of U.S. leadership in the international economy; increasing competition for world markets in manufactured goods from Western Europe, Japan, and other countries; increasing demands from third world providers of raw materials; and the movement of U.S. capital to more profitable production sites abroad. The competitive difficulties of U.S. manufacturing have contributed to the continuing decline in the proportion of manufacturing in the GNP and to the increase in output that originates in services. Many have argued that this shift to services is necessarily accompanied by a decline in average wages and a tendency toward a bifurcated income distribution (Bluestone and Harrison, 1983; Bluestone, Harrison, and Gorham, 1984; AFL–CIO, 1984).

These structural changes are reflected in a remarkable lack of economic progress for many people, at least on some indicators. Real incomes have not risen for U.S. families since 1970, although they rose substantially in the decade of the 1960s. Unemployment in 1982–84 was at its highest levels since the Great Depression.

This uneven economic performance, increases in military spending, and the tax cuts of Reagan's "supply-side" national fiscal and monetary policies have combined to produce an enormous deficit in the federal budget accounts. Though they are certainly exacerbated by the current administration's policies, the factors generating pressure for cuts in social welfare spending have a longer history. Federal social welfare outlays as a proportion of GNP actually peaked in 1976 at 12.1 percent, the year Carter was elected (Erie, Rein, and Wiget, 1983). Even with cuts in discretionary programs and slower growth in entitlements such as social security, the deficit looms large and is expected to remain so if tax policy or military spending policy is not reversed or moderated. Both continuing to live with a large deficit and taking drastic action to reduce it threaten prospects for sustained economic recovery. The long-term roots of the current fiscal crisis, then, lie in the generalized restructuring of the U.S. economy that has occurred over the past several decades. The future capacities of the U.S. economy are unclear, but the public expectation of substantial social welfare spending that has been generated by public programs developed over this same period is likely to create continued demand for social services, despite current pressures to reduce the deficit.

The real change in social welfare spending comes not from the recent Reagan cutbacks but from the previous, more gradual evolution that increased federal social welfare spending from 4 percent of GNP in 1950 to 11.5 percent in 1979 (Erie, Rein and Wiget, 1983). This long-term growth in social welfare spending has had significant effects on women's abilities to live independently of men outside of traditional families. The current cutbacks, I think, have to be seen not only as an attempt to discipline labor generally by reducing the social wage (an attempt made necessary by long-term economic difficulties), but also as an attempt to reassert patriarchal control and to turn back gains made by women in this same period. Reductions in social programs have the effect of forcing many back into traditional family forms for economic support, health care, child care, and so on. It must be recognized that the dynamics of state policy stem from gender struggle as well as from class conflict. Social structures and social policies have these dual determinants.

RECENT DEMOGRAPHIC CHANGES

Equally as striking as the postwar changes in U.S. economic structure and economic position vis-à-vis other countries are the postwar demographic changes that have occurred in fertility, family and household formation, and women's labor force participation in the United States. Briefly stated, since 1950 women are delaying marriage and childbearing, having fewer children over their lifetimes, and spending more time over their lifetimes living alone or as heads of their own households—living neither with parents or husbands. And, of course, women's participation in the labor force is at an all-time high. Let us look at some of these changes in more detail.

It continues to be true that by far the vast majority of women, and men, marry. For those between the ages of thirty-five and forty-four in 1980, over 90 percent had been or were currently married, a proportion that represents a modest increase since 1900 for both men and women. But compared to the immediate postwar baby-boom years, marriage is increasingly being delayed. For example, of those women between the ages of twenty and twenty-four, about 30 percent had never married in 1950; by 1980, fully 45 percent had not. Young women thus have more time before marriage to pursue higher education or work in the labor market than they had in 1950 and more time to live on their own (but they continue to have less such time than men, who marry on the average 2.5 years later) (Bianchi and Spain, 1984).

Divorce, as well as marriage, is now more prevalent than it was in 1950. Although the total rate of marital dissolution (death and divorce) has been fairly stable for the past one hundred years, divorce rates have generally increased as death rates have declined. Divorce rates were relatively constant in the postwar period until about 1965; since 1965 divorce rates have more than doubled. It is estimated that half of first marriages now occurring will end in divorce.

Table 2.1. **Distribution of Households across Family Types, March 1984**

	Number (thousands)	Percent
All households	85,407	100%
All families	61,997	72.4
All families with children less than 18 years old	31,046	36.3
Married couples with children	24,339	28.5
only husband in labor force	9,362	11.0
only wife in labor force	489	0.6
both husband and wife in labor force	13,899	16.3
neither husband nor wife in labor force	590	0.7
Female head with children less than 18 years old	5,907	6.9
Male head with children less than 18 years old	0.799	0.9
All families without children less than 18 years old	30,951	36.1
Married couples, no children	25,751	30.1
Female head, no children	3,971	4.6
Male head, no children	1,229	1.4
All nonfamilies	23,410	27.4
Female head	13,658	15.9
living alone	12,425	14.5
with nonfamily	1,233	1.5
Male head	9,752	11.4
living alone	7,529	8.8
with nonfamily	2,223	2.6
(All living alone)	(19,954)	(23.3)

SOURCE: U.S. Bureau of the Census, 1985b: tables 5, 18, 21; pp. 87–92, 171, 200.
NOTE: Of married couples with children, 38% have only the husband in the labor force, and in 57%, both husband and wife are in the labor force.

And although remarriage is common, the proportion of adult women who were currently married declined from 67 percent in 1950 to 59 percent in 1980 (Bianchi and Spain, 1984). The decline has been greater for black women than for white women. Espenshade (1985) recently estimated that a black woman, on the average, can now expect to spend only 22 percent of her life in marriage and a white women only 43 percent.

Coupled with the fact that women live longer than men, and thus are likely to find themselves alone at the older end of the age range, these data regarding delayed marriage and increased divorce combine to generate a very large increase in the proportion of women

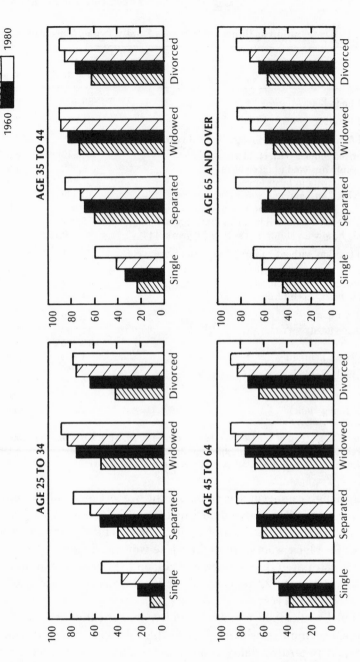

Figure 2.1. Percentage of Women Maintaining Households: 1950–1980

Source: Bianchi and Spain, 1984: fig. 2

living alone and/or not in families. The proportion of all households that were one-person households increased from 13 percent of the total in 1950 to 22 percent in 1980 (Kitagawa, 1981). As Table 2.1 shows, of 20 million single-person households in 1984, nearly two-thirds were women living alone (U.S. Bureau of the Census, 1985b). The increase in living alone is occurring at all ages but is particularly striking for the youngest and oldest women. Between 1940 and 1970, for young women eighteen to twenty-four years of age, the proportion living outside families (either alone or with unrelated individuals) increased from 11 to 17 percent of all women in that age group. For older women, those over sixty-five, the proportions living alone more than doubled, from 13.3 percent to 33.4 percent (Kobrin, 1976a and 1976b). As Figure 2.1 shows, women in all unmarried statuses at all ages are increasingly heading their own households.

During the same period, women have also experienced a decrease in the time spent over their life cycles in childbearing and childrearing. More women are having children, but they are having them later and closer together and are having fewer of them. For example, although childlessness has declined for all women, women between twenty-five and twenty-nine had twice the childlessness rate in 1980 as in 1960 (Bianchi and Spain, 1984). Between 1950 and 1980 the total fertility rate fell from 3.1 children per woman to 1.8, well below the 2.1 rate necessary for population replacement. For most women, childbearing has become increasingly compressed within a span of only a few years' duration.

With the increase in nonmarriage, a significant and growing proportion of women are bearing children outside marriage. Between 1940 and 1970, the fertility rate for unmarried women between the ages of fifteen and forty-four rose from seven births per 1,000 women to twenty-six per 1,000; the increase in extramarital fertility occurred at all ages. Since 1970 there has been some slowing in the rate of increase, and even in some years actual decreases in extramarital fertility rates for some demographic groups. But the number and proportion of childbirths outside marriage has continued to increase, as the number of unmarried women has also increased and fertility within marriage has decreased. Differences between black and white women are especially striking with respect to extramarital fertility. Between 1940 and 1976, the number of births per 1,000 un-

Table 2.2.   **Teenage Birth Rate and Out-of-Wedlock Birth Rate, by Race (Births per thousand females aged 15 to 18)**

Race	1982		1970	
	Birth rate	Out of wedlock	Birth rate	Out of wedlock
All races	53	29	68	22
White	45	18	57	11
Black	97	87	148	97

SOURCE: Moore, 1985: table 2.

married women between the ages of fifteen and forty-four rose from four to thirteen for white women and from thirty-six to eighty-three for blacks. In 1976, 50 percent of all the births that occurred to black women occurred outside marriage; for whites the figure was 8 percent (Kitagawa, 1981). Although extramarital fertility has increased over this period for both black and white women, it is important to remember that fertility has decreased for black women just as it has for white women; in fact their fertility rates are converging (Hogan, 1983).

Recently, considerable media and public policy attention has been paid to teenage pregnancy. Actually, fertility has been falling among teenagers just as it has been for all women (see Table 2.2). But fertility outside marriage has increased for young white women (while, since 1970, it has decreased for blacks). Despite this convergence in extramarital birth rates among black and white teenagers, the levels are very much higher for blacks. As shown in Table 2.2, in 1982 for black teenagers the rate was eighty-seven births per 1,000 unmarried females aged fifteen to nineteen, while for whites it was eighteen per 1,000.

To some extent the greater fertility outside marriage and at younger ages of blacks compared to whites represents a different order of marriage and parenting. For first marriages between 1970 and 1974, for example, 38 percent of black women experienced childbirth before marriage compared to 6 percent of white women. As noted above, however, black women can nevertheless expect to spend less of their lifetimes in marriage and fewer of them will marry than white women. Recent estimates suggest that marriage over a lifetime will occur at a lower rate for black women than for white (77 percent versus 92 percent; Hogan, 1983).

The racial differences in fertility and marriage result in the by now familiar statistic that many more black children than white live with their mothers only. Among blacks, more children under eighteen now live with their mothers only than with both parents (Bianchi and Spain, 1984). Among all families with children under eighteen in 1984, 48.8 percent are single-parent-female among blacks, in contrast to 14.7 percent among whites (U.S. Bureau of the Census, 1985b: Table 5). Because early childbirth has negative consequences for women's educational attainments and lifetime earnings, and because black women may face greater labor market barriers than white women, rates of poverty are approximately double among black single-parent-female families than white ones (in 1982, 56 percent versus 28 percent), and of course the incidence of poverty is higher for single-parent-female families (40 percent in 1982) than for husband-wife or single-parent-male (9 percent in 1982) (Ford Foundation, 1985: Table 3).

As noted, however, the tendency for women to form and head households on their own has increased tremendously over the past thirty years in all age groups across all nonmarried statuses (see Figure 2.1). And while heading families or households means poverty for some women, in general the tendency to form households is associated with the increases in economic well-being that make it possible, particularly the large increases in the labor force participation of women of all ages. Even the fact that young women with early first births establish their own households rather than live with their parents can be seen as an indicator of increased resources. And although a larger proportion of poor families are headed by women alone than heretofore (48 percent in 1979 versus 23 percent in 1959), actually a decreasing proportion of such households are poor. In 1959, 42.6 percent of families headed by women alone were poor; twenty years later the percent of such families who were poor had fallen to 30.4 (U.S. Bureau of the Census, 1985a: Table 1).

In sum, the experiences of marriage and childbearing have become more universal for women over the course of the twentieth century (and for childbearing, particularly since 1940), but as fertility has fallen and divorce has increased, living in families and raising children has become limited to a shorter period of the average woman's life. A substantial and increasing proportion of women raise children in households that do not include a husband or male partner. At any point in time, fewer people are living in marriages. Overall between 1950 and 1980, husband-wife couples decreased from 78 percent of all households to 61 percent (Bianchi and Spain, 1984). Single-person households have increased dramatically, and increasing numbers of couples are living in nonmarriage relationships. Thus, a general diversification of family and household types has occurred. Table 2.1 provides a general overview of family and household structure in the United States in 1984. (We cannot tell, of course, from the census data on which these figures are based to what extent people maintain important familial ties beyond households with either blood or fictive kin.)

Over this same period, as women's fertility has declined and household types have diversified, women's educational attainment and labor force participation have increased dramatically. Changes in educational attainment for women in the post—World War II period have been less dramatic than changes in labor force participation, but nonetheless substantial. For example, women have historically

Table 2.3. **Percentage of Bachelor's Degrees Awarded to Women by Discipline, 1966 and 1981, Selected Fields**

Discipline	1966 (%)	1981 (%)		1966 (%)	1981 (%)
Agriculture	2.7	30.8	Health	76.9	83.5
Architecture	4.0	18.3	Home economics	97.5	95.0
Biological sciences	28.2	44.1	Mathematics	33.3	42.8
Computer and information			Physical sciences	13.6	24.6
sciences	13.0[a]	32.5	Psychology	41.0	65.0
Education	75.3	75.0	Social sciences	35.0	44.2
Engineering	0.4	10.3	Economics	9.8	30.5
English and English			History	34.6	37.9
literature	66.2	66.5	Sociology	59.6	69.6
Foreign languages	70.7	75.6	All fields	39.9	49.8

SOURCES: U.S. Department of Health, Education and Welfare, Office of Education, "Earned Degrees Conferred: 1965–66"; U.S. Department of Education, National Center for Education Statistics, "Earned Degrees Conferred, 1980–81."
[a]Data are for 1969, the earliest year available.

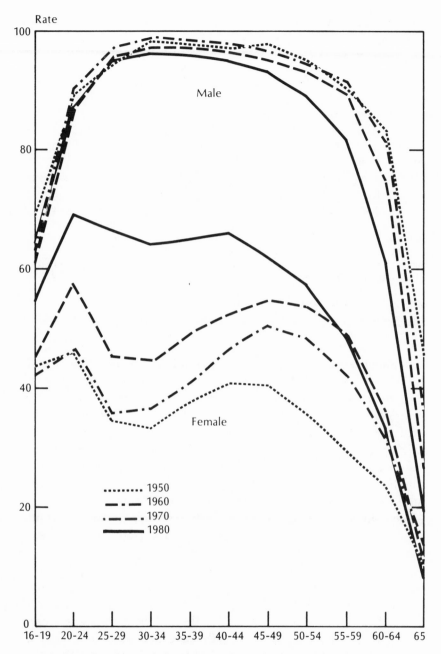

Figure 2.2. Labor Force Participation Rates, by Age and Sex: 1950 to 1980
Source: Bianchi and Spain, 1984: fig. 4

Table 2.4. **Labor Force Participation Rate of Women**

Year	Birth cohort	20–24	25–29	30–34	35–39	40–44	45–49	50–54	55–59	60–64	65–69	70
						Age group						
1955	1931–35	46.0	35.3	34.7	39.2	44.1	45.9	41.5	35.6	29.0	17.8	6.
1960	1936–40	46.2	35.7	36.3	40.8	46.8	50.7	48.8	42.2	31.4	17.6	6.
1965	1941–45	50.0	38.9	38.2	43.6	48.5	51.7	50.1	47.1	34.0	17.4	6.
1970	1946–50	57.8	45.2	44.7	49.2	52.9	55.0	53.8	49.0	36.1	17.3	5.
1975	1951–55	64.1	57.0	51.7	54.9	56.8	55.9	53.3	47.9	33.3	14.5	4.
1980	1956–60	69.2	66.8	64.1	64.9	66.1	62.1	57.8	48.6	33.3	14.7	4.
1985	1961–65	71.8	71.4	70.3	71.7	71.9	67.8	60.8	50.3	33.4	15.1	4.

SOURCES: For 1955–1975: U.S. Department of Labor, Bureau of Labor Statistics. *Perspectives (
working women: A Data Book.* Bulletin 2080. (Washington, D.C.: Government Printing Offic
October 1980.) For 1980 and 1985: Employment and Earnings, January 1981 (Annual Da
table 3). Employment and Earnings, January 1986 (Annual Data table 3).
NOTE: Labor Force Participation Rates of Women, 20 years and over, by age, annual average
selected years, 1955–1979.

had lower college completion rates than men, but by 1981 college
enrollment rates were approximately equal for men and women, and
the subjects they study have also been converging (see Table 2.3). In
1980, nearly half the bachelor's and master's degrees conferred were
awarded to women; by 1985, women earned over a third of the doc-
toral degrees—a substantial increase over 1950. For the population
over age twenty-five, a statistic that reflects past as well as current
trends, 20 percent of the men versus 13 percent of the women have
completed college (these proportions have approximately tripled
since 1950 for both sexes) (Bianchi and Spain, 1984).

Labor force participation rates, it is now well known, have increased dramatically since 1950 for every age group of women except those over age sixty-five (see Figure 2.2). And increases have
been greatest among women of childbearing age and among women
who have children under six (their rate of labor force participation
has nearly quadrupled). As Table 2.4 indicates, there is no longer a
dip in labor force participation during the childbearing years. Average expected years of work at birth have increased from twelve
years to twenty-nine years between 1940 and 1979–80 (Smith, 1982
and 1985). Women, collectively, are earning more money than ever

44

before (even though their average earnings relative to men have not increased), simply because more women are in the labor force for more of their lives than formerly. Women are thus contributing more financially to the support of themselves and their families; many are entirely self-supporting. Through increased labor force participation, women probably have access to more economic resources, independently from men, than ever before in human history.

INTERPRETATION OF CHANGE

One response to all these changes is to certify a family crisis and to bemoan the increased exploitation of women who must support households and children on their own or who bear the brunt of the speed-up that occurs when both adults must work outside the home. But another interpretation, one that I develop and support, is to see these changes as largely positive for women because they contribute to women's increased autonomy from men and their increased economic independence, whether or not they live with men. These changes probably raise women's own standards of living, since having their own sources of income probably allows them literally to spend more money on themselves. As Barbara Bergmann has pointed out, even though women earn less than men, their own earnings can bring them a standard of living comparable to that provided by men in the 1950s. Even with respect to total hours worked by women (housework plus wagework), women are probably better off now than they were just ten years ago. When women enter the labor market, total time spent working increases because wage work is added to housework: even though time spent on housework decreases substantially (from about fifty-five hours to thirty-five hours per week), the combined total represents a work week of about sixty-five to seventy hours. In the past few years, however, several studies show that housework time for working women has fallen, not because husbands are picking up more, but because women are simply doing less (Hartmann, 1981b).

It is somewhat risky, of course, to infer a great deal about changes in gender relations from aggregate data such as these. My argument

45

amounts to saying that patriarchy is weakening, and that women have benefited from these observed changes in living arrangments. But not all women have benefited equally. The fact that single black women who head households with children on their own are especially likely to be in poverty raises the issue of interpretation starkly. Does this greater autonomy from men represent choice or necessity? Is family break-up caused by poverty? Does it result from abandonment by men? These are important issues that the available research cannot yet resolve. Nevertheless, I believe my argument is sustained in its main points by what we now know.

Increased Autonomy for Women

The changes observed in the aggregate demographic data support the contention that changes in the degree, extent, and form of male domination have occurred. Three types of changes are considered: the trend toward nonmarriage and toward women maintaining households alone; the changes within marriage; and changes in responsibility for children.

First, as we have seen, the diversification of family forms has led to women having greater autonomy from men in their living situations; this is reflected in larger numbers of women living alone or heading families. The choice to maintain an independent household as a single woman has become common and socially acceptable. Only a minority of divorced women headed their own households in 1950, but most do so now. The possibility of "doubling-up" or living with other family members still exists, but it is no longer necessary. With the elderly, we have come to recognize and accept their desire to be independent, to live separately from adult children. Surely the average thirty-year-old divorced woman prefers to live on her own, too, rather than with her parents, for example. That more do live on their own, then, seems to be a superior choice, "revealed preferred," as an economist would say, chosen in preference to not doing so. Even among low-income women, maintaining a household on one's own generally became more possible over this period. A review of the literature on the impact of welfare policies on household formation shows that welfare programs do facilitate the establishment of a household once a new family has been formed, although they do not generally encourage births (Wilson and Neckerman, 1985). As further evidence of the impact of increased resources, the cutbacks in social welfare programs after 1981 were observed to coincide with a decrease in the rate of new household formation among young adults.

If it is relatively easy to conclude that maintaining one's own household once one becomes a single parent or is divorced is a preferred choice, it is more difficult to say that divorce itself, or parenthood without a male partner, is a result of choice, especially choice by women. Yet here too I would argue that evidence suggests it often is a woman's choice. First, divorce has increased over time as incomes have risen. People seem to want more divorce when they can afford it. The negative income tax experiments of the late 1960s indicate that guaranteed incomes did increase the rate of separation and divorce among poor families. In essence, the income supplement allowed many to escape from unsatisfactory marriages. More recently, Bane (1985) has found that for black women, undergoing a transition to a single-parent-female household is not associated with a transition to poverty status in a majority of cases; rather, poor black women heading their own households tended to be poor in their prior households as well. This finding suggests that it is not abandonment by males that makes these women poor. Rather, given their poverty, many apparently choose to live apart from men and head their own households. And as Petchesky (1984) notes, the increased tendency for unmarried teenage women who have become pregnant to raise their babies on their own (if they decide not to terminate their pregnancies) is an indicator of their increased freedom not to be forced into unwanted early marriages. While some young women may want to catch a man and marry, many do not, nor do they choose abortions or adoption. Instead, they apparently believe that they have the capability to raise and support a child. Many older, single, professional women are choosing to have children without men (as noted, extramarital fertility is increasing for women of all ages). And women with the highest incomes and the best educations have the highest rates of divorce. In my opinion, these developments are on the whole indicators of the preferences of many women for an unmarried state. We also know that women living without men do less housework, with and without children; the presence of

47

men in the household seems to create about eight hours of additional housework for women per week (Hartmann, 1981b). Is it not likely that faced with men's intransigence with respect to taking on more housework (housework by men, on average, has barely increased, despite women's increasing wage-work), and given that women have always been the primary child rearers anyway, that the increased propensity of all women to form their own households is in many ways a matter of choice?[1]

A second set of observations about changes in the shape of male domination concerns changes within marriage. Women are achieving greater equality with men; through wage earning, they are changing family consumption patterns toward purchases that benefit them and toward greater personal consumption (Rainwater, 1979); they are doing less housework; and their greater willingness to leave marriages may be bringing about some improvements within marriages. As Spalter-Roth shows in a recent dissertation (1984), income per hour of labor (including both wage work and housework) has increased considerably for married women over the decade of the 1970s because their wage work has increased; their return per hour has increased relative to their husbands' as well. Further, an increasing proportion of women earn more than their husbands—12 percent in 1981 (Bianchi, 1983) versus 10 percent in 1976 (U.S. Bureau of the Census, 1978).

A third kind of evidence concerns children and here the picture is more mixed. Perhaps most important, parents' responsibility for children has probably declined because they have fewer of them, closer together, and they themselves live longer; responsibility for minor children constitutes a smaller portion of adult lives than heretofore. Decreased fertility and increased control of fertility through contraception and abortion is especially liberating to women.[2] Intensive childcare represents a much more predictable and much shorter period of a woman's life. Beyond that, however, women have come to bear more of the responsibility for children alone, as single parenting has increased. On the one hand, this indicates their increased ability to do so. The right to have children without being dependent on men is no doubt important to many women. On the other hand, it indicates men's lessened responsibility for children, both in their daily care and financially. Few men pay child support faithfully after

48

divorce or separation. This failure has clearly had a negative economic impact on women and children.

We also note that as children reach adolescence and young adulthood they have more opportunities to establish independence from their families of origin. Through college attendance, work, and/or delayed marriage, they often have a period of several years when they are living on their own. As Petchesky (1984) notes, some of the hysteria over pregnancy among teenagers has to do with the fact that pregnancy outside marriage is visible evidence of their independence.

We do not know enough about all of the ramifications for men's, women's, and children's lives, but taken together they do suggest that in general men exercise less authority over women and children in families than heretofore.

I would argue, then, that to the extent that there is a family crisis, it is by and large a healthy one, particularly for women. Even if it were not heathy, however, these changes are here to stay and are likely to continue in the same direction. Women are not going to go back home. The rapid changes we have been experiencing in family organization and in women's employment do cause hardship. Wage-working women with young children work long hours between work and family care. Many newly divorced women, especially older women who did not expect to support themselves, are left without labor market skills or experience. Some single women with children live in poverty, and/or bear the total burden of financial support and physical and emotional care of their children. And as we have noted, many men seem to have abrogated their responsibilities for children. Nevertheless, although some of the changes have negative implications, especially for particular groups of women, furthering these changes and reducing their negative implications will work to women's advantage.

Alternative Interpretations

A variety of alternative interpretations of these developments have been offered and will be discussed here briefly, some in more depth than others.

First, Ehrenreich has argued in *Hearts of Men* (1983) that many middle-class men may have left wives to lead more personally fulfilling, especially sexually fulfilling, lives. Her review of *Playboy* depicts a strident theme of ditching the wife for a sexy new woman. In her view, women's independence has been more the result than the cause of men's abandonment behavior. Tricked by a new sexual morality that worked against them, women, left by men, had to learn to fend for themselves. It is, of course, very difficult to say which came first (and perhaps it is unnecessary), but it should be remembered that marriage was not fulfilling for many women either, as early women's liberation literature described at length. Educated, middle-class women felt trapped, stifled—these were precisely the women with some ability to survive on their own; perhaps they often initiated leaving. And the sexual revolution made sexual exploration by women more acceptable; in particular, it increased the sexual experience of women before marriage.

Second, some have argued that the apparent gains for women, increased employment and increased wages, have come at the expense of men, or at least that at the same time men have lost jobs and earnings (see the Bluestone and Kuhn chapter in this volume). In the past few years, for example, women's earnings have risen from 59 percent to 64 percent of men's earnings; but rather than representing a true increase for women, the improvement in the ratio could represent a deterioration for men. But there have definitely been some real labor market gains for women. They have entered professional, technical, and managerial jobs in large numbers, especially in the 1970s. During the 1970s, for the first time there was a substantial decrease in the index of sex segregaton of occupations; having hovered around 65 since 1900, the index fell to about 60 in 1980, a proportionate decrease of 10 percent (Reskin and Hartmann, 1986). It should also be pointed out that more equality is not necessarily bad, even if it comes at the expense of men. If men on the average earn a dollar less per hour, and women a dollar more, the working class as a whole has not lost (assuming there are equal proportions of men and women in the labor force for this simple example).

Third, some have argued that the dramatic changes observed in family life have been the result neither of women's nor men's choices, but have been forced choices necessitated by difficult economic circumstances (Currie, Dunn, and Fogarty, 1980). It is argued that the deepening capitalist crisis demands speed-up from workers and their families, and causes downward pressures on workers' wages to restore competitiveness. Women, especially married women, enter the labor market because two incomes are needed to support a family (due to inflation and wage erosion) or because their husbands have become unemployed (or reemployed at a low-wage job, having lost a high-wage manufacturing job). All must work harder simply to survive; neither men nor women progress toward autonomy.

This scenario probably does describe reality for some families (especially those of high-wage male blue-collar workers who have experienced substantial wage and job losses since 1980, such as those described by Bluestone and Kuhn in this volume), but it is probably not an accurate picture for many who work in other sectors. In growth sectors (and in the economy overall, unemployment has decreased since 1984), workers may feel less pressed. Many progressives emphasize strategies to restore lost jobs and preserve those remaining through greater public control over investment decisions. In addition to preserving jobs in the industrial sector, however, it is also important to think about strategies for the new jobs; such strategies will be of greater benefit to women workers. If the newly available jobs pay less than those that have disappeared, one remedy is certainly organization—improving the conditions in the new jobs. In any case, women have made real gains in the labor market, and the increased contributions women make to family incomes have improved the prospects for gender equality at home.

The new arrangement for married couples, both men and women working for wages and women doing most of the housework, does amount to speed-up for women. The New Right is not entirely wrong in protesting this speed-up. Perhaps having one job, rather than two, was easier for women; having men to support them was a traditional and honorable means of economic survival for many women for many years. But it is a less secure route to economic survival than it once was. What is at issue, then, is how women subjectively experience these changes. Is the potential control a woman has over her economic future, when she works for wages (even at lower-paid women's jobs) a sufficient benefit to offset the hardship of the dual burden? I believe many women think so, though I cannot review evidence to support this claim here. In my view women are seeking wage work, not primarily because a deteriorating economy forces

51

them to, but because they see it as a better strategy for personal economic security than the formerly available strategy of being dependent on a well-chosen man.

A fourth interpretation takes as given that many women have achieved some degree of autonomy from patriarchal control in the family (that the family has declined as a locus of men's control over women) but asks to what extent women may have traded one form of patriarchal control for another—a more diffused and generalized patriarchal control of the economy and public policy sometimes called public or collective patriarchy (Brown, 1981, and Spalter-Roth and Zeitz, 1981). Patriarchy has always been a social system, a system in which men's private power over women in families has been buttressed by such important social institutions as the church, the courts, the police, the legislatures, and so on. Those who stress the shift in patriarchal control from family to the institutions of the larger society help to broaden our understanding of patriarchy's social influence. Patriarchy does not operate only within the family (though it still operates there as well, despite some of the more optimistic observations made above), or only within the sex-gender system as narrowly construed to refer to biological and social reproduction. The sex-gender system, in this case the patriarchal sex-gender system, is everywhere.

In this view, women, having escaped from some family-centered patriarchal control, still face such control in their daily lives because economic and political systems are structured by gender: these structures include low-paid female job ghettos, lesser legal and civic rights, and public support programs (welfare, social security, unemployment insurance, health care) that treat women differently and less generously than men. Men, it can be argued, are less likely to be lords and masters at home (having determined that the costs of such a fiefdom are too high), but they are still more likely to exercise control in public domains—not only by controlling state policy, but also in the marketplace and in social life. In a way, the previous dominant form of patriarchy—male breadwinner, wife and kids at home—is being replaced with a new version—the swinging single male buying whatever services he needs and having sexual access to many women, on the one hand, and the single mother, working to support children or on welfare, on the other. The new version also

52

includes the dual-career couple in which the wife is "super mom" and suffers from the double day, while the husband still maintains some patriarchal privileges (like not doing housework).

In this new scenario, the costs of family breakdown (the costs of the new male freedom) have been shifted to the state, much as O'Connor (1973) argued that the capitalist class was able throughout the post–World War II period to transfer many of the costs of doing business (education, training, research and development, etc.) onto the state, thereby generating a fiscal crisis of the state. The growth of the welfare state can be seen as a similar shift, transferring the costs of individual patriarchy to the state. The primary cost of family-centred patriarchy has been the financial support of dependent wives and children. These private costs become social when the system of private patriarchy breaks down: women are widowed or deserted, women have children outside marriage, and so on. Over time, additional costs, such as those of taking care of the elderly, or of educating college-age children, have also been shifted to the state.

But further shifts of patriarchal costs (and control) to the public sector seem unlikely for several reasons. First, some men may feel they have little access to patriarchal benefits through the marketplace (young men and lower-paid male workers) and they may resist the shift of patriarchal authority to policy makers. Second, the recent exacerbation of the fiscal crisis, which has resulted in the Reagan administration's attempt to relocate some of the costs of dependent care back in the family, may prevent further cost shifting, as much as some men might prefer it at least in the short run. Third, women's increasing political power is likely to influence the role of the public sector. Costs may be shifted to the state, but to the extent that women can exercise influence, patriarchal control may not follow. The state may come increasingly to serve women's interests as well as, or instead of, men's. The development of the state (as well as the development of the economy) must be understood as a result not only of capitalist relations and class struggle but also of patriarchal relations and gender struggle.

Obviously, we cannot know with certainty which interpretation of the significant changes that have been observed in family structure and women's economic participation is most accurate. Equally obviously, one or another interpretation will prove most convincing according to the particular circumstances under consideration. Women have experienced these changes differently from one another depending on their race, class, and individual histories. Clearly some have lost and some have gained in the transformations in economic and gender relations that have taken place. Continuing change, too, will produce further winners and losers. But on the whole, I believe these changes have been progressive for women and are likely to continue to prove so.

ROOTS OF CHANGE, SEEDS OF FURTHER CHANGE

It may be instructive to consider one of the changes discussed above, women's increased labor force participation, in order better to understand the sources of change. The increase in women's labor force participation can be seen as a result of contradictions inherent in an earlier accommodation of gender and economic relations. Specifically, the previous, pre–World War II arrangement of patriarchal capitalism (or capitalist patriarchy) contained the seeds of the current changes, and the current situation will lead to further changes. I have argued elsewhere (Hartmann, 1981a) that in the twentieth century a partnership between capitalism and patriarchy emerged in which the interests of both were served by allowing women a secondary place in the wage labor market, which kept them dependent on men and thus assured men of their continued services.[3] Women's place in the labor market has been characterized by the sex segregation of jobs and by low wages. Women's place in the labor market should be seen primarily as the result of patriarchal gender relations (operating in this case in a capitalist production environment).

Prior to World War II, the majority of married women did not work in the labor market; female-dominated jobs were populated by single women, young and old, who had to support themselves.[4] The labor of married women, though it often contributed to cash income via various forms of homework, was largely family-centered in childcare and housework. Married women generally relied on their

54

husbands' incomes. When they worked, they were viewed as secondary earners; their positions as wives in some sense justified their lower wages. Thus, by ensuring a pool of low-wage workers (wives and by extension, all women), patriarchy created an attractive pool of additional workers who could be drawn into capitalist relations on favorable terms for the capitalists. As women are drawn into the labor market, the work they formerly did at home also became increasingly available on the market. The service sector grows because the availability of cheap female labor provides the supply and because the use of women in the labor market rather than at home also provides the demand for replacement services (fast-food replacing home cooking, for example).

In this way, the enormous growth of the service sector, an important aspect of the structural transformation discussed here, can be seen as a direct result not only of capitalist development but also of patriarchal relations. Without the availability of large numbers of low-wage women workers, it is not clear that capitalist expansion would have taken this direction so strongly. The growth of much of the business service sector is required by a shift toward large-scale, multinational business with its consequent need for more communication, management, record keeping, and so forth. Women's labor allows this shift to occur. And the shift toward the commercialization of personal services is required by women's increased labor force participation. Changes in economic structure, then, can be seen as the result of changes in gender relations as well as in class behavior.

Hence, capital may be gaining in the centuries-old struggle between capital and men over the deployment of women's labor power (and men may be losing). More of women's labor power is being deployed outside the home, where it is not under the direct control of fathers and husbands. Moreover, I would argue, women, too, are gaining in this struggle.[5]

The increased labor force participation of women also sets the stage for further transformation. As women work more and work more continuously over their lifetimes, they have come to challenge their low-wage, secondary positions. The women's movement has contributed to this general process of consciousness-raising concerning the value of women's work. Two examples of this challenge are the development of the comparable worth strategy and the beginnings of large-scale clerical worker organizing.

The comparable worth strategy challenges the relative pay levels of men's and women's jobs—nurses and plumbers, librarians and engineers, secretaries and sales representatives. Comparable worth is a direct assault on the economic, social, and cultural system that has undervalued women's work relative to men's. Such claims are usually initiated when groups of women workers begin to investigate the relative wage levels of men's and women's jobs at their workplace, the qualifications required for the jobs, and the methods of setting pay. Arguments are then couched in terms of entire groups of women workers being underpaid. (Treiman and Hartmann, 1981). The most significant part of this type of campaign may be its ideological and consciousness-raising elements. Such studies convince some women who might not have thought about it or articulated it that their jobs are underpaid, that they do deserve more for the work they do. Moreover, by bringing the bases for wage differentials into the realm of public discussion, comparable worth campaigns politicize the wage determination process. In both these ways, such campaigns set the stage for the unionization of women.

But the more revolutionary aspect of the comparable worth strategy arises because it creates the possibility that women will be able to support themselves financially on equal terms with men. Such an eventuality would revolutionize gender relations and create the possibility of true autonomy for women. Moreover, by raising issues about how women's work is valued, obvious parallels are drawn to the undervalued work women do in the home. Whether in a capitalist wage labor market or a socialist one, issues of the value of the work performed traditionally by men and by women must be raised. Such questions directly challenge patriarchal norms and patriarchal power bases.[6]

While capitalists would undoubtedly have continued to profit from women's secondary position in the labor market, women's own challenge to their secondary status creates a new opportunity for working-class unity between men and women. Men are being presented with a second chance to incorporate women into the labor market as equals. This progressive response to the changes we have observed

56

can improve women's and children's lives more than a return to greater economic dependence on men. Men, and society in general, should have greater responsibility for children, and women should have higher incomes. While men have something to lose from this approach, in the long run they also stand to gain.

CONCLUSION

To conclude, let me outline briefly the progressive social policies that would enhance women's ability to be self-sufficient, clarify what I am not arguing in this essay, and comment on the importance of understanding social change as the outcome of both gender and class struggle.

Employment-related policies that would be important to women's advancement toward autonomy include increased collective bargaining and unionization, continued emphasis on equal employment opportunities and affirmative action, and, of course, comparable worth. For these policies to be effective, consistent full employment must be achieved. This in turn will no doubt require greater public control over what have generally been up to now private investment decisions. Improving working conditions on the job will also require a greater degree of employee involvement in work decisions. Hence, advancing women's specific interests as workers will also lead to the enhancement of workers' rights and economic prospects in general. Moreover, that women have greater responsibility than men for children needs to be recognized, and social programs to ameliorate the effects of this difference must be developed. Policies to provide subsidized child care, parental leave, and so forth will at least initially benefit women more than men, but they obviously benefit male parents as well.

A central demand that should be raised and supported by feminist and progressive groups now is for universally available free child care. Because childbearing has become more universal and is limited to a shorter period of adult life, achieving consensus about supporting families for this limited period should become increasingly possible. Social security provides a useful analogy; it supports people

57

for a limited (though growing) period of their lives, and everyone pays for it through payroll taxes. Universal, employment-related parental insurance financed via a payroll tax could provide parental leaves as well as funds for child care. Child care itself could be available free (or at modest cost in addition to the normal payroll tax) to the actual current users.

In general, I believe most benefits should be tied to employment or participation in training programs. As working for wages increasingly becomes the norm for all women, the fact that poor, young, minority women are "stockpiled" on welfare programs increasingly disadvantages them. They, like all women, need to learn labor market skills and progress toward self-sufficiency. Of course, not everyone is able to work, and social programs that provide a decent standard of living for those unable to work are needed as well.

In my view, enhancing economic autonomy for women so that they need not be dependent on individual men should be the central goal of the women's movement; greater social responsibility for children is a critical component of that goal. One would also hope that individual men would adjust to the new realities and take on their share of child care and housework.

I am *not* arguing that women, who would be able to be truly economically autonomous with these new arrangements, would not choose to live with or even marry men. They might. They might also choose to live in groups or with other women or alone. But whatever their choices they would be less coerced by economic considerations than they are presently. Marriage would no longer be the central path to economic survival that it now is. I am also not arguing that the transition to this new arrangement has been painless. Some women have been negatively affected. But I am arguing that social policies such as those described above can do much to ameliorate the negative effects. In the long run we will gain more than we lose.

I want to close by explicitly arguing against the tendency to believe that everything that happens in capitalist societies is the result of capitalist development and only capitalist development. Even structural transformations that are most often thought of in economic terms—foreign competition, industry shifts, declining productivity—are in fact shaped by both gender and class relations. The reindustrialization issue itself can be seen as an attempt to preserve and reestablish the male sector of the economy. Lane Kirkland's recent unabashed, enthusiastic support for highly capital-intensive pursuits like the shale oil projects in the mountain states can be seen as a rather backward-looking approach—if the sectors where unions have been strong can grow, he seems to be thinking, then unions can grow. Kirkland apparently believes it would be easier to reindustrialize America than to learn how to unionize new kinds of workers.[7] It seems inevitable that fewer and fewer men will have "macho" jobs in the economy—those associated with hard physical labor and rugged working conditions. With technological change and sectoral shifts, more and more men will, like women, work in the service sector. The recent emphasis on sex role research, the new androgynous personality, and so forth, might be seen as an effort to retrain men for "women's" jobs, or at least to make these jobs increasingly ideologically acceptable to men. Although men will increasingly enter the service sector, I would not expect sex segregation in the labor market to be eliminated entirely over the next few decades; that will require many, many years. But the lines between blue-collar and white-collar jobs and professional and support jobs will most likely blur. These developments hold the promise of progressive change if we can develop new strategies that build upon them. Just as the increased mobility of capital noted by Bluestone and Kuhn calls forth new solutions, so might these sectoral and structural shifts. The new solutions will undoubtedly require a new consciousness on the part of men as well as of women.

Not only is there a tendency to attribute everything to capitalism in thinking about economic change, but there is an accompanying tendency to view capitalist crises as necessarily negative. There can be no question that budget cuts, unemployment, and poverty make people's lives worse and that women are particularly severely affected by them; inasmuch as these are the short-run effects of the current crisis, they are serious and unhappy results. But the longer structural transformation that is also under investigation here has had and will continue to have many positive effects, particularly for women, inasmuch as it entails fundamental changes in gender relations as well. Placing gender relations at the center of the analysis causes us to have a very different view of the transformation. There is potential now for continued truly revolutionary changes in our intimate lives and in women's ability to be economically autonomous (perhaps for the first time in human history). These are important, progressive changes. The only question is whether we as a society are ready for them.

Notes

I WOULD LIKE to express my appreciation to Lourdes Benería and Catharine Stimpson for insisting that I do this paper; members of my study group in Washington, D.C., especially Phyllis Palmer and Roberta Spalter-Roth, for trenchant discussions of many of the issues raised in this paper; several colleagues, Micaela di Leonardo, Judith Stacey, Lourdes Benería, and Catharine Stimpson, for particularly close readings of the first draft and many helpful suggestions; and several groups, in addition to the attendees at the Conference on Structural Transformation, whose spirited argument and probing questions have helped clarify the argument: the Women's Studies Forum at the University of Pennsylvania and groups at the University of California at Los Angeles, University of California at Berkeley, Evergreen State College, Bucknell University, and Harvard University. I would also like to thank Lucile DiGirolamo of the National Research Council staff, and Gillian Marcelle, an intern with the council, for assistance in completing this paper. The views expressed, however, are mine, and not those of the National Academy of Sciences.

1. Elaine McCrate (1984) has recently formalized these notions in a feminist model of a non-clearing marriage market.

2. It is important to keep in mind that the legal right to abortion is only slightly more than a decade old; and the right to contraceptives is only about twenty years old.

3. During the periods of the emergence of capitalism and the industrial revolution, wage labor became the dominant mode of economic survival, a mode that challenged earlier family-centered production systems and created a challenge to men's continued control of women's labor power and to women's ability to continue to contribute to the economic support of their families. That challenge was resolved by the establishment of family wages (at least as the ideal), which allowed men to support their wives and children at home, retaining the advantages of the deployment of women's labor power at home (Hartmann, 1976; 1981a).

4. Many poor women and minority women did work in the labor market, even when they were married, and many married women earned money at home. In general, the "patriarchal accord" was less relevant for poorer and minority men, since, in the patriarchal hierarchy, they enjoyed fewer patri-

archal privileges than majority men. They often did not have wives at home. But even in these groups it was believed that men should be the primary earners.

5. Contrast this feminist interpretation with that of Karl Kautsky (1971: 26), an important socialist of his day: "The capitalist system of production does not in most cases destroy the single household of the workingman, but robs it of all but its unpleasant features. The activity of woman today in industrial pursuits . . . means an increase of her former burden by a new one. *But one cannot serve two masters.* The household of the working-man suffers whenever his wife must help to earn the daily bread." Apparently one type of slave these socialists were not interested in liberating was women.

6. The issue of comparable worth also fundamentally alters our understanding of the way the labor market operates. In earlier work on job segregation, for example, I essentially assumed that some jobs have low wages, and, through a process of struggle between men and women, those are the ones allocated to women. But another way to look at the same result—women in low-paid jobs—is to see it as the result of an attempt to devalue whatever it is that women are doing and to pay it less. In this view, the pay levels of jobs themselves are seen to be the result of gender struggle on the job. Just as Marxists have increasingly begun to look at class struggle as it occurs directly on the shop floor as well as in the larger society, feminists have to look at gender struggle in the workplace—how new jobs get allocated to each sex, how their pay levels are determined, and so on. This perspective can lead to a transformation of accepted Marxist theories. As Philips and Taylor (1980) point out, Harry Braverman's book *Labor and Monopoly Capital* (1974), emphasizes only class struggle: it is always in the interest of capital to divide workers and to deskill as many components of the job as possible. Taylor and Philips argue, however, that the process of deskilling is sometimes only apparent: the jobs may not actually require less skill, rather they are labeled unskilled and devalued. Male workers often play a large role in the process of devaluing and labeling women's work and in determining relative wage rates. Wages are gendered for both women and men.

7. Rothschild (1981) has criticized this view fairly thoroughly; growth rates in the industrial sector would have to be very great over the next several years in order to bring about any reversal of the secular trend toward the service economy.

Reference List

AFL–CIO. 1984. *Deindustrialization and the two tier society: Challenges for an industrial policy.* (Washington, D.C.:) Industrial Union Department, AFL–CIO.

Bane, Mary Jo. 1985. The politics and policies of the feminization of poverty. Paper prepared for the Colloquium on The Changing Situation of Black Americans and Women: Roots and Reverberations in U.S. Social Politics since the 1960s, University of Chicago, April 26–27.

Bianchi, Suzanne M. 1983. *Wives who earn more than their husbands.* Special Demographic analyses CDS–80–9. Washington, D.C.: GPO.

Bianchi, Suzanne M., and Daphne Spain. 1984. *American women: Three decades of change.* Special Demographic Analysis CDS–80–8. Washington, D.C.: GPO.

Blaustein, Arthur I. 1982. *The American promise: Equal justice and economic opportunity.* New Brunswick, N.J.: Transaction Books.

Bluestone, Barry, and Bennett Harrison. 1983. *The deindustrialization of America.* New York: Basic Books.

Bluestone, Barry, Bennett Harrison, and Lucy Gorham. 1984. *Stormclouds over the horizon: Labor market crisis and industrial policy.* Brookline, Mass.: Economic Education Project.

Bluestone, Barry, and Sarah Kuhn. 1983. Paper presented at the Conference on Women and Structural Transformation: The Crisis of Work and Family Life, Rutgers University, New Brunswick, November 18–19.

Braverman, Harry. 1974. *Labor and monopoly capital: The degradation of work in the twentieth century.* New York: Monthly Review Press.

Brown, Carol. 1981. Mothers, fathers and children: from private to public patriarchy. In *Women and revolution,* edited by Lydia Sargent, 239–67. Boston: South End Press or London: Pluto Press.

Currie, Elliott, Robert Dunn, and David Fogarty. 1980. The new immiseration: stagflation, inequality, and the working class. *Socialist Review* 54 (November–December): 7–31.

Ehrenreich, Barbara. 1983. *The hearts of men.* Garden City, N.Y.: Anchor Press/Doubleday.

Erie, Steven E., Martin Rein, and Barbara Wiget. 1983. Women and the Reagan revolution: thermidor for the social welfare economy. In *Families, politics, and public policy: A feminist dialogue on women and the state,* edited by Irene Diamond, 94–119. New York: Longman.

Espenshade, Thomas J. 1985. Marriage trends in America: estimates, implications, and underlying causes. *Population and Development Review* 11(2): 193–245.

Ford Foundation. 1985. Women, children, and poverty in America. Working Paper New York NY (January).

Hartmann, Heidi I. 1976. Capitalism, patriarchy, and job segregation by sex. *Signs* 1, 2 supplement (Spring): 137–169.

Hartmann, Heidi I. 1981a. The unhappy marriage of Marxism and Feminism. In *Women and revolution,* edited by Lydia Sargent, 1–41. Boston: South End Press or London: Pluto Press.

Hartmann, Heidi I. 1981b. The family as the locus of gender, class and political struggle: the example of housework. *Signs* 6 (Spring): 366–394.

62

Hogan, Dennis P. 1983. Demographic trends in human fertility and parenting across the life-span. Paper prepared for the Conference on Biosocial Life-Span Approaches to Parental and Offspring Development, sponsored by the Social Science Research Council, Elkridge, Maryland, May.

Kautsky, Karl. 1971. *The class struggle*. New York: W. W. Norton.

Kitagawa, Evelyn M. 1981. New life-styles: marriage patterns, living arrangements, and fertility outside of marriage. *Annals of the American Academy of Political and Social Sciences* 453 (January):1–27.

Kobrin, Frances E. 1976a. The fall in household size and the rise of the primary individual in the United States. *Demography* 13 (February):127–38.

Kobrin, Frances E. 1976b. The primary individual and the family: changes in living arrangements in the United States since 1940. *Journal of Marriage and Family* 38 (May):233–39.

McCrate, Elaine. 1984. The Growth of Nonmarriage among U.S. Women: An unanswered question for the new family economics, and an alternative. Department of Economics, University of Massachusetts, Amherst (October).

Moore, Kristin A. 1985. Teenage pregnancy: The dimensions of the problem. *New Perspectives* 17 (Summer):11–15.

O'Connor, James. 1973. *The fiscal crisis of the state*. New York: St. Martin's Press.

Petchesky, Rosalind Pollack. 1984. *Abortion and women's choice: The state, sexuality, and reproductive freedom*. New York: Longman.

Phillips, Anne and Barbara Taylor. 1980. Sex and skill: notes toward a feminist economics. *Feminist Review* 6:79–88.

Rainwater, Lee. 1979. Mothers' contribution to the family money economy in Europe and the United States. *Journal of Family History* 4(2):198–211.

Reskin, Barbara F. and Heidi I. Hartmann, eds. 1986. *Women's work, men's work: sex segregation on the job*. Washington, D.C.: National Academy Press.

Rothschild, Emma. 1981. Reagan and the real economy. *The New York Review of Books* 28(February 5):12–18.

Smith, Shirley J. 1982. New worklife estimates reflect changing profile of labor force. *Monthly Labor Review* 105 (March):15–20.

Smith, Shirley J. 1985. Revised worklife tables reflect 1979–80 experience. *Monthly Labor Review* 108(August):23–30.

Spalter-Roth, Roberta. 1984. A Comparison of the living standards between husbands and wives in dual-earner couples, 1968–1979: A feminist analysis. Ph.D. dissertation. The American University, Washington, D.C.

Spalter-Roth, Roberta M. and Eileen Zeitz. 1981. Production and reproduction of everyday life. In *Dynamics of world development,* edited by Richard Rubinson, 193–209. Beverly Hills, Calif.: Sage Publications.

Treiman, Donald J. and Heidi I. Hartmann, eds. 1981. *Women, work, and wages: Equal pay for jobs of equal value*. Washington, D.C.: National Academy Press.

Wilson, Willam J. and Kathryn M. Neckerman. 1985. Poverty and family structure: the widening gap between evidence and public policy issues. In *Fighting poverty: What works and what doesn't,* edited by S. Danziger and D. Weinberg, 232–282. Cambridge, Mass.: Harvard University Press.

U.S. Department of Commerce. Bureau of the Census. 1985a. *Characteristics of the population below the poverty level: 1983.* Current Population Reports. Series P–60. No. 147 (February). Washington, D.C.: GPO.

U.S. Department of Commerce, Bureau of the Census. 1985b. *Household and family characteristics, March 1984.* Current Population Reports, Series P–20, No. 398. Washington, D.C.: GPO.

U.S. Department of Commerce, Bureau of the Census. 1978. *Money income in 1976 of families and persons in the United States.* Current Population Reports. Series P–60, Number 114. Washington, D.C.: GPO.

3

The Demise of Domesticity
in America

Alice Kessler-Harris and Karen Brodkin Sacks

Incremental changes in our economy may seem to be of little consequence for ordinary people, and yet, added together, they may produce unforeseen and radical results. In this paper, we want to take a historical view of deindustrialization and the current structural transformations in America's political economy to see how they are altering women's traditional roles. We believe that changes now in process will ultimately restructure family forms and gender relations, and open the possibility of transforming some of our social institutions. The changes described by several authors in this volume alter the way women and men think about themselves and about each other in relation to both the home and work. These emerging self concepts will tend to challenge nuclear family relationships as we know them. Specifically, we seek to explore the consequences for all of us when women act on new perceptions.

Our approach is grounded in recent data from the social sciences. It now seems apparent that the current structural transformation has increased female employment and male unemployment. The visible and immediate impact of this change is to alter the balance of power within families as they come to depend more heavily on women's wages. The most remarked-upon consequences of this changed power balance have been a sharp rise in divorce rates, in single-parent households, and in the pauperization of women. While family breakdowns constitute the most striking short-term trend, a longer-term qualitative analysis reveals a history that shows such breakdowns as parts of larger restructuring processes. Here women have been the main actors in creating new rules for family relation-

65

ships, new forms of household organization, and, perhaps, even new relations between families and wage work, and families and the state. We are witnessing a new stage in that process today, as we see a ripening of the contradiction between the realities of family life and the ideology by which these realities have been interpreted and channeled. That ideology, the domestic code, is being directly confronted, not only by self-styled feminists, but by large numbers of women who seek the rewards of the marketplace while denying any connection with feminism.

Before exploring these issues we want to stress that we use the terms "deindustrialization" and "structural transformation" in their traditional sense, meaning the movement to a service economy from our specific vantage point in time and culture. We are guilty, therefore, of a certain amount of ethnocentrism. For clearly the international capitalist economy is not becoming deindustrialized; rather the United States has lost its hegemony in basic industries, and many American corporations are locating an increasing portion of their production in the third world. From a third world perspective, industrialization is the norm. Our perspective comes from that part of the metropolis that consists of native-born women whose kin and immediate families are resident in the United States. Similarly, structural transformation has different possible meanings in different parts of the world. In some places, the dominant shift is from subsistence to capitalist or commercial agriculture; in others, from primary production or extraction to heavy manufacturing. In still others, notably the old industrial nations, the term refers to a shift in the kinds of jobs in which the waged workforce engages—from the production of goods to the production of "services." We use structural transformation in this latter sense.

The current transformation in what is produced, where it is produced, and by whom, is part of a continuing process by which the spread of capitalism has reshaped the world's political economy. In the United States, this penetration is now converting formerly unwaged and informal economic activities, such as meal preparation, child care, and the care of the aged, into profit-making enterprises. The result is to place women, whose lives are most immediately touched by these activities, at the forefront of change, and to pose questions for their families that may challenge the structure of capitalism itself.

SHIFTS IN THE BALANCE OF FAMILY POWER

For most of the American working class for most of its history, the wage of even the principal (male) earner was inadequate to raise a family. As interpreted by labor unions and social reformers in the past, the demand for a "living wage" often meant that a man's wage be adequate to sustain a whole family. The current feminist movement has pointed out the double-edged nature of that demand, however (Hartmann, 1976; Humphries, 1977; Sen, 1980). On the one hand, such a wage provided married women with some economic security and limited the number of family members required to engage in alienating labor. On the other, the sexist assumption that men were the only legitimate wage earners increased wives' dependency on husbands and provided a basis for the intrafamily oppression of women. It also denied women without husbands access to a living wage. As Wandersee notes, "One of the basic facts of family economics during the early twentieth century was that most working-class males, and many of those in the middle class, were not paid enough to support their families according to the American standard of living." (1981:1). Even with the success of unions in heavy industry, it is debatable whether a single wage ever covered the costs of rearing a family in more than a minority of cases. But for most of the past, women were able to make up the differential between the male wage and the cost of survival through their own and community resources in ways that did not alter family relationships. The structural transformation of the last twenty-five years has made that no longer possible.

A variety of family strategies contributed to household well-being prior to World War II. Daughters and sons as well as husbands were typically wage-earners. Indeed, the vast majority of poor and working-class parents found themselves dependent on their children's wages to keep their households afloat and expected their children to contribute to the collective endeavor. In addition, mothers, wives, and other non-wage-earning adults in the family participated in what has come to be called an informal economy, where they provided significant amounts of cash for family needs and stretched family income with their unwaged labor. These earning efforts, as the new scholarship in feminist and working-class history has demonstrated, were often hidden and unrecognized in terms of informal and casual enterprises—generally a mixture of petty entrepreneurial sales and service activities, such as taking in piecework or laundry at home, baking goods for sale, peddling, or running a small store.

Large proportions of working-class wives and mothers took in lodgers. They thus provided to the unmarried of the working-class community some of the domestic services they performed directly for their own families, and made a cash contribution to the household budget as well (Jensen, 1980; Pleck, 1979; Smith, 1979). In the steel and coal regions of the midwest, as in the mushrooming cities of the East, boarders could contribute a significant share of a family's income. For example, some 40 percent of all families of immigrant steel workers in Homestead, Pennsylvania, in the early twentieth century took in boarders. With one to four lodgers in a four-room house, a family could add about 25 percent to its income (Byington, 1911). In New England communities of Polish silk and cotton mill workers, four out of five people lived in houses with boarders (Lamphere, et al., 1980). Taking in boarders created larger households, and sometimes, when the boarders were women, increased the availability of domestic labor. In addition, boarding gave single members of the community a set of social places and links they might not otherwise have had. Significantly, this effort to bring cash into the household provided women with key roles in building working-class communities at the same time as it reinforced their home-centered roles.

The same might be said for most jobs in the informal economy: they were not only consistent with women's conventional roles at home, they reinforced them. Far from altering the balance of family relations, they perpetuated the notion that women could extend family income by being good wives and loyal family members. Moreover, they tied women into networks of kin and neighborhood activities that in turn tied the family into the social and economic life

68

of the community, reinforcing the family's position within it and providing a larger context for women's hard work. We see such networks in studies of Italian and Jewish immigrant communities and more recently in analysis of urban black families, Appalachian families, and third world families (Kessler-Harris, 1982; Caulfield, 1974; Cohn, 1977; Stack, 1974; Yans-McLaughlin, 1977).

The transition in the economy since World War II has made wage work more available to women and reduced the incentive to continue informal earning activities. Produce and poultry, as well as clothing, can be bought more cheaply than produced at home. Large franchised chains reduce the possibility of women starting their own little grocery stores. At the same time, the commoditization of services has made such goods more easily bought by those to whom wives and mothers formerly provided them. Many fewer working-class mothers earn cash by boarding, cooking, washing, or sewing for others. The trade-off for women who need to supplement family incomes is the part-time job, where they earn wages to provide services their mothers or grandmothers would have offered from their own homes.

But what seems like a simple trade-off—women using their own wages to purchase the ready-to-eat or ready-to-wear commodities they no longer produce at home—in fact erodes men's domestic power and authority over them. By commoditizing new areas of domestic life, from cooking to child care and nursing the aged, capitalism simultaneously reduces the scope of private housework and undermines husbands' control over wives' labor power. At one level, increased reliance on commodities releases women from the excessive isolation of the home and thus has a feminist aspect. It may also represent women's decisions about how they wish to use their wages, offering the possibility of some autonomy and the potential for ameliorating their ever-increasing burdens (Spalter-Roth, 1983).[1] At another level, by placing women in positions parallel to husbands who earn wages, it deprives husbands of the unwaged labor from which they have historically benefited, and thus of the self-esteem and privileges that have historically accompanied "supporting" a family (Rubin, 1976).

In addition, in the process of undermining male domestic privileges, women's actions are raising equally subversive questions about wages themselves: for what labor are wages paid and are they really the "private property" of those to whom they are paid? These are not entirely new questions. Historically, struggle between husbands and wives occurred over whether the husband had use of "his" wages, or whether the wife had first claim on them because of her responsibility for buying food and children's clothing and paying the rent. The nineteenth-century women's rights movement engaged itself with this issue, and the conflict infused the temperance movement with much of its vitality among the North American and English proletariat (Bordin, 1981; Paulson, 1973; Blocker, 1985). For women especially, liquor embodied the evils of a philosophy that gave wage-earners ownership of their wages as private property. In contrast, a family-ownership philosophy underlay the practice of "tipping," where all earners of the household put their wages in a family pot to be allocated, usually by the mother, or by whomever played the role of household administrator (Humphries, 1977; Tilly and Scott, 1978).

Contemporary feminist analysis focusing on white families stresses the extent to which the wage has traditionally covered the cost of reproduction of the whole family and class of wage earners as well as the maintenance of those who actually earn the wages. Black families have depended more heavily on the wages of women as well as of men. With more wives and mothers of small children heavily involved in the wage labor force, the gender dimensions of the wage conflict have become more visible, such that women increasingly see wages as their private property and use them to assert their rights to autonomy and to resist subordination to husbands, as did wage-earning daughters in the nineteenth century. Yet mothers and wives lack the mobility of fathers and daughters, because mothers still tend to bear responsibility for dependent children. In this context, two contradictory aspects of wages-as-private-property become apparent. On the one hand, wages represent a basis for resisting gender and generational subordination within the family (a longer tradition for black families); on the other hand, they provide women with the opportunity to avoid family situations altogether. Today's wage-earning women seem to be resisting subordination more than rejecting a give and take that is part of family life. Men are less able to demand obedience from wives.

70

These conflicts are sustained and exacerbated by rising levels of white as well as black male unemployment in the face of more available (although poorly paid) jobs in sectors normally defined as female. For many families this implies increasing reliance on the female wage and increasing difficulty in defining it as merely supplemental. Intermittent campaigns to take women out of the workforce and to construct a nuclear family under the rule of a male breadwinner, such as have been undertaken by the Reagan administration, seem to have fallen prey to the need for two wage earners in the family. Also, as jobs in traditionally male areas decrease, conventional notions of masculinity are less effective in frightening men away from paid jobs in traditionally female occupations. Intrafamilial negotiations over power have emerged as the norm. What is to be decided first in family after family and finally in the sphere of social policy is whether the increasing discordance between the wages women actually earn and their traditionally subordinate roles in relations to husband and family can any longer be contained. This raises the question of what it means to be a wage earner and what wage-earning implies about "woman's place."

WHAT IS HAPPENING TO "WOMAN'S PLACE?"—OR CHALLENGES TO THE DOMESTIC CODE

Families have been said to be based on the complementarity of opposites in everything from economics to temperament. The conventional dichotomy of society into a home or family sphere of love and emotion as women's place and responsibility, and a public sphere of power and work as men's, is often called the domestic code (Welter, 1966). The edges of both spheres are unravelling as current economic shifts influence the ways people behave.

The domestic ideology, or domestic code, is an interpretation about what work is and what it is not, about who works and who does not; about what a man is and does, and what a woman is and does. These ideas have become a part of our way of talking and thinking about our lives to each other and ourselves. They have ordered the family and defined social possibilities for men and women. And they have

71

now become the basis of structural conflicts that have divided the genders and generations in both the family and factory (Ryan, 1981).

The domestic code provided a rationale for the reciprocally confirming notion that women who belonged at home lacked the impetus and ambition to make their way in the workforce, and therefore behaved in ways that justified their disadvantaged places in comparison with men. Women, who earned about 60 percent of male pay, were given the argument that their wages need not be large enough to support a family. And if poor pay and discrimination discouraged them from seeking jobs at all, rational observers suggested that this only proved that women were in fact better suited to the home.

Such circular reasoning provided easy justifications for employers to exploit women, for public policymakers to ignore those who asked for benefits and higher wages and for organized labor to refuse to take such demands seriously (Kessler-Harris, 1975:164). A favorite example comes from the American Association for Labor legislation, which in 1916 proposed a national health insurance scheme that would have, among other things, paid hospital expenses of pregnant women who withdrew from the workforce in the weeks immediately before and after childbirth. Critics protested that such generosity would give potential mothers an incentive to seek jobs, and the proposal was immediately withdrawn.

Despite the steadily growing dependence on wages of adult women for family survival in the working class and in much of the middle class, the domestic code has insisted that women's most essential role is that of wife-and-mother. The rise of post–World War II domesticity was based on a widely shared consensus that the health of the American economy depended heavily on women returning to the home and leaving their relatively well-paid wartime jobs to men. In return, these men were supposed to support their wives and children in a higher, middle-class lifestyle in the new suburbs that psychologists and financiers alike were promoting as integral to a solid peacetime economy. An especially virulent version of the domestic ideology emerged in this milieu: it insisted that women no longer "needed" to work, and thereupon denied them even the minimal privileges of work (advancement, health benefits, equal pensions, and so forth). They were admitted to jobs in which they were needed but in which career possibilities were blocked or nonexistent.

72

Like the attempt to negate the existence of a working class, which occurred in the same period and which assigned to those who lived in the suburbs middle-class attitudes and aspirations, these 1950s attitudes hid women who desired careers and salaries instead of wages. Women whose lifestyles did not conform to these expectations were viewed as deviants to be cured of their ills lest they set bad examples to others (Ehrenreich and English, 1979; Farnham and Lundberg, 1947; Ryan, 1979; Weisstein, 1970). They were depicted in the media as social problems, the causes of a variety of social sins from homosexuality and juvenile delinquency to the deterioration of American values and the Great Depression.

We now know that the imposed domesticity of the fifties masked the reality of what women were actually doing. Most of the Rosie the Riveters of World War II did not leave the workforce when they were forced out of their wartime jobs (Anderson, 1981; Gabin, 1982; Trey, 1972). Instead, they found other jobs in offices, hospitals, and banks, in nonunionized small factories, and in a variety of personal services. To be sure, these jobs did not pay as well as those the women lost and they preserved the traditional segmentation of the labor force. Yet the permanent expansion of women's workforce participation and the shift in government policy to encourage training women for certain kinds of jobs began in the wake of cold war needs for what Women's Bureau head Frieda Miller described as maintaining "the skills acquired by two and a half million women in wartime." (Kessler-Harris, 1982:304).

Behind the image of working-class prosperity lay the reality that working-class families needed more than one paycheck to participate in the more expensive suburban lifestyle. Part-time work, "mothers' shifts," seasonal jobs that allowed "vacations" when the kids were out of school all helped these "deviant" women disguise themselves as proper homemakers. During the 1950s the proportion of wives and mothers in the wage labor force grew by one third.

As more women went out to work, those women who had been earning wages all along appeared less deviant. Wage work became acceptable if it was presented as an extension of women's family responsibilities and as lacking any element of personal ambition. As any fan of Doris Day movies well knew, every smart woman who made it to the top gave up her career as soon as Mr. Right came

73

along. As the media portraits altered and the paradigms of social science shifted to encompass the new realities, black women, married and single, who had always worked in higher proportions than white women, moved to the forefront. In the context of a new affirmation supported by an emerging civil rights movement, they asserted their real economic roles, demanded government policies that acknowledged labor force discrimination, and insisted on educational opportunities for their children. In some ways they were the vanguards of the then-still-incipient women's movement.

These contradictions matured throughout the 1950s until, by the early sixties, the domestic code that had confined women's increasing workforce participation to narrow spheres and had limited their aspirations to "helping out at home" began to break down. Helped by the meritocratic and egalitarian consciousness that emerged from the struggle for civil rights and against the Vietnam War, women began to demand the rewards of hard work. Those who left their homes out of financial need wanted the promotions and high wages that were the normal rewards of hard work. By the mid-1970s, these women began to organize themselves into groups like Women Office Workers, Union Wage, and the Coalition of Labor Union Women to fight for equal pay for equal work, clearer job definitions, and access to promotions. Women who left home out of the search for satisfaction wanted the personal fulfillment that jobs promised. They hoped to teach or do social work in "helping" settings. Instead, they entered a tightening job market where social services were being cut back to the point where workers could not help clients; they could only police them. In both cases, women ran up against the barriers of the occupational ghetto rooted in notions that women belonged at home. The search for fair treatment in the workplace demanded that America come to terms with whether women's family roles needed to be so rigidly prescribed. The ever-increasing numbers of wage-earning women who confronted work roles governed by outdated notions of domesticity that limited and defined their relationships to the concept of family and their families added their voices to those of the young people and minorities of the 1960s who demanded that the society live up to its rhetoric.

Given the persistence of women's continuing relationships to paid work and given the structural sources out of which women's complaints arose, the domestic code is increasingly anachronistic. It contradicts the experience that families require prodigious amounts of unpaid work as well as increasing amounts of paid labor from women. And it sustains male attempts to hang on to patterns of behavior that emerged in families where women's unwaged labor predominated. To eliminate distinctions between the sexes seems particularly threatening in a society where other elements are in such flux. What is at stake is nothing less than the issue of whether woman's place is in the home.

WHAT IS A GOOD WOMAN?—OR WOMEN'S SELF-DEFINITION APART FROM FAMILY ROLES

To examine the material realities that push women into the workforce and that undermine the family's ability to keep them at home is to urge a re-vision of women's economic responsibilities and jobs. As wage work becomes the life labor of women as well as of men, and as women begin to insist on its rewards, their behavior and expectations of waged and unwaged work change. The result is to alter the way the "family" functions.

Women workers now make up almost half of the American labor force, and as some of the other papers in this volume indicate, they are the large majority of workers in some of the fastest-growing and lowest-paying industries, such as electronics manufacturing, hospitals and nursing homes, fast foods, data and word processing. More women head families and are the sole supports of children than ever before. The threat of consistently high unemployment makes women's earnings central even in families where a man is also working. The typical woman today is a wage worker in a job that pays poorly, gives her little possibility for advancement, and little control over her work or decision-making power in her work. The typical hourly wage-worker today is a woman. One recent analysis of the American class structure using such criteria concludes that women now make up the majority of the working class, and that together with minority men, women and minorities comprise a large majority of the American working class (Wright, Costello, et al., 1982).

As women are forced more intensively into wage labor, they develop a consciousness of themselves as doubly exploited at home and in the factory or office. While in the past women who entered wage work could protect themselves with the assumption that this role was temporary and that their identities resided in their home roles, the recognition of work as a permanent part of their lives no longer permits such self-deception. If honor and dignity now reside for women, as for men, at least to some extent in their paid work, then struggles for recognition on the job and for some element of control will become an increasing part of women's lives. The unity of home and work—of the social and economic spheres—will be established.

The result then is a series of struggles around both home and work. Women's collective action and overwhelming support for pay equity and active efforts against sexual harassment are affirmations of women's developing sense of self. Yet the rewards of success are seen to come at the expense of men, raising the level of competition between the sexes. While women workers are increasingly concerned about the impact of their double days on children, they still try to carry both wage labor and the unpaid labor of raising children and other dependents. Women's activism in joining trade unions (women are half of all new union members since the 1960s), and in litigating and agitating for workplace justice on a wide variety of fronts suggests that there is at least a potential for their transforming traditional notions about family and work and about men's and women's relationships. The steps needed for this transformation include demands for employer payments for family-oriented benefits—health insurance for pregnancy and birth, paid parenting leaves, paid time off for dependent care, paid child care, and shorter and more flexible working days.[2] These kinds of demands imply that women are using their roles as workers not to free themselves from family roles, but to sustain the social responsibilities formerly undertaken by families and defined as private affairs or nonwork. They are beginning to transform women's family tasks into responsibilities to be shared.

Women who insist on the freedom to perform successfully at work demand the same freedom in their personal behavior. To do well on the job while maintaining households with children requires a new subjective sense of self as well as new shared social definitions of women's objective needs. Thus behavior earlier seen as natural and described as dependent and gentle or—feminine—no longer appears natural at all to women who see such a stance as inhibiting their performance at work. The positive responses to such new self-perceptions appear in more expressive sexualities, in openness toward lesbianism and rejection of heterosexual relationships, in rising divorce rates, in increasing numbers of women who choose motherhood without marriage, and in a more tangible sense of independence on the part of young girls. The image of a "good" woman changes. And some of these changes meet no opposition from among men relieved of the need to be "good" men—or to provide entirely for their families (Ehrenreich, 1983). Yet insofar as notions of femininity provided the substructure on which the framework of domesticity (and therefore gender segmentation in the workforce and male dominance in the family) was built, its wholesale abandonment threatens to reveal the ideological nature of the current insistence on divisions into private and public spheres. It threatens in short, to open to the public eye the daily reality of a unified labor. This is because successful engagement with wage work for women and men who wish also to maintain satisfying family lives requires the cooperative work of both sexes, and perhaps of several generations organized in households and families of various kinds. The cultural language and behavior that denies this unity must inevitably be called into question.

THE FAMILY AND SOCIETY

These new perceptions, however, raise fundamental questions about the nature of the family in relation to the community and to kin, and about its function in maintaining social order. From the perspective of traditionalists, such questions are enormously threatening, suggesting not only the demise of the family but the end of respect for the values that the family had sustained. In the last few years we have seen the emergence of powerful groups like "Stop ERA," the "Committee for the Survival of a Free Congress," and the "Moral Majority" dedicated to making divorce less accessible, prohibiting abortions, and creating "pro-family" coalitions. In the end, such goals must involve removing women from all but the most menial jobs. As we have seen, this process runs counter to current economic and occupational trends. The result is a struggle around emerging values, which, we suggest, traditionalists will inevitably lose—at least in the long run.

In families these struggles grow out of women's new relationships to income and the way they influence community life. As we have seen, from a working-class woman's perspective, her ability to provide services and cash for household needs by her entrepreneurial activities has been slowly eroded since World War II. Working-class women have been pressed and encouraged to give up their autonomous income-generating activities for wage labor—at minimum wage as often as not—for the very corporations that undermined their unpaid labor at home. The suburbanization of their communities together with the growth of a service sector that provides women with both jobs and consumer services reduces the strength of informal kin and neighborhood support networks. Unlike earlier income-generating activities and jobs, new jobs for women conflict in time and space with family and community life. As wage-earning women pass into these jobs, community-based, informal economic activities can be expected to break down.

There are two sides to this process. On one side is a loss of kin-based and community activities built around women's entrepreneurial activities, and a simultaneous atomization into small household political economies. The decline—in number and real wages—of many working-class men's jobs has placed families under heightened economic pressure. Attempts to survive economically have led fathers to leave home in search of work and mothers to contribute a relatively larger share of the family's cash needs through their waged labor.

On the other side, women's decreased economic dependence on husbands has occurred simultaneously with an increase in the number of adult wage-earning sons and daughters who remain in the parental household. The same pressures that lead husbands to abandon family responsibilities may encourage young adults to share them. Economic pressures, most notably the cost of housing, seem to be at the root of a variety of domestic arrangements including group houses of unrelated adults with or without children, adult sons and daughters remaining in the parental house, adult children returning to the parental house as single parents on the breakup of their marriages, and couples with children living with the parents of one of them. All of these combinations involve adults of both genders and different generations in a single unit of economic cooperation, creating models of extended family survival that sustain larger kin networks.

A growing body of post–World War II studies of working-class family and kinship stresses the importance of economically based kin relations in attempts to cope with and surmount the divisive and disintegrative pressures that come from the intensification of a wage economy (Rapp, 1978, reviews much of this literature; see also Caulfield, 1974; Stack, 1974; Tilly and Scott, 1978). They emphasize the variety and importance of extended kinship and friendship networks for coping with poverty and economic insecurity whose source is primarily capitalist wage labor relations. Black families have faced these atomizing pressures for a long time because they have had the lowest-paid and least secure jobs, and they have historically had less access than whites to land or other forms of productive property. The extended kin networks that join many small households together, often over great distances, and that form the basis of non-nuclear family households, have been well-documented in black working-class communities. As some analysts are pointing out, they are becoming increasingly common among whites, as they respond in similar ways to similar pressures.

In the past, local kin and community links provided a significant basis of support for sustained workplace resistance among wage-earning daughters and other kin. For example, Kessler-Harris (1981: 91) credits family support networks with helping women garment workers in New York City hold a key and turbulent strike for three months in 1909. This "Uprising of 20,000" was the victory that established a union in a garment industry made up of many scattered, small-scale shops—an amazing feat of organizing and unity. And Nancy MacLean (1982) extends this analysis to the importance of women's networks both in the strike and in the subsequent building of the International Ladies Garment Workers' Union (ILGWU). Organizing this scattered and diverse workforce clearly demanded significant, though largely unstudied, family and community organization. In the absence of women's informal economic activities, networks of class-based communities decrease and the kin group remains relatively isolated and less able to defend women's and men's class interests.

Isolation of the broader kin group is encouraged by some of the same forces that lead to new forms of family as well as by federal and state policies. The diminished economic power of some men relative to women under current economic circumstances has led to increased divorce rates, an increase in single-parent households, and to the related feminization of poverty that further atomizes family and household ties (Pearce and McAdoo, 1981). To shore up the nuclear family, policymakers urge state intervention—and the state in fact provides support, but in ways that discourage extended kin support systems (Boris and Bardaglio, 1983). Reciprocity and community self-provision still survive in many working-class neighborhoods, but since World War II those neighborhoods have been undermined by suburbanization, urban renewal, and increased penetration of capitalist economic relations.

In the past women were able to exert a certain amount of pressure vis-à-vis the state in their family roles because households were parts of locally based kin networks in more or less tightly integrated working-class communities. While women-centered networks sustained community support for strikes, they also reinforced the separation of work and family, even as they reinforced women's association with the latter. When women challenged employers and the state in this way, they could still maintain a self-image of themselves as domestic beings. Today, working-class communities have been dispersed and considerably weakened vis-à-vis the state. Women have taken many of the family-related concerns they once dealt with through community self-help to the workplace with them. These issues, from pay equity with its implied demands for adulthood, to dependent health and child care, are now being transformed from private responsibilities of individuals to demands for social responsibility from corporations and the state in bearing the economic costs of social reproduction, or family life.

As women come to perceive "family" issues as social and public ones, they move beyond the community to the national arena. These perceptions are shared—and acted upon—across the political spectrum, even among those to whom they are anathema. Thus right-wing and right-to-life women join with the left and with feminists in demanding that the state deal with reproductive issues and with child and dependent care. The irony is that the right-wing paradoxically demands state intervention against a whole range of issues they assert ought to be private decisions. What we witness then is a manifestation of the shift from kin responsibility to shared adult social responsibility, and a corresponding shift in locus from community struggle to workplace and state-centered arenas. But since the core of the struggle revolves around who will have social power and how it will be used, the shifts in class and gender relations produced by recent economic trends are likely to produce particularly virulent battles. These struggles are being waged at a time when families have to confront the state directly and individually, as the larger community structures that women maintained and that have previously acted as buffers and brokers give way under the pressures of maintaining households in the context of the amount of time devoted to wage work.

CONCLUSION

The sum of these effects is to undermine the shared values, or "meaning system" (Parkin, 1971) by which men and women have defined their roles. The current turmoil creates a new kind of consciousness among women, which, minimally, appears to defuse the notion that women work for the sake of the family, and at its extreme can introduce for some women an autonomous and aggressive independence. Still other women will attempt to bring the familial ideals of cooperation and nurturance to bear upon what they hope will be a newly rearranged workforce.

81

But as we have seen, the new relations of women to family and production also move the locus of struggle from community to the workplace and alter the perception of issues from familial to social change. Around the political implications of these issues working people polarize, some defending the traditional family, others legitimizing various family forms. Both groups seek to encourage the state to act on their behalf. In response, the state intervenes to reinforce traditional roles while it simultaneously insists on formal equality for women. This contradiction cannot long persist. But action in either the direction of traditional roles or in that of a more than formal equality will create its own, perhaps shattering response. We believe the result will be new family relations, new relations between men and women, and a radical transformation of the relationship of family (in all its diversity) to political economy and the state.

Notes

1. In contrast to Vanek's earlier studies, Spalter-Roth's study of time spent in housework and wage work between 1970 and 1980 indicates that women decreased their housework hours with increased wagework, while men increased theirs slightly.
2. This comes at a moment in time when the prospect of continuing high unemployment and low wages reduce the capacity of all workers to influence their working lives.

Reference List

Anderson, Karen. 1981. *Wartime Women*. Westport, CT: Greenwood Press.
Blocker, Jack S. 1985. Separate paths: Suffragists and the women's temperance crusade. *Signs* 10 (Spring): 460–476.
Bordin, Ruth. 1981. *Woman and temperance: The quest for power and liberty 1873–1900*. Philadelphia: Temple University Press.
Boris, Eileen, and Peter Bardaglio. 1983. The transformation of patriarchy: The historic role of the state. In *Families, politics and public policy: A feminist dialogue on women and the state,* edited by I. Diamond, pp. 70–93. New York: Longman.

Byington, Margaret. [1910] 1974. *Homestead: The households of a mill town.* Pittsburgh: University of Pittsburgh Press.

Caulfield, Mina. 1974. Imperialism, family and cultures of resistance. *Socialist Revolution* 29:67–85.

Cohn, Miriam. 1977. Italian–American women in New York City: 1900–1950, work and school" in *Class, sex and the Woman Worker,* edited by M. Cantor and B. Laurie, pp. 120–143 Westport: Greenwood Press.

Ehrenreich, Barbara, 1983. *Hearts of men: The American dream and the flight from committment.* New York: Doubleday.

Farnham, Marynia, and Ferdinand Lundberg. 1947. *Modern women: The lost sex.* New York: Harper and Bros.

Gabin, Nancy. 1982. 'They have placed a penalty on womanhood': The protest actions of women auto workers in Detroit-area UAW locals, 1945–1947. *Feminist Studies* 8,2:373–398.

Humphries, Jane. 1977. Class struggle and the persistence of the working class family. *Cambridge Journal of Economics* 1:241–258.

Jensen, Joan. 1980. Cloth, butter and boarders: Women's household production for the market. *Review of Radical Political Economics* 12, 2:14–24.

Kessler-Harris, Alice. 1975. Where are the organized women workers? *Feminist Studies* 3, 1–2:92–110.

Kessler-Harris, Alice. 1981. *Women have always worked.* Old Westbury: Feminist Press.

Kessler-Harris, Alice. 1982. *Out to work: A history of wage-earning women in the United States.* New York: Oxford University Press.

Lamphere, Louise, Ewa Hauser, Dee Rubin, Sonya Michel, and Christina Simmons. 1980. The economic struggles of female factory workers: A comparison between early and recent French, Polish and Portuguese Immigrants. Proceedings of a conference on Educational and Occupational Needs of White Ethnic Women. Washington, D.C.: National Institute of Education.

MacLean, Nancy. 1982. *The culture of resistance: Female institution-building in the ladies garment workers' union 1905–1925.* Occasional Papers in Women's Studies, University of Michigan.

Parkin, Frank. 1971. *Class, inequality and the political order.* New York: Praeger.

Paulson, Ross. 1973. *Women's suffrage and prohibition: A comparative study of equality and social control.* Glenview, IL: Scott Foresman and Company.

Pearce, Diana, and Harriett P. McAdoo. 1981. *Women and Children: Alone and in poverty.* Washington, D.C.: National Advisory Council on Equal Opportunity.

Pleck, Elizabeth. 1979. A mother's wages: Income earning among married Italian and black workers. In *A heritage of her own,* edited by N. F. Cott and E. Pleck, pp. 367–392. New York: Simon and Schuster.

Rapp, Rayna. 1978. Family and class in contemporary America: Notes toward understanding of ideology. *Science and Society* 42, 3:278–300.

Rubin, Lillian. 1976. *Worlds of pain: Life in the working-class family.* New York: Basic Books.

Ryan, Mary. 1979. *Womanhood in America.* New York: Franklin Watts.

Ryan, Mary. 1981. *Cradle of the middle class: The family in Oneida County, New York 1790–1865.* Cambridge: Cambridge University Press.

Smith, Judith. 1979. Our own kind: Family and community networks in Providence: In *A heritage of our own,* edited by N. F. Cott and E. Pleck, pp. 393–411. New York: Simon and Schuster.

Spalter-Roth, Roberta. 1983. Differentiating between the living standards of husbands and wives in two-wage-earner families, 1968 and 1979. *Journal of Economic History* 43, 1:231–240.

Stack, Carol. 1974. *All our kin: Strategies for survival in a black community.* New York: Harper Colophon.

Tilly, Louise, and Joan Scott. 1978. *Women, work and family.* New York: Holt, Rinehart and Winston.

Trey, J. E. 1972. Women and the war economy—World War II. *Review of Radical Political Economics* 4, 3:1–17.

Vanek, Joann. 1974. Time spent in housework. *Scientific American,* November, 116–121.

Wandersee, Winifred. 1981. *Women's work and family values 1920–1940.* Cambridge: Harvard University Press.

Weisstein, Naomi. 1970. Kinde, Küche, Kirche as scientific law: Psychology constructs the female. In *Sisterhood is powerful,* edited by R. Morgan, pp. 205–219 New York: Vintage Books.

Welter, Barbara. 1966. The cult of true womanhood 1820–1860. *American Quarterly* 18, 2 pt.1:151–174.

Wright, Eric, Cynthia Costello, David Hachen, and Joey Sprague. 1982. The American class structure. *American Sociological Review* 47, 6:709–726.

Yans-McLaughlin, Virginia. 1977. *Family and community: Italian immigrants in Buffalo, 1880–1930.* Ithaca: Cornell University Press.

Placing Deindustrialization in Perspective

George Sternlieb and Carole W. Baker

One of the curious phenomena of our age is the prevalence of self-flagellation. "The sky is falling" is a philosophy that has always had its supporters, perhaps because it provides an opportunity essentially for abdicating responsibility for making things work, perhaps as a rationalization of personal frustration.

Rarely, however, has the contrast between doom-and-gloom and reality been more telling than in the recent analyses of basic trends in the economy. Certainly, there are vast areas of confusion; in recent years forecasting has been much more noted for its incompetence than its effectiveness. But as we turn to the very subtitle of this conference, "Crisis of Work and Family Life," and review the definition of crisis, i.e., a turning point, we might do well to recall the movies of the thirties when the term was used in the context of an acute disease. Then it was understood that a crisis pointed either toward improvement or terminal deterioration. Today a much greater level of uncertainty is suggested as to what the future holds for America's labor force—both male and female.

The tremendous surge in the labor force, marked particularly by the increased participation of women, the transformation of the economy from agriculture to manufacturing and now to services, and the increasing dominance of the last element are factors that have leaped ahead of our abstractions about how Americans make their living. When this discrepancy is placed within the context of a homogenized world labor market, the conceptual tools of the past are found distinctly wanting, and the threat of the unknown sometimes produces near-hysterical reactions.

The very rise of the current women's movement, borne by the vigor of economic transformation, and perhaps even preceding and abetting it as well, may have accentuated the crisis of confidence in America's nearly totally masculine political/industrial leadership. The new economy is overrunning the masculine blue-collar bastions of heavy industry. Yet at the same time, it is increasingly receptive to women. But for how long? Are the changes we see now in the workforce and in job composition transient? Or rather, are they a matrix of things to come?

The theme of this chapter is that the macroeconomic data on employment, while raising some issues about what it is that Americans will do so uniquely well in the future to justify their standard of living, have little within them based on historical trends to the present to support a Spenglerian thesis of the decline of the West. Instead, they suggest that the economy has done a remarkable job of absorbing large numbers of new workers and that the post–World War II era has been a time of unparalleled opportunity for women. This note of optimism, however, must be tempered with an awareness that very real economic and social stresses remain, including declining productivity and inequalities of wages.

The sequence of the presentation in this paper involves first an overview of the economy and its structural transformation as reflected in employment data. This is followed by an analysis of changes in the labor force, particularly focusing on the employment of women and perhaps even more strikingly on the changing experience between the sexes in relation to layoffs and job losses. After a brief view of the gender lag in salaries, we conclude with a modest coda on some trends of the future.

THE ECONOMY: STRUCTURAL TRANSFORMATION

Table 4.1 provides a simplified data base that affords insight into the economic transformation in America from 1940 to 1984. Two major changes are evident: first, changes in total employment, and second, changes in manufacturing activity. The former parameter provides overwhelming evidence of the incredible absorptive ca-

Table 4.1. **Trends in Manufacturing, Durable and Non-durable Goods Employment United States 1940–1984**

Year	Total non-agricultural employment Thousands	Manufacturing employment Thousands	Manufacturing employment Percent	Durable goods employment Thousands	Durable goods employment Percent	Non-durable goods employment Thousands	Non-durable goods employment Percent
1940	32,361	10,985	33.9	5,363	16.6	5,622	17.4
1945	40,374	15,524	38.4	9,074	22.5	6,450	16.0
1950	45,197	15,241	33.7	8,094	17.9	7,147	15.8
1955	50,641	16,882	33.3	9,541	18.8	7,341	14.5
1960	54,189	16,796	31.0	9,459	17.4	7,337	13.5
1965	60,765	18,062	29.7	10,405	17.1	7,656	12.6
1970	70,880	19,367	27.3	11,208	15.8	8,158	11.5
1975	76,945	18,323	23.8	10,688	13.9	7,635	9.9
1980	90,406	20,285	22.4	12,187	13.5	8,098	9.0
1981	91,105	20,173	22.1	12,117	13.3	8,056	8.8
1982	89,630	18,848	21.0	11,112	12.4	7,736	8.6
1983	89,978	18,678	20.8	10,932	12.1	7,747	8.6
1984	94,156	19,590	20.8	11,635	12.4	7,954	8.4

SOURCES: U.S. Department of Labor, Bureau of Labor Statistics, *Employment and Earnings, United States, 1909–1978* Bulletin 13 12–11, (Washington, D.C.: U.S. GPO, 1979.) U.S. Department of Labor Statistics, *Supplement to Employment and Earnings, Revised Establishment Data.* (Washington, D.C.: GPO, 1982.) U.S. Department of Labor, Bureau of Labor Statistics, Employment And Earnings," vol. 30, no. 3; vol. 31, no. 3; vol. 32, no. 3. (Washington, D.C.: GPO, 1985.)

NOTE: Based on data from Establishment Reports. Includes all full-time and part-time employees who worked during or received pay for any part of the pay period reported. Excludes proprietors, the self-employed, farmworkers, unpaid family workers, domestic servants, and armed forces.

pacity of America's economic structures over the last generation. The vitality of the post–World War II economy is effectively demonstrated by the figures for total nonagricultural employment. Those who scoffed at Henry Wallace's call for 60 million jobs and who feared a return to the Depression years with the end of World War II, saw 70 million people employed in 1970. Even this figure was eclipsed in the decade from 1970 to 1980 with a total job growth of nearly 20 million. While job growth suffered in the downturn of 1982–1983, the absolute decline was relatively trivial, the revival in 1984 without parallel. In the three decades since the mid-1950s, employment has doubled!

Table 4.2. Comparative Employment Data: United States, West Germany, and Japan

		1970	1982	Percent change
Total labor force (total civilian labor force)	United States	85,959 (82,771)	112,384 (110,204)	30.74
	West Germany	26,817 (26,318)	27,455 (26,923)	2.37
	Japan	51,530 (N.G.)	57,740 (N.G.)	12.05
Civilian employment	United States	78,678	99,526	26.49
	West Germany	26,169	25,090	−4.13
	Japan	50,940	56,380	10.67

SOURCE: Organization for Economic Cooperation and Development *Labour force statistics 1962–82* (Paris, 1984).
NOTE: Includes self-employed, other nonpayroll employed, unemployed

Putting this into an international perspective, from 1970 to 1982 (Table 4.2), U.S. employment grew by 26.49 percent, whereas Japan's grew only 10.67 percent, and West Germany's actually declined. In Japan and West Germany, the absolute growth in the labor force was considerably smaller than the gains in the working-age population. In the United States, however, the labor force expansion far exceeded the growth in the working-age population. In general, then, the United States economy has performed remarkably well in absorbing the burgeoning baby-boom generation, both male and female, into the workforce.

The second change, in manufacturing activity, reflects the transformation from a national economy dominated by manufacturing to a postindustrial or service economy. In the last twenty-five years, manufacturing employment has essentially been static at roughly the 19 million mark, plus or minus 6 percent. Even within the manufacturing sector, there has been some shift of employment from production to nonproduction personnel as shown in Table 4.3. Moreover, current forecasts suggest a near halving of national manufacturing employment by the turn of the century.

As the manufacturing sector wanes, the enormously vigorous

growth of total employment indicates the flourishing of other sectors of the economy. Trends in wholesale and retail trade, services, and government employment (Table 4.4) show an increase of jobs in the wholesale and retail trade sector in excess of 5 million from 1970 to 1980, and even more strikingly, a near doubling in services employment from 1970 to 1984. By the latter date there were over 20 million employed in this sector from a baseline of only 11½ million. And clearly, despite protestations to the contrary, government employment as a percentage of the total has remained relatively constant in the face of a variety of efforts and statements to alter it.

A clearer picture of restructuring within the services sector is sketched out in Tables 4.5 and 4.6, which give the distribution of services employment. The growth of health services employment, which doubled from barely three million in 1970 to over six million in 1984, symbolizes the structural change involved in this sector.

Also especially noteworthy has been the growth of the business and legal services industry—including the classic accounting firms, law firms, advertising firms, and consultants. This area has seen a doubling of employment since 1970. Educational services, however, at least at the elementary school level, have been relatively static— a victim of the baby-bust generation.

While the time series are insufficient in some cases to give a long-term perspective, the data do provide support for this basic thesis: as the U.S. economy was undergoing a structural transformation from manufacturing to a postindustrial or service economy, it did remarkably well in creating new jobs and in absorbing large increases in the labor force. But much of this growth was accommodated by service industries and other postindustrial economic sectors, which to date have been least amenable to productivity-increasing measures. Unfortunately, then, just as newcomers were flooding the labor force, American economic growth was faltering, which in turn forced even more workers into the job market. The two-worker household has thus increasingly become, not a generator of luxury, but a necessity for sustenance at a constant rather than augmented level of amenity. It is with this awareness that we turn to a closer examination of what the restructuring of the American economy has meant in terms of opportunities for the labor force in general and for women workers in particular.

89

Table 4.3. **Production Workers in the U.S. Economy 1940–1984**

Year	Total non-agricultural employment			Manufacturing employment		
	All employees (thousands)	Production employees[a] (thousands)	Percent production employees	All employees (thousands)	Production employees (thousands)	Percent production employees
1940	32,361	N/A		10,985	8,940	81.4
1945	40,374	N/A		15,524	13,009	83.8
1950	45,197	34,349	76.0	15,241	12,523	82.2
1955	50,641	37,500	74.0	16,882	13,288	78.7
1960	54,189	38,516	71.1	16,796	12,586	74.9
1965	60,765	42,278	69.6	18,062	13,434	74.4
1970	70,880	48,156	67.9	19,367	14,044	72.5
1975	76,945	50,991	66.3	18,323	13,043	71.2
1980	90,406	60,331	66.7	20,285	14,214	70.1
1981	91,105	60,881	66.8	20,173	14,021	69.5
1982	89,630	59,587	66.5	18,848	12,782	67.8
1983	89,978	59,925	66.6	18,678	12,696	68.0
1984	94,156	63,300	67.2	19,590	13,455	68.7

SOURCES: U.S. Department of Labor, Bureau of Labor Statistics, *Employment and Earnings United States, 1909–1978* Bulletin 13 12–11, (Washington, D.C.: GPO, 1979). U.S. Departmen of Labor, Bureau of Labor Statistics, *Supplement to Employment and Earnings, Revised Estab lishment Data.* (Washington, D.C.: GPO, 1982). U.S. Department of Labor, Bureau of Labor Sta tistics, "Employment and Earnings," vol. 30, no. 3; vol. 31, no. 3; vol. 32, no. 3 (Washingtor D.C.: GPO, March 1985).

NOTE: Based on data from Establishment Reports. Includes all full-time and part-time em ployees who worked during or received pay for any part of the pay period reported. Exclude proprietors, the self-employed, farmworkers, unpaid family workers, domestic servants, an armed forces.

LABOR FORCE: GROWTH AND CHANGE

Few periods in history can match the incremental increase in the size of the workforce over this last generation. From 1969 to 1979, the total United States population aged between fifteen and sixty-four years increased by nearly one in four. The employment tabulations documenting this phenomenon are illustrated in Table 4.7. The average annual growth in nonfarm payroll employment in the United States from 1960 to 1975 was over the 1.5 million mark. From 1975 to 1980, years of relative stagnation, the annual gain ac-

Durable goods employment			Non-durable goods employment		
All employees (thousands)	Production employees (thousands)	Percent production employees	All employees (thousands)	Production employees (thousands)	Percent production employees
5,363	4,477	83.5	5,622	4,463	79.4
9,074	7,541	83.1	6,459	5,468	84.8
8,094	6,705	82.8	7,147	5,817	81.4
9,541	7,548	79.1	7,341	5,740	78.2
9,459	7,028	74.3	7,337	5,558	75.8
10,405	7,715	74.1	7,656	5,719	74.7
11,208	8,055	71.9	8,158	5,989	73.4
10,688	7,557	70.7	7,635	5,485	71.8
12,187	8,492	69.7	8,098	5,772	71.3
12,117	8,301	68.5	8,056	5,721	71.0
11,112	7,364	66.3	7,736	5,418	70.0
10,932	7,246	66.3	7,747	5,450	70.3
11,635	7,846	67.4	7,954	5,610	70.5

tually increased to over 2.6 million. Indeed, in absolute numbers, the latter period registered a staggering employment increase in excess of 13 million persons. And, between 1980 and 1984, employment continued to increase, growing by almost 4 million workers. To absorb these numbers without generating massive unemployment has truly been a remarkable accomplishment of the American economy.

As the workforce was burgeoning, we have seen that the various components of the economy were undergoing crucial alterations. The evolution of the United States into a postindustrial economy saw a restructuring of the economy whereby many of today's jobs can be handled by either sex. Even within the manufacturing segment there has been some shift of employment from production to nonproduction personnel (shown in Table 4.3)—a case of paperwork replacing physical labor, offering more employment opportunities for women.

The employment figures in Table 4.8 trace clearly the changing structure of the economy. First, employment in the manufacturing sector declined in relative importance, while private nonmanufacturing activity virtually doubled, with a growth increment in excess

Table 4.4. **Trends in Wholesale and Retail Trade, Services and Government Employ ment 1940–1982**

	Total non-agricultural employees	Wholesale and retail trade employment		Services employment		Government employment	
Year	Thousands	Thousands	Percent	Thousands	Percent	Thousands	Percent
1940	32,361	6,750	20.8	3,665	11.3	4,202	13.0
1945	40,374	7,314	18.1	4,222	10.4	5,944	14.7
1950	45,197	9,386	20.8	5,357	11.8	6,026	13.3
1955	50,641	10,535	20.8	6,240	12.3	6,914	13.6
1960	54,189	11,391	21.0	7,378	13.6	8,353	15.4
1965	60,765	12,716	20.9	9,036	14.9	10,074	16.6
1970	70,880	15,040	21.2	11,548	16.3	12,554	17.7
1975	76,945	17,060	22.2	13,892	18.0	14,686	19.1
1980	90,406	20,310	22.5	17,890	19.8	16,241	18.0
1981	91,105	20,551	22.6	18,592	20.4	16,024	17.6
1982	89,630	20,551	22.9	19,001	21.2	15,788	17.6
1983	89,978	20,513	22.8	19,680	21.9	15,744	17.5
1984	94,156	21,787	23.1	20,662	21.9	15,969	17.0

SOURCES: U.S. Department of Labor, Bureau of Labor Statistics, *Employment and Earning United States, 1909–1978* Bulletin 13 12–11, (Washington, D.C.: GPO, 1979). U.S. Departmer of Labor, Bureau of Labor Statistics, *Supplement to Employment and Earnings, Revised Esta lishment Data.* (Washington, D.C.: GPO, 1982). U.S. Department of Labor, Bureau of Labor Sta tistics, "Employment and Earnings," vol. 30, no. 3; vol. 31, no. 3; vol. 32, no. 3 (Washingto D.C.: GPO, March 1985).

of 29 million jobs. Second, the government sector advanced very rapidly from 1960 to 1975, although expansion has slowed dramatically since that time. And finally, by 1984 barely one in four of all nonfarm payroll jobs in the United States were in manufacturing, while private nonmanufacturing jobs accounted for over 60 percent of the total. It is the latter sector that encompasses the new postindustrial jobs that have expanded in parallel with (or facilitated) the surge of women into the labor force and to which we now turn our attention.

Women in the Labor Force

The vitality of the economy, as evidenced by the growth of total employment, coupled with the emergence of the postindustrial economy, whereby many if not most jobs can be handled by either men or women, have made this an opportune time for women to enter the workforce in large numbers. But it is not only that opportunities have presented themselves; changes in attitude toward women in the workplace have been essential in overcoming a significant barrier to women's broader involvement. Some women have always worked, of course, often out of economic necessity. But today as women enter the working world, an ever-widening range of occupational choices is open to them.

The evolving pattern of the female role in the labor force is illustrated in Table 4.9 that contrasts the proportion of women employed versus total employment in various industrial segments for 1970, 1981, and 1984. There has been an enormous expansion in female employment as a proportion of the total—by 1984 over 43 percent of the 100 million persons employed in the United States were women. Even in manufacturing, whose total labor force remained relatively stagnant in the fourteen years after 1970, the share of jobs held by women shifted up abruptly to the one-in-three mark.

What is most striking, however, is that it is in the growth segments of our economy, notably wholesale and retail trade and services, that increasing numbers of women can be found. Wholesale and retail trade, and particularly retail trade, have long had a respectable share of women employees. The service industries, including the rapidly expanding business and professional services, have seen a doubling of employment since 1970, and women are entering these fields in ever-increasing numbers. Moreover, there is very clear evidence of a growing dispersion of these jobs as the campus-office park in suburbia and, indeed, in exurbia, begins to become a major presence. This is particularly convenient for women who seek work near their homes.

Further indicated in Table 4.9 is the other side of the coin—that is, the jobs secured by default of other opportunities—and these are the employment areas that have declined. Private household employment, for example, typically a low-paying and low-status effort, has fallen as a whole, and since 1970, so has the proportion of women employed in this sector. As women enter the boardrooms, they are discovering how hard it is to find other women to clean the

Table 4.5. **Trends in Services Employment 1960–1984**

Year	Total service employment Thousands	Personal service[a] employment Thousands	Personal service[a] employment Percent	Business services[b] employment Thousands	Business services[b] employment Percent	Health services[c] employment Thousands	Health services[c] employment Percent
1960	7,378	894.2	12.1	777.7	10.5	1,547.6	20.0
1965	9,036	985.4	10.9	1,138.9	12.6	2,079.5	23.0
1970	11,548	989.0	8.6	1,675.5	14.5	3,052.5	26.4
1975	13,892	860.9	6.2	2,041.9	14.7	4,133.8	29.8
1980	17,890	900.7	5.0	3,092.0	17.3	5,278.0	29.5
1981	18,592	913.9	4.9	3,255.0	17.5	5,555.1	29.9
1982	19,001	924.5	4.9	3,298.2	17.4	5,776.5	30.4
1983	19,680	937.2	4.8	3,595.0	18.3	5,948.4	30.2
1984	20,662	995.9	4.8	4,002.5	19.4	6,068.2	29.4

SOURCES: U.S. Department of Labor, Bureau of Labor Statistics, *Employment and Earnin*, *United States, 1909–1978* Bulletin 13 12–11, (Washington, D.C.: GPO, 1979). U.S. Departme of Labor, Bureau of Labor Statistics, *Supplement to Employment and Earnings, Revised Esta lishment Data.* (Washington, D.C.: GPO, 1982). U.S. Department of Labor, Bureau of Labor St tistics, "Employment and Earnings," vol. 30, no. 3; vol. 31, no. 3; vol. 32, no. 3 (Washingtc D.C.: GPO, March 1985).

Table 4.6. **Trends in all Other Services Employment as a Percent of Total Services Employment 1960–1984**

Year	Hotels and other lodging places Thousands	Hotels and other lodging places Percent of total	Auto repair services and garages Thousands	Auto repair services and garages Percent of total	Miscellaneous repair services Thousands	Miscellaneous repair services Percent of total	Motion pictures Thousands	Motion pictures Percent of tota
1960	N/A		N/A		N/A		189.6	2.6
1965	N/A		N/A		155.0	1.7	185.1	2.0
1970	N/A		N/A		188.7	1.6	204.1	1.8
1975	898.4	6.4	438.8	3.2	217.5	1.6	205.7	1.5
1980	1,075.8	6.0	570.9	3.2	288.8	1.6	216.9	1.2
1981	1,118.6	6.0	572.3	3.1	296.2	1.6	217.0	1.2
1982	1,099.2	5.8	579.5	3.0	294.3	1.5	211.8	1.1
1983	1,120.4	5.7	586.9	3.0	271.0	1.4	208.6	1.1
1984	1,254.2	6.1	673.1	3.3	303.5	1.5	219.9	1.1

SOURCES: U.S. Department of Labor, Bureau of Labor Statistics, *Employment and Earning United States, 1909–1978* Bulletin 13 12–11, (Washington, D.C.: GPO, 1979). U.S. Departme of Labor, Bureau of Labor Statistics, *Supplement to Employment and Earnings, Revised Esta*

Educational services employment		Membership organization employment		All other services[c] employment	
Thousands	Percent	Thousands	Percent	Thousands	Percent
616.1	8.4	N/A	N/A	3,542.4	48.0
772.1	8.5	N/A	N/A	4,060.1	44.9
939.6	8.1	N/A	N/A	4,891.4	42.4
1,000.9	7.2	1,452.3	10.4	4,402.2	31.7
1,138.2	6.4	1,539.3	8.6	5,941.8	33.2
1,173.2	6.3	1,529.0	8.2	6,165.8	33.2
1,180.5	6.2	1,534.8	8.1	6,286.5	33.1
1,207.3	6.1	1,521.9	7.7	6,470.2	32.9
1,219.4	5.9	1,503.6	7.3	6,872.4	33.3

[a]Personal services includes laundry, cleaning, beauty shops, and funeral services.
[b]Business services includes advertising, credit reporting and collection, mailing, reproduction, building services, and computer and data processing services.
[c]All other services includes hotels and motels; auto repair services; miscellaneous repair services; motion pictures; amusement and recreation services; legal services; engineering and architectural services; and accounting, auditing, and bookkeeping services.

Amusement and recreation		Legal services		Social services		Miscellaneous	
Thousands	Percent of total	Thousands	Percent of total	Thousands	Percent of total	Thousands	Percent of total
N/A		144.0	2.0	N/A		N/A	
N/A		181.5	2.0	N/A		N/A	
N/A		236.0	2.0	N/A		N/A	
396.8	4.3	340.3	2.4	689.9	5.0	723.5	5.2
763.5	4.3	497.7	2.8	1,134.3	6.3	977.4	5.6
772.6	4.2	532.4	2.9	1,156.6	6.2	1,044.7	5.6
837.1	4.4	566.4	3.0	1,183.2	6.2	1,061.3	5.6
843.1	4.3	602.4	3.1	1,251.0	6.4	1,064.9	5.4
840.0	4.1	646.9	3.1	1,307.0	6.3	1,133.3	5.5

lishment Data. (Washington, D.C.: GPO, 1982). U.S. Department of Labor, Bureau of Labor Statistics, "Employment and Earnings," vol. 30, no. 3; vol. 31, no. 3; vol. 32, no. 3 (Washington, D.C.: GPO, March 1985).

Table 4.7.   **United States Total Employment Change: 1960 to 1984 (Thousands)**

| 1960 | 1975 | Change: 1960–1975 | | Average annual change |
		No.	%	
54,189	76,945	22,756	42.0	1,517.1

| 1975 | 1980 | 1984 | Change: 1975–1984 | | Average annual change |
			No.	%	
76,945	90,406	94,156	17,211	22.4	1,912.3

Source: U.S. Department of Labor, Bureau of Labor Statistics, *Employment and Earnings,* (Washington, D.C.: GPO), monthly.
Note: Employees on non-agriculture payrolls as of March of the respective years; excludes self-employed and unpaid family workers; excludes Hawaii and Alaska. Intraperiod growth increments: 1960–1965, 6,576; 1965–1970, 10,115; 1970–1975, 6,065; 1975–1980, 13,461; 1980–1984, 3,750.

Table 4.8.   **United States Employment Change by Sector: 1960 to 1981**

| | 1960 | 1975 | Change: 1960 to 1975 | |
			No.	%
Total	54,189	76,945	22,756	42.0
Manufacturing	16,796	18,323	1,527	9.1
Private non-manufacturing	29,040	43,936	14,896	51.3
Government	8,353	14,686	6,332	75.8

| | 1975 | 1980 | 1984 | Change: 1975 to 1984 | |
				No.	%
Total	76,945	90,406	94,156	17,211	22.4
Manufacturing	18,323	20,285	19,590	1,267	6.9
Private non-manufacturing	43,936	53,881	58,597	14,661	33.4
Government	14,685	16,240	15,969	1,284	8.7

Source: U.S. Department of Labor, Bureau of Labor Statistics, *Employment and Earnings,* (Washington, D.C.: GPO), monthly.
Note: Employees on nonagriculture payrolls as of March of the respective years; excludes self-employed and unpaid family workers; excludes Hawaii and Alaska.

Table 4.9.   Employment, by Industry: 1970 and 1981

	1970		1981		1984	
Industry	All employees (thousands)	Percent female	All employees (thousands)	Percent female	All employees (thousands)	Percent female
Total employed	78,678	37.7	100,397	42.8	105,005	43.7
Agriculture, forestry, fisheries	3,567	17.0	3,518	19.7	3,321	19.7
Mining	516	7.0	1,118	15.2	957	17.2
Construction	4,818	4.9	6,060	8.2	6,665	8.4
Manufacturing	20,746	27.7	21,817	31.7	20,995	32.6
Transportation, communication, and other public utilities	5,320	21.2	6,633	26.5	7,358	25.8
Wholesale and retail trade	15,008	23.8	20,524	46.9	21,979	47.4
Wholesale trade	2,672	22.4	4,016	25.7	4,212	27.4
Retail trade	12,336	45.8	16,508	52.0	17,767	52.2
Finance, insurance, real estate	3,945	50.4	6,133	58.5	6,750	57.7
Banking and other finances	1,697	57.7	2,721	66.7	3,032	64.4
Insurance and real estate	2,248	44.9	3,413	51.9	3,720	52.1
Services[a]	20,281	60.6	29,360	60.9	32,214	60.7
Business services	1,403	40.4	2,518	44.7	3,630	47.7
Automobile services	600	8.7	989	12.4	11,186	11.2
Personal services[a]	4,276	75.5	3,914	72.5	2,931	67.4
Private households	1,782	88.9	1,276	84.7	1,243	85.5
Hotels and lodging places	979	68.0	1,197	65.8	1,347	66.1
Entertainment and recreation	717	33.9	1,107	39.4	1,260	38.6
Professional and related services[a]	12,904	63.7	20,201	65.7	21,174	66.4
Hospitals	2,843	77.4	4,186	76.4	4,288	76.5
Health services	1,628	71.1	3,476	75.6	3,646	75.8
Elementary, secondary schools			5,439	70.9	5,347	70.0
Colleges, universities	6,126	62.0	2,147	49.8	2,209	49.4
Public administration[b]	4,476[c]	31.5	5,233	36.0	4,766	40.2

SOURCE: U.S. Bureau of Labor Statistics, *Employment and Earnings,* (Washington, D.C.: GPO), monthly and unpublished data.

Includes industries not shown separately

Includes workers in uniquely governmental activities, e.g., judicial and legislative

Not strictly comparable with later years due to reclassification between "Professional and related services" and "Public administration" houses they have left behind. Welfare and a range of job alternatives are the working middle-class mother's rivals for household help.

Employment in educational services has slowed, at least at the junior levels. Long a profession in which females predominated, elementary and secondary-school teaching in particular face a diminution of opportunities in the near future in light of the shrinking school age population base.

Viewing these findings from a market perspective, even if women's share of employment by sector of the economy were suddenly to become stagnant, the proportion of women employed within the overall economy would continue to increase. The sectors in which women are most deeply involved are growing, while those in which their participation is at a much lower level have tended to be relatively stagnant.

Obviously, the millenium is not at hand—but these data should be viewed from the perspective that in the not-so-distant past, employment of women outside the home was essentially confined to schoolteaching—and even that was threatened during times of economic stress—witness the Depression.

Now attitudes toward women in the workplace have changed, and their accepted roles have suddenly expanded. For example, the Rutgers graduate accounting program accepted its first female applicant less than twenty years ago; current enrollment by women is now close to the halfway mark. A generation ago, women lawyers outside of family practice were a rarity; now they are an ever-growing fact of life. And we could go on. These changes have been accomplished at a time of rapid growth of newcomers to the job market—courtesy of the baby boom, a negative period from a demographic point of view. Progress will be fostered as the United States moves into a far slower period of labor force growth. By mid-1995, the impact of the "baby bust" generation will result in a near halving of the annual accession rate of job seekers (Sternlieb and Hughes, 1984). Women in a period of booming availability have won a share of the job market. Now their acceptance will be even more rapid as America becomes labor short.

Startling as the notion might be at first, the structural transformation of the economy may turn out to be a more painful process for men than for women employees, both present and prospective. Evidence on this point can be derived from the differences in layoffs and in job losses between the sexes.

Layoffs and Job Losses

One of the impressions we often have of women in the labor force is one concerning the marginals—the last-hired and first-fired—partaking of all of the trauma of the secondary labor force within the dual labor market structure. While certainly this kind of marginalization may well be the case in relation to any of a number of job activities, judging from macroeconomic data on this point, the generalization as a whole does not hold water. As shown in Tables 4.10 and 4.11, when job losers by sex and age are reviewed for 1982, for example, a classic recession year, women suffered far less than males did both in terms of percentages of total unemployment and in attributing their unemployment to layoffs and to permanent separations. And this trend continued into 1984's recovery year.

This relative success on the part of woman may well be evaluated as unique to the rifleshot recession, with its focal point on heavy industry—steel and autos, particularly—long a stronghold of masculine prerogatives. The data, however, indicate that while historically women have had higher unemployment rates than men, the surge in the total number of women employed even in years of recession has bypassed men. Thus, in the recession of 1975, while male employment rose by less than a million in absolute numbers, female employment actually exhibited an increase of more than 1.5 million (see Table 4.11).

Furthermore, when men lose their jobs, in general they suffer from lengthier layoffs than women do (see Table 4.12). Not only are men laid-off for longer periods of time, but when unemployment data are reviewed by industry, we also find that, with few exceptions, men are far more likely than women to be laid-off or permanently separated, i.e., fired (see Table 4.13).

These findings may be explained partially by the lower pay levels of women, or perhaps by their greater adaptability and flexibility within the labor market as second-wage earners. But certainly the

Table 4.10. **Job Losers, by Sex and Age, 1982, 1984: Annual Averages**

	Layoffs					
	Number (thousands)		% of total unemployment due to layoffs		% of total un- employment of eac population group[a]	
Characteristics	1982	1984	1982	1984	1982	1984
Total, 16 years and over	2,127	1,171	100.0	100.0	22.4	13.7
Teenagers	111	64	5.2	5.5	5.6	4.3
Men	1,394	739	65.5	63.1	27.4	18.8
Women	622	368	29.2	31.4	17.2	11.8

SOURCE: U.S. Bureau of Labor Statistics, *Employment and Earnings,* (Washington, D.C.: GPO), vol. 30, no. 1, January 1983; vol. 32, no. 1, January 1985.

Table 4.11. **Trends in Employment Rates, by Sex, 1960–1984**

	Men			
Year	Labor force[a] (thousands)	% of population	Unemployed (thousands)	Rate[b]
1960	48,870	84.0	2,486	5.4
1965	50,946	81.5	1,914	4.0
1970	54,376	80.6	2,238	4.4
1973	56,900	79.5	2,275	4.2
1974	57,397	79.2	2,714	4.7
1975	58,899	78.4	4,442	7.7
1976	58,756	78.0	4,036	6.7
1977	59,959	78.1	3,667	6.3
1978	61,151	78.3	3,142	5.1
1979	62,215	78.2	3,120	5.0
1980	62,932	77.8	4,267	6.8
1981	63,486	77.4	4,577	7.2
1982	63,979	77.0	6,179	9.7
1983	64,580	76.8	6,260	9.7
1984	65,386	76.8	4,744	7.3

SOURCE: U.S. Bureau of Labor Statistics, *Employment and Earnings,* (Washington, D.C.: GPO), vol. 30, no. 1, January, 1983; vol. 32, no. 1, January 1985.
[a] Includes Armed Forces.

Other Jobs Losers

Number (thousands)		% of total unemployment due to permanent separations		% of total unemployment of each population group[a]	
1982	1984	1982	1984	1982	1984
4,141	3,250	100.0	100.0	43.6	38.1
348	207	8.4	6.4	17.6	13.8
2,571	2,061	62.1	63.4	50.5	52.4
1,222	982	29.5	30.2	33.8	31.6

NOTES: Includes persons on layoff and persons whose employment ended involuntarily who immediately began looking for work.
[a] Total unemployment includes job losers, job leavers, reentrants, and new entrants.

Women				Total	
Labor force[a] (thousands)	% of population	Unemployed (thousands)	Rate[b]	Non-institutional population[a] (thousands)	Labor force[a] (thousands)
23,272	37.8	1,366	5.9	119,759	72,142
26,232	39.3	1,452	5.5	129,236	77,178
31,583	43.4	1,855	5.9	140,272	85,959
34,855	44.8	2,089	6.0	149,423	91,756
36,274	45.7	2,441	6.7	151,841	93,671
37,553	46.4	3,486	9.3	154,829	95,452
39,069	47.4	3,369	8.6	157,817	97,825
40,705	48.5	3,324	8.2	160,688	100,664
42,731	50.0	3,061	7.2	163,541	103,882
44,343	51.0	3,018	6.8	166,460	106,558
45,611	51.6	3,370	7.4	169,349	108,543
46,829	52.2	3,696	7.9	171,774	110,315
47,894	52.7	4,499	9.4	173,939	111,873
48,646	53.0	4,457	9.2	175,891	113,226
49,855	53.7	3,794	7.6	178,080	115,241

[b] Percent of civilian labor force for 1960, 1965, 1970, 1973. For 1974–1984, percent of labor force, including armed forces.

Table 4.12. **Job Losers' Duration of Unemployment, by Sex (in percent)**

| | Layoffs | | | | | |
| | Total | | Men | | Women | |
Duration	1982	1984	1982	1984	1982	1984
Job Losers						
Number (in thousands)[a]	2,127	1,171	1,394	739	622	368
Percent	100.0		100.0		100.0	
Duration of unemployment (in percent)						
Less than 5 weeks	40.3	46.1	38.7	43.7	41.0	46.5
5 to 14 weeks	31.2	27.8	31.0	27.6	31.3	28.7
15 to 26 weeks	15.3	12.5	16.3	13.5	14.4	12.1
27 weeks and over	13.2	13.6	14.0	15.2	13.2	12.6
Mean Duration (weeks)[b]	13.6		14.2		12.4	

SOURCE: U.S. Bureau of Labor Statistics, *Employment and Earnings,* (Washington, D.C.: GPO), vol. 30, no. 1, January 1983; vol. 32, no. 1, January 1985.
NOTE: Includes persons on layoff and persons whose employment ended involuntarily who immediately began looking for work.
[a]Total number includes job losers of both sexes 16 years and older; figures for men include job losers 20 years and older.
[b]The mean duration was estimated using the midpoints of the number of weeks in unemployed categories: 52 weeks was the assumed midpoint for the 27 weeks or more category.

trauma of recession, judging from these data, tends to be less for women as wage-earners than for men, regardless of the antecedents of the variation.

Wages

Concern has been growing over the fact that, even allowing for differences in senority, work experience, and the like, women's wages continue to lag seriously behind those of men. This gap is far from trivial, as is witnessed in Table 4.14. Furthermore, in a study of men and women workers in specific occupations, only 4 percent of the wage difference between the sexes could be explained by the shorter occupational tenure of women, leaving a substantial portion

		Other Job Losers			
Total		Men		Women	
1982	1984	1982	1984	1982	1984
4,141	3,250	2,571	2,061	1,222	982
100.0		100.0		100.0	
25.3	26.8	22.7	24.4	27.1	27.8
31.1	28.1	30.4	26.8	31.4	29.8
20.0	16.7	20.4	16.4	20.0	18.1
23.6	28.4	26.4	32.4	21.5	24.2
19.7		21.2		18.7	

of the total wage gap unaccounted for (Rytina, 1982). Certainly it is possible that some part of the remainder may be attributed to worker and job characteristics not analyzed in the study, but it is even more likely that the differences are due to sex discrimination.

We suggest that wage inequalities may represent (consciously or otherwise) one of the penalties of "buying in," i.e., of overcoming prejudice by undercutting the market. Thus the disparities should largely be reduced over time—witness the shift up in ticket prices of the newcomers to the airline industry after they develop their own market shares. This is happening for black women whose earnings have been converging with those of black men—from 55 percent in 1955 to 76 percent in 1981. But for white women, the gap with regard to white men's earnings has widened: In 1955 white women earned 65 percent of what white men earned, but by 1980 they earned only 59 percent (Spain and Bianchi, 1983). If we pursue the airline analogy further, this is the price of increased female accession rates to the labor force: Women employees could be hired at a discount when the pool of applicants seemed neverending. They had to "buy into the market." This will be decreasingly the case in the future. Clearly, concern over wage discrepancies are appropriate;

Table 4.13. **Job Losers by Industry and Sex, 1982**

Job losers	Percent of total unemployment due to layoffs and permanent separations		Percent of total unemployment in each industry due to layoffs and permanent separations	
	Men	Women	Men	Women
Layoffs, total	100.0	100.0	27.4	17.2
Mining	4.3	0.3	43.6	30.2
Construction	20.7	2.1	32.2	23.4
Manufacturing	49.4	58.8	42.7	36.4
Durables	41.2	31.7	48.0	38.3
Nondurables	8.2	27.1	27.4	34.4
Transportation and public utilities	7.2	3.1	33.9	23.2
Wholesale and retail trade	7.4	13.4	13.4	9.8
Finance, insurance and real estate	0.4	2.1	6.0	7.9
Services	4.9	11.8	12.3	9.3
Government	2.2	6.6	9.9	11.0
Permanent separations, total	100.0	100.0	50.5	33.8
Mining	2.4	0.4	44.4	57.6
Construction	19.0	2.2	54.6	49.3
Manufacturing	28.4	29.8	45.2	36.3
Durables	19.5	15.7	41.8	37.5
Nondurables	8.9	14.0	54.8	35.0
Transportation and public utilities	5.8	2.4	50.0	35.6
Wholesale and retail trade	17.5	25.5	58.3	36.6
Finance, insurance and real estate	2.3	4.9	62.7	37.8
Services	13.0	22.3	60.3	34.7
Government	6.6	10.1	55.3	33.0

SOURCE: *Monthly Labor Review,* 106, 9 (September 1983): 8.
NOTE: Excludes agricultural wage and salary workers and self-employed and unpaid family workers.

Table 4.14. **Median Income by Sex, 1983**

Occupation	Women	Men	Ratio female/male
Managerial	$18,277	$30,476	60
Professional	19,202	29,547	65
Technical support	16,555	24,573	67
Administrative support (incl. clerical)	13,473	20,833	65
Sales	11,979	23,128	52
Crafts	13,245	21,520	62
Operatives	11,182	18,525	60
Transportation and movers	13,595	19,380	70
Laborers	11,858	15,183	78
Private household	6,296	*	—
Other services	9,465	14,695	64

SOURCE: U.S. Department of Commerce. Bureau of the Census. *Current Population Reports: Consumer Income* Series P–60, No. 145, August 1984.
NOTE: Median wage and salary income of full-time, year-round workers.
*Sample too small to produce data.

women are still a long way from achieving equal pay for equal work. The reasons are a subject for further research (Haggstrom et al., 1984).

CONCLUSION

The macroeconomic data presented here clearly show favorable trends for women: Their participation in the workforce has expanded enormously; they are heavily represented in the growth segments of American economic activity; their rate of unemployment is smaller than that for men; and they are less likely than men to be laid-off or fired. Yet, these findings must be tempered with the awareness that this progress is often accompanied by stress. In this case, ironically at the very time when the restructuring of the economy and changes in attitudes toward women in the workplace offer women employment opportunities unprecedented in our nation's history, the slowdown in productivity has made an increased number of workers per household necessary in order to support "the good life."

The real problem, of course, arises for nonelite, single wage-earners. Their apotheosis is the single woman, especially if she is heading a household. For such women, economic reality is bleak, because sustenance requires two incomes. Compounding the problem for women, as we have seen, is the continuing inequality in wages, resulting in a disproportionate incidence of poverty among women heading households. Even though women as workers have flourished, they may suffer as men do from the effects of the decline in male blue-collar job opportunities—whether the effect of the decline comes about by reducing a family's standard of living or in some cases by contributing to a family's break-up.

An awareness of the failures of the American socioeconomic system, however, should not cause us to be obsessed by failure nor should it blind us to the economy's real, if partial, successes. Widening opportunities and changing attitudes prompt us to revise the conventional wisdom. For American women at this stage in the country's economy, it is simply incorrect to say that "the sky is falling." Instead, American women find more within their grasp than at any time in our history.

Notes

THE AUTHORS would like to acknowledge the contribution of Charles M. Wilhelm, James W. Hughes, and Edward Duensing.

Reference List

Bednarzik, Robert W. "Layoffs and permanent job losses: Worker's traits and cyclical patterns." 1983. *Monthly Labor Review.* 106 (September): 3–12.

Haggstrom, G. W., L. J. Waite, D. E. Kanouse, and T. J. Blaschke. 1984. *Changes in the lifestyle of new parents.* Santa Monica, Ca.: Rand Corporation.

Organization for Economic Cooperation and Development (OECD). 1984. *Labor force statistics 1962–82.* Paris: OECD.

Rytina, Nancy, 1982. "Tenure and the male-female earnings gap." *Monthly Labor Review* 105 (April): 32–34.

Spain, Daphne, and Susanne M. Bianchi. 1983. "How women have changed." *American Demographics* 5 (May): 19–25.

Sternlieb, G., and J. W. Hughes. 1984. *Income and jobs: USA.* New Brunswick, N.J.: Center for Urban Policy Research.

U.S. Department of Commerce. Bureau of the Census. 1984. *Current population reports: Consumer income,* Series P–60, No. 145 (August).

U.S. Department of Labor. Bureau of Labor Statistics. 1979. *Employment and earnings, United States, 1909–1978,* Bulletin 13, 12–11. Washington, D.C.: GPO.

U.S. Department of Labor. Bureau of Labor Statistics. 1982. *Supplement to employment and earnings, revised establishment data.* Washington, D.C.: GPO.

U.S. Department of Labor. Bureau of Labor Statistics. *Employment and earnings.* (Monthly) Washington, D.C.: GPO.

PART II

Historical Perspectives on Change

5

Women Workers and the Labor Movement in Hard Times: Comparing the 1930s with the 1980s

Ruth Milkman

On 17 April 1982, the president of the United States blamed the rise in unemployment under his administration—then at a postwar high of 9 percent and soon to climb still higher—on women workers. "Part of the unemployment is not as much recession as it is the great increase in the people going into the job market, and, ladies, I'm not picking on anyone, but because of the increase in women who are working today and two-worker families and so forth," Reagan told reporters (*New York Times,* 1982b). At a time when many of the administration's critics were beginning to compare the deep economic slump of the early 1980s to the Great Depression, Reagan himself invoked an ideology that had enjoyed widespread popularity during the 1930s in suggesting that the influx of women into the workforce, and especially married women, was responsible for the problem of unemployment.

It is very tempting to compare the impact of the economic downturn of the 1980s with the Great Depression. Certainly there are many parallels. In both periods, the unemployment rate was significantly higher for men than for women, because the occupations and industries in which men are concentrated—especially heavy manufacturing and construction—were affected most severely. In both periods, too, spouses reversed "traditional" roles in many families, with women bearing an increased burden of family support. And one can unearth other recent statements like the one just cited, scapegoating women workers for the severity of the slump.

And yet, what is most striking about women's relationship to the

111

economic crisis of the 1980s when considered against the background of the 1930s experience is that the ideological assault on female employment now lacks the popular legitimacy it enjoyed in the
earlier period. When Reagan trotted out the standard argument in
1982, he was immediately denounced by the AFL-CIO, among others; and perhaps more significantly, he quickly abandoned his position as it became obvious that it had minimal popular appeal.

Even in the Great Depression, as I have argued elsewhere, the
ideological assault on female workers did not produce a wholesale
expulsion of women from the labor force. Because of the rigidity of
occupational sex-typing and of job segregation, employers rarely
substituted men for women, and women's unemployment remained
relatively low—as was also the case in the "Reagan Recession" of
the early 1980s (Milkman, 1976). But in the 1930s, both the general
public and the labor movement strongly supported the notion that
women, and especially married women, should be denied employment opportunities so long as male unemployment remained a serious problem. Today, in contrast, support for that point of view is
conspicuously absent. The popular scapegoats for the economic problems of the 1980s are, on the one hand, outside the borders of the
United States—the Japanese, and the OPEC countries—and, on the
other hand, the big industrial unions, especially in high-wage industries like auto and steel, which are widely supposed to have demanded "too much" from management, leading firms to shift investments elsewhere. So, insofar as workers are being blamed for the
high rate of unemployment, they are overwhelmingly male workers,
organized in strong industrial unions—ironically, the very unions
born in the late 1930s.

This chapter examines the impact on women as workers and as
family members, the recent economic downturn, and the economic
restructuring presently underway against the background of the
1930s, with particular attention to the role of the labor movement in
the two periods. The first section presents an overview of employment and unemployment patterns in each period, emphasizing the
increased centrality to the U.S. economy of "women's work" in service and clerical occupations. The second section discusses the impact of high unemployment on women in families in the two periods
in the context of the historical transformations that have occurred

112

in the intervening decades. Building on this background, the third part of the paper presents an explanation for the contrast between the two periods, that is, the ideological shift bringing greater popular legitimacy to women's employment. Then, in a fourth section, I turn to a comparison of the relationship of women workers to the labor movement in the two periods, stressing the recent feminization of the unions, on the one hand, and the impact of the economic downturn on organized labor as a whole, on the other. The conclusion explores the possibility of a revitalization of the labor movement in a form that would give women workers and their specific concerns a greater role than in the past, one commensurate with their increased importance in the economy.

WOMEN AND UNEMPLOYMENT IN THE 1930s AND THE 1980s

Throughout the postwar period (except during the 1982–1983 recession), women's unemployment rate in the United States has exceeded men's by a significant margin, according to the official government figures. This can be explained in terms of sex differences in job turnover, in movement in and out of the labor force ("frictional unemployment"), and in opportunities for occupational mobility. In spite of these factors, however, the sex gap in unemployment rates has narrowed significantly in each postwar recession because of the fact that "male" occupations, on the average, are more cyclically sensitive than "female" occupations (Niemi, 1974).

In the early 1980s, as unemployment climbed to a new postwar high, male unemployment rose first to the level of female unemployment, and then still higher, exceeding the female rate for the first time since the 1930s. At the peak, in December 1982, the adult male unemployment rate was 10.1 percent, while the female rate was 9.2 percent (*Monthly Labor Review*, 1983). In 1930, similarly, male unemployment was recorded at a rate of 7.1 percent, while the female rate was 4.7 percent (U.S. Department of Commerce, 1930b, 2:13–18). While the two sets of figures are not strictly comparable, it is clear that in both instances the relatively low rates for women were

113

due to their concentration in occupations less affected by the economic contraction. In durable goods manufacturing, where three-fourths of the workforce is male, unemployment peaked at 17.1 percent in December 1982, whereas in finance and service industries, where women make up 60 percent of the workforce, the peak was 7.9 percent.[1] The same situation prevailed in the 1930s. In both periods, the sexual division of labor remained intact, as the overwhelming majority of employers continued to treat male and female labor as noninterchangeable (Milkman, 1976).

The economic contraction of the 1980s differs from that of the 1930s and also from all previous postwar recessions in one critical respect. While the industries hit hardest by unemployment in the Great Depression (and later recessions) ultimately revived, and their employment levels generally rose over the postwar period, many of the jobs lost in the manufacturing sector during the economic downturn of the 1980s will never be restored. For even before the sharp rise in unemployment in the 1980s, manufacturing employment growth had levelled off, and service employment, much of it female, had become the fastest growing part of the economy. Service employment grew three times as fast as manufacturing during the 1970s. Between 1973 and 1980, over 70 percent of private sector employment growth was in services and retail trade, and the majority of the new jobs were filled by women (*New York Times,* 1987d; Rothschild, 1981; Smith, 1984; Kuhn and Bluestone, this volume).

In the 1980s, what had been a relative decline in manufacturing employment became an absolute drop, but this was essentially the acceleration of a preexisting trend. While male workers have always been more vulnerable to short-term, cyclical unemployment because of their concentration in goods-producing industries, in the 1980s, that vulnerability has become a long-term, and in some instances even a permanent condition, in the face of the recomposition of the occupational structure now underway and the changing position of the United States within the international division of labor.

Of course, those women who are employed in declining industries are also vulnerable to long-term displacement. In such nondurable goods-manufacturing industries as textiles, clothing, leather products, and food, the secular trend in employment is also unfavorable, and here the majority of the workers affected are female (Rosen,

114

1982). So far, the net effects (although not necessarily the specific ones) of this decline have been offset by the rapid growth of clerical and service employment, supplemented by rising employment in such new high-tech industries as electronics, because all of these sectors are predominantly female. But there have also been some predictions of a decline in growth in services and office work with the increased application of microprocessor-based technologies (Gregory, 1982: esp. 88; National Council on the Future of Women in the Workplace, 1984: 6–7). In this scenario, women workers would no longer be "protected" by their concentration in these fields of work, as they have been in the past.

Most projections, however, are for continued growth in the service sector and for sluggish manufacturing growth, most of it in new "sunrise" industries. There is likely to be some recovery in manufacturing, but in such industries as autos and steel, even optimistic employment projections are well below prerecession levels. Service employment is expected to account for 39 percent of the new jobs created in the next twelve years, according to U.S. Bureau of Labor Statistics projections, while manufacturing is expected to account for 14 percent of new jobs. Moreover, most of the specific occupations expected to produce large numbers of new jobs are female-dominated. The ten fastest growing occupations in the 1980s, according to BLS projections, will be: secretaries, nurses' aides and orderlies, janitors and sextons, sales clerks, cashiers, professional nurses, truck drivers, fast-food workers, general office clerks, and waiters and waitresses (Carey, 1982; *Wall Street Journal,* 1983; *New York Times,* 1983d). Most of these are "pink collar jobs," employing predominantly women at relatively low wage rates.

The process of occupational recomposition is indeed increasing the number of low-wage jobs, while employment is declining most sharply in high-wage, blue-collar industrial jobs (e.g., autos and steel), where wage concessions have also been particularly extensive. The occupational structure as a whole is becoming increasingly polarized between well-paid professional and managerial jobs at one end and low-wage manufacturing, service, and clerical jobs at the other (Kuttner, 1983; Turner et al., 1984; Kuhn and Bluestone, this volume). While this phenomenon is not directly linked to the sexual division of labor, it has tended to affect men's wage levels more than

115

women's (which were low to begin with), so that the sex gap in earnings actually narrowed slightly during the economic downturn of the 1980s (*New York Times,* 1983e). Thus not only in regard to unemployment levels, but also with regard to wage rates, women workers have been hurt less by the recession than men.

Since the economic restructuring now underway involves extensive application of new technology as well as reorganization of the labor process in many industries, it is conceivable that a greater proportion of jobs in service industries will be filled by male workers than in the past—because shifts in the sexual division of labor are often occasioned by changes in job definitions. But so far, the 1980s has brought very little substitution of men for women (nor, for that matter, substitution of women for men, which one might expect in the face of a profitability crisis).[2] Indeed, this stability in the sexual division of labor is the main continuity between the 1930s and the 1980s in regard to the effects of each economic contraction on women workers.

On the other hand, there have been dramatic changes in the relationship of women to the labor market during the intervening half-century, most obviously and importantly, the huge increases in female labor force participation. In 1930, only 24 percent of the adult female population was in the labor force, as compared to 52 percent in 1980. The change has been even more pronounced for married women, whose labor force participation rate more than quadrupled over this fifty-year period, from 12 percent in 1930 to 50 percent in 1980. (U.S. Department of Commerce, 1930a, 4:69; see also U.S. Department of Labor, 1981b). Seen in this light, the continuing resilience of job segregation is especially remarkable. Clearly a far larger number of women workers are "protected" today than in the 1930s by the fact that the economic downturn affects male-dominated jobs disproportionately. And while job segregation itself has decreased only marginally with the increases in women's labor force participation, the position of women in the larger society, and particularly in the family, has been radically altered. In comparing the impact of the crisis of the 1930s on women within the family to the effects of the economic restructuring and contraction of the 1980s on that dimension of women's experience, one would expect to find far less

116

continuity than in women's relationship (as workers) to unemployment itself.

CHANGING FAMILY PATTERNS AND ECONOMIC DECLINE

By the 1970s, married women's employment had become a "normal" feature of family life, and mothers were even more likely to be in the labor force than were married women without the economic burdens of children (Hayghe, 1982). The situation in 1980 contrasts sharply with the one fifty years earlier in this respect. In 1930, employment for married women, and particularly for mothers, was still predominantly a product of poverty or misfortune. The "family wage," as an ideal and as a practice, still reigned supreme, although there had already been a small influx of wives from middle-income families into the workforce during the 1920s, anticipating the trend that would accelerate in the postwar decades (Wandersee, 1981: chap. 4).

However, primarily because of continuing job segregation by sex, the growth in employment among married women in recent years has not eliminated female subordination in the family (although employment does significantly enhance the power of wives vis-à-vis their husbands). And women in "traditional" (husband-wife) families, whether they are employed outside the home or not, are subject to many of the same pressures wives faced in the Great Depression if their husbands are hit by unemployment. This is particularly true today in the industrial heartland—the steel, auto, and rubber-based industrial communities of the Northeast and Midwest—where plant closings and employment cutbacks have dramatically altered the lives of men accustomed to high wages and secure (if cyclically unstable) employment. The situation of men and women in these communities in the 1980s closely parallels that which inspired the classic sociological portraits of the effects of (male) unemployment on families in the 1930s. Although today the wives are much more likely to have been employed before their husbands suffered job

117

losses, the effects of male unemployment still involve a "role reversal" similar to that of the 1930s.

While there have been few detailed studies of the social, psychological, and health-related effects of unemployment in the 1980s, the available data unambiguously suggest that family life is dramatically altered under the impact of long-term male unemployment. The specific effects include increased marital conflict, alcoholism, child and spouse abuse, emotional stress, and a variety of mental and physical health problems. On the national level, rising unemployment is associated with rising suicide and homicide rates, prison and mental hospital admissions, and heart- and liver-disease rates. Compounding these problems is the fact that unemployed workers often lose their health insurance benefits along with their jobs, so that they are unable to secure the medical care that they are more than ever likely to need (*Wall Street Journal,* 1982; Brenner, 1976; Ferman and Blehar, 1983; Bluestone and Harrison, 1982: chap. 3; Lien and Rayman, 1982; Rosenblum, 1984).

Poverty is another critical social effect of unemployment on families. While wives can often find jobs when their husbands cannot, the net result is that many families accustomed to reliance on high male incomes are forced to depend exclusively on relatively low female earnings. Just as in the Depression, men and women in this situation today "didn't choose to trade roles, they've been forced to trade," as Harvey Brenner has pointed out (quoted in *Wall Street Journal,* 1982; see also Milkman, 1976). In both periods, the "role reversals" have tended to reinforce traditional roles rather than encourage egalitarianism, since the situation is primarily associated with an extremely negative experience: economic deprivation. The unemployed men in this situation are typically desperate to resume the role of breadwinner, while their wives face pressures from several conflicting directions, as they struggle both to increase their earnings and to maintain their marriages.

There are a number of other parallels to the 1930s in the situation of families affected by male unemployment today. Once again, women face pressure to conserve sharply reduced family income by substituting their own unpaid labor for purchased goods and services— a pressure intensified by inflation as well as by reduced family income. And, in another pattern reminiscent of the 1930s, some

118

families have "doubled up," with two generations sharing a dwelling, in response to skyrocketing housing costs. The psychological pressures on wives, who typically feel responsible for the emotional well-being of the whole family, have also increased, just as they did in the Depression (*New York Times,* 1982f; 1982g; 1983a; *Wall Street Journal,* 1982). In short, in traditional husband-wife families, the impact of male unemployment on women seems to closely resemble the classic 1930s pattern, despite the transformations that have occurred in the intervening period.

But what of the large population of women who do not live in conventional families? As a result of the increased divorce rate and the higher number of "never married" women, the number of single-parent households has grown very rapidly in recent years. Most single parents are women, and their earnings tend to be low as a result of continuing job segregation by sex. This is the basis of the much-publicized "feminization of poverty" of the past decade, a problem that the economic downturn of the 1980s has intensified (*Monthly Labor Review,* 1978; Ehrenreich and Stallard, 1982; *New York Times,* 1983c). In addition, the number and proportion of households comprised of one person (never married, divorced, or widowed) has grown: in 1980, nearly a fourth of all households were of this type (Skolnick and Skolnick, 1983:2; Hartmann, this volume).

There are more women living outside of "traditional" husband-wife families today than there were in the 1930s, but the extent of the contrast between the two periods is far smaller than popular stereotypes of the "family crisis" would suggest. In 1940, 11 percent of all families were "female-headed," compared to 13 percent in 1975 and 16 percent in 1982. (Johnson, 1978:33; U.S. Department of Labor, 1982). Families of this type have always been disproportionately represented among the poverty population, in the Great Depression as much as today. On the other hand, the growing number of employed women who do not live in conventional families and who also do not have children enjoy relatively high incomes today (Hacker, 1983). This suggests a positive aspect of the changes in family patterns that have occurred in the postwar period, one that is sometimes neglected in the "feminization of poverty" discussion: the extent to which women today can choose not to marry at all, or to leave unsatisfactory marriages. This "choice" does entail serious economic

119

penalties for women raising children, particularly for those foregoing marriages to middle-class men. (Though it should also be noted that the "feminization of poverty" notion does tend to obscure the extent to which poverty remains associated with class and race positions.)

Hard times increase the economic difficulties of life outside marriage, and so, just as in the Great Depression, the downturn of the 1980s has produced a decline in the divorce rate, for the first time in twenty years (*New York Times,* 1982e). More generally, the net effect of the 1980s recession on the position of women in relation to the family has been to reinforce "traditional" arrangements. Nevertheless, women can (and do) still choose an independent existence to a far greater extent than they could fifty years ago, and that is by far the most important contrast between the 1980s and the 1930s in this area. To be sure, the end of the "family wage" and the fact that employment is now "normal" for married women has not meant the end of inequality between the sexes—far from it, as both the "feminization of poverty" and the conservatizing consequences of "role reversals" in husband-wife families attest. But what was irrevocably altered with the rapid rise in women's participation in the labor force over the past half-century is the ideology defining women's rights vis-à-vis paid work. With the rise of the two-income family, on the one hand, and the resurgence of feminism (itself partly a product of the expanded role of women in the workforce) on the other, it is no longer possible in the 1980s, as it was in the 1930s, to win popular support for an assault on women's rights to employment opportunities.

THE END OF THE "FAMILY WAGE" IDEOLOGY

The 1930s, as has now been well documented, was a period of antifeminist backlash directed, above all, against women's right to work. Not only were women "blamed" for the unemployment crisis, but explicit prohibitions on female employment, in most cases directed against married women, were instituted by many employers. While the extent of female labor force participation, including that of married women, actually increased during the depression decade, one would never have suspected it from the ideological consensus that crystallized in the early 1930s in opposition to women's employment (Humphries, 1976; Scharf, 1980).

The idea than a man should earn a "family wage" sufficient to support his wife and children as well as himself had long been popular in the American working class, among both men and women. The feminist notions of work for women as a desirable pursuit, which flourished in the 1920s, were a middle-class phenomenon. Even though many poor and working-class women did in fact work outside their homes in this period, this was seen as an unfortunate necessity, due only to the fact that the family wage ideal had not yet been realized. And for married women particularly, paid work was a sign of misfortune, not of emancipation, in the prewar working-class community.

The depression of the 1930s, which brought such extensive unemployment to men, breathed new life into the family wage ideal, and all but submerged the nascent middle-class feminism of the 1920s. The New Deal gave short shrift to the plight of the unemployed woman, even though a substantial contingent of "social feminists" was part of the Roosevelt administration. And in the labor movement, above all, the family wage ideal was frequently invoked in the 1930s, by both the CIO unions and the AFL—although the new industrial unions did organize women workers to an unprecedented degree at the same time.

It was only in the postwar period that the "family wage" ideal began to be eroded, after the expansion of the female labor force had exhausted the supply of single, divorced, and widowed women, so that married women and then even mothers were incorporated into the wage labor force in large numbers. This ideal died a slow death, but in the inflationary 1960s and 1970s as the expanded demand "pulling" women into the labor market came to be supplemented by a new family economics "pushing" women out of the home, the "family wage" finally began to disappear (Kessler-Harris, 1982: chap. 11; Ehrenreich, 1983: esp. 2–13). With the resurgence of feminism in the 1960s and its increasing popularity in the 1970s a new egalitarian ideology took over, proclaiming women's right to equal treatment in the labor market.

While educated, middle-class women are disproportionately represented in the contemporary women's movement, working-class women have also been greatly influenced by it. If few identify themselves directly as "feminists," growing numbers readily endorse the movement's basic goals. In particular, and more than any other feminist principle, the ideal of gender equality in the labor market has won enormous popular support (Rubin, 1976: esp. 130–132; Seifer, 1973; Social Research Inc., 1973; Ferree, 1980). The ideological support for economic equality between the sexes is indeed far more extensive than the structural changes in women's actual position in the labor market would seem to warrant. In this respect, the economic crisis of the 1980s contrasts sharply with that of the 1930s, when the ideological assault on women's right to employment obscured the actuality of lower female unemployment and expanded workforce participation among women.

Insofar as popular understanding of the economic situation in the 1980s involves scapegoating workers, it is *male* workers who are being fingered with responsibility—not "as men," but as members of strong unions that have enjoyed high wage levels over the past few decades (Bluestone and Harrison, 1982:79–81). In regard to the family wage ideal, the chickens have truly come home to roost. The belief is widespread that unions have made such exorbitant wage demands that employers have been driven to shift investments to other areas, killing the proverbial goose that laid the golden eggs. Women workers are obviously blameless in this regard, since even those who are unionized are concentrated in low-wage occupations. But the composition of the labor movement is undergoing some dramatic changes. As the once-formidable strength of the industrial unions that came to power in the 1930s is being undercut in the face of job losses and "concession bargaining" in the 1980s, organized labor is undergoing an unprecedented process of feminization.

WOMEN AND THE LABOR MOVEMENT IN THE 1930s AND THE 1980s

The rise of industrial unionism in the late 1930s brought about large increases in the number of women union members, since the CIO was committed to organizing workers in mass production industries regardless of sex or skill, in a radical departure from the craft unionism that had previously dominated the U.S. labor movement. By 1940, female union membership had grown to 300 percent of the level at the beginning of the depression decade, yet the proportion of women workers organized was no higher than in 1920, the peak of union strength in the pre–CIO era, because the majority of workers in the industries on which the CIO drives concentrated were male (Dickason, 1947:71). And the CIO had no special commitment to women's concerns, largely accepting the ideology of "woman's place" that prevailed in the larger society, including the family wage ideal. The unions were more concerned with "women's issues" during the World War II years, because the economic mobilization transformed the sexual division of labor in the basic industries organized in the 1930s. But in the aftermath of the war, there was a return to the prewar situation (Strom, 1983; Milkman, 1980).

In the 1950s and early 1960s, before the implications of the increases in female labor force participation were widely appreciated, and before the rebirth of feminism, the labor movement maintained its traditional posture toward women workers. They were seen as a marginal constituency, a special group of workers in need of special forms of protection, and not as full participants in either paid work or union activity (Cook, 1968). Yet during this period, as the occupational structure was changing in composition and moving increasingly toward service employment and away from manufacturing, which was labor's stronghold in the 1930s and 1940s, the increased participation of women in the workforce was directly correlated with a decline in union membership as a proportion of the workforce, starting in the mid-1950s (U.S. Department of Labor, 1980:60).

There was some new organizing in the postwar decades, but it failed to keep pace with the growth of the workforce. By 1984, union membership had fallen to 19.1 percent of the labor force, the lowest level since the 1930s (Adams, 1985:26). The percentage of unionized women (among all employed women) also fell during the period following the mid-1950s, but the rate fell far more rapidly for men. The postwar decades were a period of feminization for the labor movement, as well as a period of declining membership strength for organized labor in the workforce as a whole. In 1956, women were 18.6 percent of union members; by 1984, they comprised 33.7 percent of the total (Adams, 1985:29; Le Grande, 1978:9).[3]

This feminization of the labor movement was not the result of any special commitment to organizing women workers *per se;* rather it was the unintended consequence of a series of piecemeal efforts to offset the general decline in union membership by organizing particular occupational groups—teachers, hospital workers, and government employees, most importantly—which happened to include large numbers of women. By 1980, nearly half of the six million organized women workers in the United Stateswere in three employment categories: educational services (29 percent), medical services (11 percent), and public administration (8 percent). Another 24 percent were in manufacturing, labor's traditional stronghold (U.S. Dept. of Labor, 1981a).[4]

At first, the influx of women into the nation's labor organizations had little direct impact on their overall character or on their institutional functioning. But in the 1970s pressures began to build for change in the unions' traditional outlook toward women workers. It was no longer possible for union leaders to ignore efforts to assert the special interests of women workers as a group within the membership, and now, what had historically been a marginal issue for the labor movement emerged as a central dilemma. Gradually, the growing pressures began to yield results. In 1973, the AFL–CIO endorsed the Equal Rights Amendment, and the following year, the Coalition of Labor Union Women (CLUW) was founded, establishing an institutional base for women in the labor movement that the major unions gradually grew to accept. Female representation in labor leadership also grew during the 1970s, especially on the local level. And unions (especially those with large female memberships) began to take up such "women's issues" as affirmative action, child care, and equal pay for comparable worth on an unprecedented scale (Foner, 1980:478–572; Bell, 1985).

These developments notwithstanding, the impact of feminism on the labor movement has remained limited in a number of crucial areas. For example, women's representation in union leadership, particularly at the upper levels, remains quite minimal in relation to the large increases in female union membership of recent years

124

(Coalition of Labor Union Women, 1980). Women's relationship to organized labor has never been an easy one, and the old difficulties have not suddenly disappeared in the wake of women's increased labor force participation or the feminist resurgence. But, in comparison to the situation in the 1930s, the extent of attention being paid to women's concerns by the unions and the likelihood of continued interest in that area, given the feminization process, is without precedent.

To be sure, this has occurred in the context of an overall decline in the strength of organized labor, both in terms of membership levels and in terms of the place of labor in the larger society. The situation is very similar to that of the labor movement in the early 1930s, before the rise of industrial unionism. Even before the economic downturn of the 1980s, the organized labor movement was in deep trouble, and the assault on the unions—above all on the industrial unions built in the 1930s—has further eroded its strength. Deindustrialization has brought deunionization in its wake; and "concession bargaining" has confirmed the popular impression that union demands for wages and benefits are themselves the cause of the nation's economic troubles (*New York Times,* 1982a; 1982c; Freedman and Fulmer, 1982; Slaughter, 1983).

Concession bargaining, like the broader crisis of organized labor, has been concentrated in the manufacturing sector of the economy where women's presence is in any case relatively marginal. That the entire labor movement has been thrown on the defensive as a result of the assault on what was once its strongest sector has affected organized women workers as well. But, in the longer run, the decline of the industrial unions seems likely to enhance the position of women workers in the labor movement. Minimally, the feminization of union membership serves to guarantee that the unions will defend women's rights to employment.

During the Great Depression of the 1930s, the labor movement began to take a more inclusive posture toward women workers, not only because of the development of industrial unionism, but also out of fear that employers would use women's labor to undercut that of men (Kessler-Harris, 1982:268–269). But in that period, unionists, like working men and women themselves, remained ambivalent about women's right to employment. The conflict between the "family wage" ideal and the principle of nondiscrimination that was so fundamental to industrial unionism was ever-present, and this conflict was resolved differently in different situations. Some unions defended women's right to employment while lamenting its necessity; others, including the CIO unions, fought for prohibitions against married women's employment, following the logic of the family wage principle (Milkman, 1987: chap. 3).

In the 1980s, union leaders are still not entirely lacking in ambivalence regarding the greatly enlarged female workforce, and feminists within the labor movement have quite rightly complained that the labor movement has lagged behind the larger society in regard to women's rights. But there can be no return to the pre–World War II situation, and it is inconceivable that unions would be part of a backlash against women's employment rights, even if such a backlash were to emerge as a serious problem. If that is the case now, when the fortunes of organized labor are at their lowest ebb in half a century, the situation would be even more favorable if the labor movement were to be revitalized, as it was in the late 1930s. Any such revitalization would have to involve organizational initiatives in the expanding parts of the economy where women are heavily employed.[5] Despite the feminization of union membership that has already occurred, only 14 percent of the female labor force is unionized (Adams, 1985:30). Just as the rise in female labor force participation precipitated the demise of the family wage ideology in the society as a whole, so the feminization of the labor movement can provide the basis for a full-scale alliance between the unions and the nation's women workers.

CONCLUSION

Comparing the situation of women workers in the 1930s and the 1980s reveals both continuity and change in the relation of women to economic crisis. The persistence of job segregation by sex is the major continuity between these periods; from this stem the many parallels between the two periods in relation to unemployment by sex and also in the impact of the economic contraction on families. And yet what seems far more important is the shift between these two periods in the legitimacy of female employment, a product of the increased scale of women's proletarianization (albeit on unequal, segregated terms) and in the ideological impact of the feminist resurgence itself. Politically, this shift offers an enlarged potential for alliances between workers across gender lines, and even for alliances between feminists and unionists. Of course, whether or not that potential is realized will depend on many unpredictable factors, among them whether or not the labor movement itself can again become a major political force. But the transformations of the past half century do ensure that women workers will not be faced with an assault on their employment rights, as they were in the 1930s, at the very least. And under favorable political circumstances, those same transformations could be the basis for a renewal in the labor movement within which feminism could play a historically unprecedented role.

Notes

1. *Monthly Labor Review,* 106 (Feb. 1983): 62. Figures on the sex composition of these industry groups are from U.S. Department of Labor, 1981b.

2. Evidence for the 1980s has yet to be analyzed in detail, but there is abundant analysis of the 1960s and the 1970s, suggesting only a modest decline in the extent of occupational segregation by sex, most of it in the professions. On the 1960s, see Blau and Hendriks, 1979; and for the 1970s, Beller, 1984.

3. The data for these two years are not strictly comparable because of changes in Labor Department methods, but there is no mistaking the direction of the trend.

4. The breakdown for 1984, using different methods, was reported by the Labor Department as follows: 46 percent in government, 21 percent in manufacturing, 13 percent in service industries, and 10 percent in wholesale and retail trade. See Adams, 1985:29.

5. For the AFL–CIO's own statement about this, see the report of the AFL-CIO Committee on the Evolution of Work, *The Changing Situation of Workers and Their Unions* (Washington, D.C.: AFL–CIO, 1985).

Reference List

Adams, Larry T. 1985. Changing employment patterns of organized workers. *Monthly Labor Review* 108 (February):25–31.

Bell, Deborah E. 1985. Unionized women in state and local government. In *Women, work, and protest: A century of U.S. women's labor history,* edited by Ruth Milkman, 280–299. Boston: Routledge and Kegan Paul.

Beller, Andrea H. 1984. Trends in occupational segregation by sex and race, 1960–1981. In *Sex segregation in the workplace: Trends, explanations, remedies,* edited by Barbara F. Reskin, 11–26. Washington, D.C.: National Academy Press.

Blau, Francine D., and Wallace E. Hendriks. 1979. Occupational segregation by sex: Trends and prospects. *The Journal of Human Resources* 14 (Spring):197–210.

Bluestone, Barry, and Bennett Harrison. 1982. *The deindustrialization of America.* New York: Basic Books.

Brenner, Harvey. 1976. *Estimating the social costs of national economic policy implications for mental and physical health and clinical aggression.* U.S. Congress, Joint Economic Committee. Washington, D.C.: GPO.

Carey, Max L. 1982. Occupational employment growth through 1990. In *Economic projections to 1990.* U.S. Department of Labor, Bureau of Labor Statistics, Bulletin 2121. Washington, D.C.: GPO.

Coalition of Labor Union Women, Center for Education and Research. 1980. Absent from the agenda: A report on the role of women in American unions. New York: Coalition of Labor Union Women. Mimeo.

Cook, Alice. 1968. Women and American trade unions. *Annals of the American Academy of Political and Social Science* 375 (January):124–132.

Dickason, Gladys. 1947. Women in labor unions. *Annals of the American Academy of Political and Social Sciences* 251 (May):70–78.

Ehrenreich, Barbara. 1983. *The hearts of men.* New York: Doubleday.

Ehrenreich, Barbara, and Karin Stallard. 1982. The nouveau poor. *Ms.* (July/August):217–224.

Ferman, Louis A., and March C. Blehar. 1983. Family adjustment to unemployment. In *Family in transition,* edited by Arlene S. Skolnick and Jerome H. Skolnick, 587–601. Boston: Little, Brown.

Ferree, Myra Marx. 1980. Working class feminism: A consideration of the consequences of employment. *The Sociological Quarterly* 21:173–184.

Foner, Philip. 1980. *Women and the American labor movement from World War I to the present.* New York: The Free Press.

Freedman, Audrey, and William E. Fulmer. 1982. Last rites for pattern bargaining. *Harvard Business Review* 60 (March/April):30–48.

Gregory, Judith. 1982. Technological change in the office workplace and implications for organizing. In *Labor and technology: Union response to changing environments*, edited by Donald Kennedy, Charles Craypo, and Mary Lehman, 83–101. University Park, Pa.: Department of Labor Studies, Pennsylvania State University.

Hacker, Andrew. 1983. Where have the jobs gone? *New York Review of Books* (30 June): 27–32.

Hayghe, Howard. 1982. Marital and family patterns of workers: An update. *Monthly Labor Review* 105 (May): 53–56.

Humphries, Jane. 1976. Women: Scapegoats and safety valves in the Great Depression. *Review of Radical Political Economics* 8 (Spring): 98–121.

Johnson, Beverly L. 1978. Women who head families, 1970–1977: Their numbers rose, income lagged. *Monthly Labor Review* 101 (February): 32–37.

Kessler-Harris, Alice. 1982. *Out to work: A history of wage-earning women in the United States*. New York: Oxford University Press.

Kuttner, Bob. 1983. The declining middle. *Atlantic Monthly* (July): 60–72.

LeGrande, Linda H. 1978. Women in labor organizations: Their ranks are increasing. *Monthly Labor Review* 101 (August): 8–14.

Liem, Ramsey, and Paula Rayman. 1982. Health and social costs of unemployment. *American Psychologist* 37 (October): 1116–1123.

Milkman, Ruth. 1976. Women's work and economic crisis: Some lessons of the Great Depression. *Review of Radical Political Economics* 8 (Spring): 73–97.

Milkman, Ruth. 1980. Organizing the sexual division of labor: Historical perspectives on 'women's work' and the American labor movement. *Socialist Review* 10 (January/February): 125–141.

Milkman, Ruth. 1987. *Gender at work: The dynamics of job segregation by sex during World War II*. Champaign: University of Illinois Press.

Monthly Labor Review. 1983. Current labor statistics: Household data. 106 (Feb. 1983): 62.

National Council on the Future of Women in the Workplace. 1984. *The invisible worker in a troubled economy: Women and the industrial policy debate*. Washington, D.C.: National Federation of Business and Professional Women's Clubs.

New York Times. 1982a The cooperative economy. 14 February.

New York Times. 1982b. Jobless rate tied to big work force. 18 April.

New York Times. 1982c. "Labor's concessions stir worried debate over shifts in power. 25 April.

New York Times. 1982d. 'Big Mac' supplants big steel as manufacturing jobs lag. 31 May.

New York Times. 1982e. Divorce appears to dip with economy. 29 September.

New York Times. 1982f. Job losses end prosperity for more families. 10 October.

129

New York Times. 1982g. Families facing recession's stresses. 14 October.

New York Times. 1983a. Married couples squeeze into parents' homes. 24 February.

New York Times. 1983b. U.S. divorces fell in '82; first decline in 20 years. 16 March.

New York Times. 1983c. Sharp rise is seen in poor children. 29 April.

New York Times. 1983d. 'High Tech' is no jobs panacea, experts say. 18 September.

New York Times. 1983e. Earnings gap is narrowing slightly for women. 3 October.

Niemi, Beth, 1974. The male-female differential in unemployment rates. Industrial and Labor Relations Review 27 (April): 331–350.

Rosen, Ellen. 1982. Hobson's choice: Employment and unemployment among blue collar women workers in New England. Social Research Institute, Boston College. Mimeo.

Rosenblum, Susan B. 1984. Health care and the unemployed. Labor Research Review 5 (Summer): 28–44.

Rothschild, Emma. 1981. Reagan and the real economy. The New York Review of Books (5 February): 40–50.

Rubin, Lillian B. 1976. Worlds of pain: Life in the working class family. New York: Basic Books.

Scharf, Lois. 1980. To work and to wed: Female employment, feminism, and the Great Depression. Westport, Conn.: Greenwood Press.

Seifer, Nancy. 1973. Absent from the majority: Working class women in America. New York: National Project on Ethnic America.

Skolnick, Arlene S., and Jerome H. Skolnick. 1983. Introduction. In Family in transition, edited by Arlene S. Skolnick and Jerome H. Skolnick. Boston: Little, Brown.

Slaughter, Jane. 1983. Concessions—and how to beat them. Detroit: Labor Education and Research Project.

Smith, Joan. 1984. The paradox of women's poverty: Wage-earning women and economic transformation. Signs 10 (Winter): 291–310.

Social Research Inc. 1973. Working-class women in a changing world: A review of research findings. New York: McFadden-Bartell Corporation.

Strom, Sharon. 1983. Challenging 'women's place': Feminism, the left, and industrial unionism in the 1930s. Feminist Studies 9 (Summer): 359–386.

Turner, Brian, et al. 1984. Deindustrialization and the two-tier society. Washington, D.C.: Industrial Union Department, AFL–CIO.

U.S. Department of Commerce. Bureau of the Census. 1930a. Fifteenth census of the U.S. Population, vol. 4, Washington, D.C.: GPO.

U.S. Department of Commerce. Bureau of the Census. 1930b. Fifteenth census of the U.S. Unemployment, vol. 2, Washington, D.C.: GPO.

U.S. Department of Labor. Bureau of Labor Statistics. 1980. Directory of national unions and employee associations, 1979. Bulletin 2079. Washington, D.C.: GPO.

U.S. Department of Labor. Bureau of Labor Statistics. 1981a. *Earnings and other characteristics of organized workers, May 1980*. Bulletin 2105. Washington, D.C.: GPO.

U.S. Department of Labor. Bureau of Labor Statistics. 1981b. *Employment and unemployment: A report on 1980*. Special Labor Force Report 244. Washington, D.C.: GPO.

U.S. Department of Labor. Women's Bureau. 1982. *Twenty facts on women workers*. Washington, D.C.: GPO.

Wall Street Journal. 1982. Conflict at home: Wives of jobless men support some families—but at heavy cost. 8 December.

Wall Street Journal. 1983. Factory job growth seen in next 12 years, but U.S. calls outlook dim in autos, steel. 19 May.

Wandersee, Winifred D. 1981. *Women's work and family values, 1920–1940*. Cambridge: Harvard University Press.

The Meaning of Unemployment in the Lives of Women

Margot B. Kempers and Paula M. Rayman

. . . our civilization is now geared to expect able-bodied women to be self-supporting. Chivalry is no longer our social frame of mind. Women must go on working outside the home, even if such banner phrases of the feminist as "economic freedom" and "equality of opportunity" may prove to be hollow sounds echoing from a vanishing era.—*Helen Field, 1931*

In the current depression . . . the most vulnerable group consists of 8 million women who support families.—*Carolyn Shaw Bell, 1983*

During congressional hearings in 1977, experts on female employment testified that the rapid influx of women into the labor force during the preceding ten years had "outdistanced theory" and urged that the range and significance of the resulting effects of this influx be given immediate and careful attention (Joint Economic Committee, 1977). Our awareness of the short-term and long-range consequences of women's presence in the labor force is only now unfolding. We have not yet developed a comprehensive understanding of what happens when women are confronted with the loss of paid employment. The limitations of our thinking about women and unemployment were sharply revealed during the back-to-back recessions that occurred between 1979 and 1982. In order to contribute to our knowledge of the ways that job loss affects the lives of women, we propose to explore the changing meanings of unemployment by reviewing social science research that has been concerned directly or indirectly with this issue. We will limit our review to two periods of severe economic dislocation—the Great Depression of the 1930s and the recessions of the early 1980s—in order to outline the state of past and present research on women's unemployment.

Conceptions and definitions of work—essential prerequisites for

133

any thorough comprehension of unemployment—have only recently been elaborated and made relevant to women's experiences. Two theoretical frameworks in particular have expanded our understanding of women's activities in the economic sector of capitalist societies. The first, the traditional Marxist critique, has explored the structure and content of labor and production by emphasizing the dehumanization of wage labor. However, this approach abstracts from age, sex, and race differences as well as from marital status and household roles (Macdonald, 1979), and consequently it denies the authenticity and complexities of women's experiences in the world of work.[1] The second framework is a feminist one. By means of a careful identification and analysis of patriarchal institutions, feminist thinking has helped to explain or modify the distinction between wage and non-wage categories of work by emphasizing the productivity and importance of each. Matthaei (1982), Hartmann (1976), and others have skillfully demonstrated the inadequacy of conceptualizing work, and by extension, unemployment, solely in terms of paid labor. They suggest that there is no such category as a "non-working woman," and instead concentrate their analysis on the relationship between market and non-market institutions.

Our comparison of unemployment research from the 1930's Depression with contemporary studies needs to begin with an acknowledgement of the dramatic shifts that have occurred within the economy since that time. For example, during the most recent recession, prime manufacturing industries with predominantly male labor forces were among those hardest hit (Bluestone and Harrison, 1982). Service sector occupations, historically staffed primarily by women, were not similarly affected. Thus, in contrast to previous recession cycles, women experienced proportionally lower unemployment rates in 1982 than men. This advantage was offset by the fact that women holding jobs in unionized manufacturing industries tended to enjoy less seniority than men and therefore were less likely to be recalled than men. Furthermore, while a slowdown of births in the 1960s provided women with greater opportunities to enter the wage labor force, more than 50 percent of working women are concentrated in low-paying service sector positions.

The ways in which entries into and exits from the labor force touch the lives of women are complex. As we considered representative studies from the Depression years and from the past fifteen years, three interrelated aspects of unemployment became clear. We will devote a section to each in this chapter. The first concerns the sociological concept of roles: What have been the social role categories of women that have guided social science research and how well do these "typified" categories fit with the actual experience of women confronted with unemployment? A handful of studies have paid attention to the varied roles that women actually perform, and we explored the findings of these studies with particular care. The second part of this chapter discusses the ways in which women have coped with the effects of unemployment: Specifically, what patterns of coping exist that appear to be characteristic of women? A preliminary conclusion underscores the important fact that all women's unemployment experiences are not similar. Therefore, in the third section, we consider the need to study the experiences of specific groups of women in order to develop a fuller and more realistic conception of female unemployment.

SOCIAL ROLES AND RESEARCH CATEGORIES

Mirra Komarovsky, the author of one of the foremost studies on unemployment, observed in 1940 that there is generally every reason to expect dislocation of life as a result of loss of work. Generally, the roles prescribed to women in studies on unemployment have been a direct function of existing social values and dominant intellectual concerns. The nature of these values and concerns has persistently prevented researchers from gaining an accurate recognition and understanding of the presence and importance of women in our society.

Long before the economic contraction of the Depression, distinctions between the various and related roles of women had crystallized. The duality of paid and unpaid labor—of productive and domestic activity—had been firmly established during the industrial revolution (Tilly and Scott, 1978), but women continued to be identified primarily with the family. This meant that women were not acknowledged as having autonomous connections with the world of

135

wage labor and later with the world of unemployment. The duality of women's lives, as domestic workers and as wage laborers, has served to orient the ways in which women have been incorporated into or excluded from unemployment studies. During the Depression, research consistently reinforced the primacy of the former role by denying the actuality of the latter. Studies on unemployment tended to identify the "real victims" of job loss as men.

In 1933, for example, Clague and Powell studied the lives of unemployed workers in the Philadelphia area; their published findings, *Ten Thousand Out of Work,* did not include any women as workers. Even though the authors were aware of the significant female presence in the Philadelphia labor force, "women were entirely eliminated from consideration." Notwithstanding, they felt that their study had identified an "average group of unemployed workers and their families, that no sampling difficulties encountered in the study seriously affected the representative character of the group, and that the data reported [were] sufficiently reliable to be accepted as social facts" (p. xviii). Seven years later Bakke completed his famous study, *The Unemployed Worker.* Here again, women were not included in the database. This exclusion was not purely arbitrary, for during the Depression it was widely accepted that the place for women was in the home; that gainful employment for women, if it was respectable, was basically a premarital function; and that when women did work, they did so for amusement or for "pin money." The concerns and approaches of a great deal of the Depression era research directly reflected the social value placed on the traditional American family with a working husband supporting wife and children. The overriding perceptions of male responsibility were strong enough to support the popular feeling that, particularly during hard times, "it was only fair that the jobs be left to men who had to support families" (Bakke, 1940). Indeed, this feeling was frequently translated into employment policies during the Depression.

However, during the Depression, the tension between the cultural ideals of what women were supposed to be doing and their actual work experiences became much more evident. A classic unemployment research project, *Marienthal, the Sociography of an Unemployed Community,* recognized this tension. Here a team of authors acknowledged the conceptual limitations of the contemporary thinking about unemployment. This study of an Austrian industrial community hit by massive unemployment in 1930 applied the term unemployment "in the strict sense only to the men of the community, for the women [were] merely unpaid, not really unemployed" (p. 7). However, the team carefully documented the ways in which the lives of women were intimately affected by and connected to the work world and the jobless world. *Marienthal* broke ground in unemployment research by revealing some of the complexities of perceptions of women's roles and responsibilities during times of economic dislocation.

Research on unemployment during the Depression was not coordinated or formally organized, and on-going records of the ways that massive unemployment affected the social institutions of the family were not kept systematically. However, several separate studies on just this problem were conducted during the later years of the 1930s. While such studies as those completed by Elderton (1931), Angell (1936), and Cavan and Ranck (1938) did have a broader focus than research concerned principally with unemployed males, these studies also were ultimately constrained by preconceived research definitions and popular social standards and perceptions. For example, Cavan and Ranck (*The Family and the Depression,* 1938) sought to measure "the ways in which families and the individual members of families adjusted or failed to adjust themselves to the depression" (p. 2). Their conclusion that well-organized families adjusted better to the Depression-induced crisis than poorly organized families can only be fully appreciated once their definitions are clarified. A well-organized family was one in which reciprocal functioning roles were clearly assigned (e.g., "If the father is in dominant control, organization in the family demands that the mother and children should be subordinate and that each member should conceive of his role as dominant or subordinate" (p. 4); well-adjusted women in this study were those who conceived of themselves as subordinate to men and who recognized men as the economic mainstays of their households. If a woman in such a family had to take on wage labor to cover for her husband's loss of income, she was encouraged to think of her work and her income as somehow not as significant as those of a man.

A notable exception to this trend was Komarovsky's *The Unemployed Man and His Family* (1940). Taking as given the patriarchal nature of society, she focused on man's predominant role as the economic provider and the connection between this role and his authority in the family. She assumed that unemployment would have significant effects on family relations. Women were recognized by Komarovsky as primary components of the power configurations of the family; she argued that in order to maintain prestige, men needed women's endorsements. In this study women were granted an important level of autonomy, but they still were understood mainly as the recipients of economic support. Nonetheless, Komarovsky changed normal theoretical concerns by exploring the support activities of women.

An important subset of Depression era studies focused directly on women by seeking to identify and explain the ways in which women wage-earners were affected by and responded to job losses. Pruett and Peters, in their study *Women Workers Through the Depression* (1934), recognized the importance of examining the status quo, because the Depression was "the first crisis occurring after women received the vote and the first to occur after women [had] secured some political experience" (p. 7). Also important was the unprecedented number of trained women in the workforce. While their findings were limited to this select group of professional women, the study was significant because of the attention it paid to the economic and psychological losses suffered directly by women as individuals. Interestingly, however, this research tended to downplay family connections, and thus while it highlighted important aspects of women's experiences that had previously been ignored, it also skewed reality by presenting a sketch of the working woman as professional, autonomous, wage-earning, white, and single.

This sketch was partly elaborated upon by the descriptive work completed by the U.S. Women's Bureau. In a regular series of pamphlets presented to the federal government, the bureau sponsored research on unemployment fluctuations; unemployed women seeking relief; effects of the Depression on female wage-earners' families; and the situation of the woman wage-earner (numbers 113, 1933; 139, 1936; 92, 1932; 108, 1936; and 172, 1939, respectively). However, while these studies generated a wealth of facts and statistics on how and where women did fit into the economy during the Depression years, they did not attempt to analyze why and how

138

women experienced the hardships connected with unemployment. The literature from the Women's Bureau did not provide a critical assessment of women's roles in society. Taken as a whole, then, Depression-era studies on women and unemployment provided more descriptions than explanations and it provided biased and incomplete descriptions at that.

Both similarities and differences exist between these studies and contemporary examinations of unemployment and women. It is immediately apparent that recent conceptualizations of workers and hence of unemployment still do not always automatically provide a space for women. For example, in a 1981 study on eastern Massachusetts engineers who had lost their jobs during the 1970s entitled *Professionals Out of Work*, women were not included. What the choice of title reveals is not just that professional occupations have long been and continue to be dominated by males, but also the more significant truth that the reported results of many studies on unemployment cannot be generalized beyond the specific groups investigated.

The shortcomings of unemployment research that investigate only the experiences of specific job or human categories is slowly being acknowledged. A 1975 Office of Economic and Community Development report concluded that while there have been vast positive qualitative and quantitative changes in the employment of women in industrial countries during the last two decades, there still remains a substantial disparity between male and female employment patterns. In the United States, up until the recession of the early 1980s, women persistently have had much higher rates of unemployment than men. To understand this, we must look beyond statistics to underlying societal values. As the report pointed out,

> because the alternative of staying at home full time is socially acceptable for women, and not for men, very likely many "unemployed" women may appear in the statistics as housewives engaged in work in the home. In contrast, men who are not members of the labor force are almost by definition unemployed. (Darling, 1975:111)

There are also indications that unemployed female manufacturing workers experience more difficulty securing reemployment, with new jobs rarely paying salaries comparable to the old ones. The re-

139

cently completed research of Snyder and Nowak (1983) on the impact of a plant shutdown in Indiana explores sex-differentiated patterns of demoralization, levels of economic insecurity, and reemployment outcomes among 150 workers. The research of Rayman and Bluestone (1982) and Rosen (1982), which anticipated some of the recent findings of Snyder and Nowak, has amplified our understanding of the short-range, negative consequences that result from the social role changes demanded in unemployment situations. Rayman and Bluestone (1982), for instance, in their study of unemployed aircraft workers, found that men were far more likely than women to take out their anger on family members during layoffs and they were also more likely to regain jobs in the industry.

This initial review highlights some of the problems that have complicated efforts to develop a full understanding of what unemployment means for women. Among the most obvious is the continual difficulty of describing the phenomenon of unemployment. Official definitions cannot capture the actual situations of many individuals—female and male—confronted with job loss. The U.S. Bureau of Labor identifies the unemployed as "those reported as having looked for work while not employed, or as having been on layoff for at least one week during the survey year," even though the length of actual unemployment may vary from a single week up to a full year (*U.S. Department of Labor Bulletin* 2222, 1985). While the bureau has broadened the scope of its categories of unemployment by including such categories as discouraged workers, transfers, and recent entrants into the wage labor force, it has not been successful in outlining the full range of ways that women in particular are connected with the contemporary wage labor force. Problems of definition are compounded by the difficulty of making sense out of the data that are available. An example taken from the Depression illustrates the point: in one study of South Bend, Indiana, just four percent of the women interviewed (95 percent of whom had earlier been regularly employed full-time in industry jobs) had full-time employment; nonetheless, three-fifths of the entire group had been reported as employed in Indiana employment statistics (U.S. Women's Bureau, Bulletin No. 108, 1936). Since "there is no way we can go back into the past and get data which were not collected at the time,"

(Joint Economic Committee, 1973: parts 1–4) longitudinal studies about women's roles in the economy have been precluded.

COPING WITH PRIVATE AND SOCIAL STRESS: "NO-WIN HEROINES"

The range and complexity of women's roles suggests that women as a group cope with the realities of unemployment in a variety of ways. Unemployment studies have taught us that regardless of whether a woman is hurt directly by unemployment through loss of her job, or indirectly (at least initially) through the loss of her spouse's job, she will seek to readjust her life by utilizing diverse mechanisms. Women also affected by unemployment tend to suffer numerous economic and health-related hardships.

Our consideration of the Depression-era research reveals that discussions on the coping strategies of women fall into one of two categories: those concerned with single women and those focused on married women. Again, this dichotomy reflects the social reality of that time when marriage was an asset for working men but a liability for women seeking paid employment. Research that conceptualized unemployment as primarily a male problem tended to recognize the woman/wife as an important support person. Attention was focused on the "women of our unemployed" according to how well or how inadequately they provided domestic care for the unemployed. Komarovsky, after identifying three meanings that unemployment had for men—the loss of role of provider in the family; the role of economic failure, with its loss of prestige implications; and the loss of daily work routines and their organizing and self-expressive capacities—documented the importance of women's supportive efforts in maintaining family cohesion. Women's abilities to reorganize budgets and spending patterns, to work for wages regardless of the physical hardships involved, and to bolster the sagging confidence and morale of "the unemployed" men were instrumental in the survival of families during the Depression (Komarovsky, 1940).

While unemployment for men meant the loss of activity, for women it meant dramatic increases in both activity and responsibility. There is abundant case material that illustrates the range of ways women changed their life patterns to compensate for their husbands' loss of income and for their consequent loss of spirit.

> Mrs. Athas has aged perceptibly since she began working. Her shoulders have become rounded and she is very fatigued. She gets up at 6 A.M., leaves home at 6:30, takes her lunch with her, and returns at 4 P.M. to do the housework and cooking for the evening meal. . . . Mrs. Athas is the one who has had the courage and fortitude. Her husband is plump and placid, but the change of the role of breadwinner has been a cause of irritation between them. . . . The mother has no recreation, no opportunity to continue her English classes, and her work on Sunday makes it impossible for her to attend church. But she declares that she is willing to do anything to have her children educated and properly fitted for work. (Case 109, Elderton, *Case Studies of Unemployment*, 1931)

Elderton's 1931 study of unemployment, sponsored by the National Federation of Settlements, described vividly the ways in which women across the country sought to cope with the effects of joblessness. Often personal possessions and jewelry were sold to help pay off family debts or simply to purchase food. Women frequently moved their families into smaller and cheaper quarters, and many times they took boarders into their already crowded homes as a means of supplementing the family income. There was little privacy and rest for the women in Elderton's study. Clothing for the entire family had to be remade and patched, and food had to be obtained, even though there was often no money with which to make purchases.

However, the importance of women as a safety net during the Depression years was not just limited to their abilities to feed, clothe, and nurture their families with imagination and compassion. Some research also pointed out that "as a last resort" women were often able to enter the paid labor force when their husbands were unable to obtain or keep paid positions (U.S. Women's Bureau, Bulletin No. 164, 1938). However, even these studies did not confront the fact that frequently the jobs women were able to obtain paid far less than comparable work for men, and that the jobs themselves were those rejected by men seeking work. This discrimination against women was dramatically exemplified in the case of a woman who went to

142

look for work at the place where her husband had been employed prior to his recent layoff: she was offered her husband's old job at half the pay (U.S. Women's Bureau, *Bulletin* No. 92, 1932).

In general, Depression-era research revealed that while women could and did obtain wage labor during times of economic contraction, it was usually in the low-wage sector of the economy. Women generally found themselves working longer hours, obtaining lower wages with respect to men (regardless of the physical exertions demanded by the workplace), and yet at the same time, women found that the range and extent of their home activities and responsibilities increased greatly. A number of Depression-era studies supported the idea that unemployment placed women in a no-win situation. Research findings suggested that a woman's leaving home for wage labor activity would have negative psychological effects on the out-of-work father and the children, and that it could ultimately lead to family disintegration (Elderton, 1931; Claque and Powell, 1933). What emerged was a tragic pattern of women taking on tremendous burdens in order to support their families fully, only to be castigated for shirking their familial responsibilities.

The unemployment census of 1930 revealed that one-tenth of all unemployed women were heads of households with dependents at that time (U.S. Women's Bureau, *Bulletin* No. 113, 1933). While the majority of unemployment studies were concerned only secondarily with women (as spouse supporters), a few studies attempted some better understanding of who these unemployed women with dependents were. As early as 1931, Emergency Work Bureaus were swamped with applications from women who had "ridden into business on the wave of great economic and professional activity which followed the [first World] war. . . . who had been in charge of offices, promoted from stenographic to secretarial, and from secretarial to executive positions," and who now, faced with being out of a job, were "not only willing but eager to take any position they could find" (Field, 1932: 352). Helen Field, while registering such women for the New York Emergency Bureau, observed that the dangers of unemployment for women extended beyond "penury and the pinch of hunger" into "personal deflation and the shrinking of one's sense of importance" (Field, 1932:352). Pruett and Peters, in their research on the unemployment experiences of over 500 members of

143

the American Women's Association, similarly found that women faced with job loss appeared willing to do "anything." The authors were cognizant of the higher levels of skill and economic resources in the group they were studying; they were aware that the professional members of the American Women's Association were more advantaged than most women. Still, their research supported the notion that women were more likely to give aid than to receive it, even if they themselves were in dire straits. The aid given was usually to extended-family members dependent upon the earnings of these women.

This kind of economic dependency on women surfaces again and again in case materials from the Depression—while they were not accorded recognition as a significant part of the wage labor force, many women in fact were responsible for the economic maintenance of their immediate and extended families. Even the independent, single, working woman labored within a framework of dependency— family members and friends relied on her for support, both economic and emotional. Studies like those completed by Pruett and Peters and the U.S. Women's Bureau (*Bulletin* Nos. 103, 1933; 164, 1938) have helped to dispel the myth that job losses for men were more severe in their consequences than those for women. In both cases, their situations were desperate.

Contemporary explorations of the ways by which women cope with unemployment have often followed the Depression-era model by focusing on men as the primary victims of unemployment. The majority of recent media accounts do not distinguish unemployed workers on the basis of sex, despite a growing awareness of the problems of overgeneralizing. There persists in contemporary research a tendency to "masculinize" the unemployed. This in turn is still reinforced by an erroneous characterization of women as secondary or supplementary wage-earners, even though one out of three breadwinners (i.e., the sole job holder in a family) is female, and even though most women of middle- and working-class status today work for pay throughout their lives (Milkman, 1976).

Notwithstanding this prevailing tendency, there are a small number of research projects designed especially to explore the meaning that unemployment has had on the lives of women during the past several decades. Rayman and Bluestone's study of unemployed work-

Table 6.1. **Physical Effects of Layoff—Gender Differences**

Physical effects	% Males	% Females	Physical effects	% Males	% Females
Headaches	8	24	Loss of appetite	9	7
Stomach trouble	15	1	Drinking more	21	0
Heart trouble	1	0	Smoking more	34	25
High blood pressure	11	0	Lack of energy	9	1
Insomnia	33	7	Other effects	11	34

SOURCE: The 206 respondents to *Out of Work* questionnaire, printed in Paula Rayman, "The Human and Social Costs of Unemployment," Consortium of Social Science Association's Occasional Papers 2, Washington, D.C., 1984.

ers in the Hartford aircraft industry (1982) has generated important information on the coping strategies of women. For example, the study presents differences between men and women in reports of the physical effects of unemployment (see Table 6.1). In-depth interviews with aircraft workers revealed the male bias of the health indices used in the administered questionnaire and enabled female respondents to discuss female-related problems that were omitted from the formal checklist of physical effects, including such problems as increasingly difficult menstrual cycles.

Repeatedly, the Hartford respondents described their unemployment experiences as a pattern of financial and health "skidding"; of downward economic mobility combined with socio-psychological dislocation. It is clear that unemployment involves more than the loss of an economic standard of living. As the case of Sara reveals, unemployment means the loss of an entire means of living, including expectations and dreams:

> Sara is a forty-seven-year-old black woman, living in public housing with her five children, separated from her husband. Originally from the south, her family came north to "make better for themselves." She was laid off in 1978 following her four years doing setups in the aircraft plant. Her foreman had been harassing her for months, timing her visits to the bathroom and accusing her of not being able to read since most "of my people are illiterate." She filed a grievance with the union, which Sara feels is very weak and does not have the clout to combat the power of the company. After a year on welfare, she found a job working swing shift at a nursing home

145

15 miles away at a salary only 50 percent of her previous job. This causes her great difficulty commuting as she relies on public transport and also greatly affects the time she can spend with her young children. Her mother, sister, and eldest daughter help out with child care. (Rayman and Bluestone, 1982: chapter 7)

Rosen's study of married blue-collar women has begun to explore the importance of job loss duration in understanding women's responses to unemployment. While many of the blue-collar women respondents engaged in seasonal work felt initially relieved at being eased out of the double-burden situation of wage labor and domestic activity, extended job loss shifted this relief into anxiety (Rosen, 1982). Both Rosen's and Rayman's work indicate that women affected by unemployment turn to various support groups. While men admit the importance of a "good wife" during times of economic hardship, fewer women report that spouse support was vital in coping with the unemployment experience (Rayman and Bluestone, 1982). Instead, women tend to maintain connections with work colleagues, often forming informal support groups, and they also tend to rely on neighborhood networks as they adjust their lives to the psychological stress and economic hardships of unemployment. Snyder and Nowak's research (1983) on the differences between male and female responses to job loss reveals that more women than men internalized the distress they felt upon losing their jobs. It suggests that stress related to job loss continues long after the actual layoff. Depression, insomnia, irritation, and loss of trust were among the consequences that laid-off women workers discussed.

Regardless of the effort expended, a married woman cannot always make up for the lost income of her husband. If she is single, a woman often has difficulties obtaining pay equal to a man. (In 1985, women still earn on the average $.60 for every dollar earned by men.) This general discrimination against women, regardless of marital status, can be compounded during times of recession, and it often means that women will find themselves cast as "no-win heroines." To illustrate this role, consider the following familiar situation: the wife of an unemployed male worker goes to work full-time; she shifts around her entire life, but is only able to bring home a fraction of what her spouse had been earning. These sacrifices and compromises notwithstanding, she still frequently has to deal with

146

tension and resentment at home—there simply is not a great deal of male sympathy and support for this type of role reversal. What Milkman (1976) has observed of the Depression remains valid today:

> To say that the unemployed father lost status in the family would seem to imply that women who assumed the role of provider gained somehow. But such a role reversal was not a simple exchange of power. Women's responsibility for providing emotional support to family members was not diminished during this period. On the contrary, the reversal of roles made this task much more difficult, for an unemployed husband demanded more support than ever before. If there was any increased recognition of woman's economic role in the family, it did not represent a gain in status, for no one was comfortable with the new state of affairs, and the reversal of roles was resented by everyone involved. (Milkman, 1976:83)

Differentiation of Unemployment Experiences

Unfortunately, faulty generalizations still mar contemporary research. Studies on "the unemployed worker" have largely been, and continue to be, sex specific—and race, class, and occupation specific—even though they are frequently introduced as applicable to the widest possible social universe. As Marianne A. Ferber (1982) recently observed in a review essay on issues closely connected to our own concerns: "It is interesting to note . . . one significant difference between studies concerned with only men as opposed to those investigating women. The latter tend to be unmistakably labeled, while the former have titles which give no hint that they are restricted to men" (293). Past and present research must be evaluated for what it actually says and doesn't say about whom; the claims of research frequently exceed the actual findings. Even though the major patterns of research and thought about unemployment has been male-specific, there is a growing recognition that women have a different set of unemployment experiences than men do, and that women's experiences differ amongst themselves.

For example, the narrow focus of unemployment research on women is evidenced dramatically with regard to race. During the Depression years, the U.S. Women's Bureau conducted nearly two hundred research projects on the experiences of women; out of the

147

handful of projects addressing unemployment issues, there was only one that examined the situation of black women workers. While "The Negro Woman Worker" (U.S. Women's Bureau No. 265, 1938) did describe, if only in Kentucky, how black women were a significant part of the labor force,[2] it did not move beyond description into an analysis of the problems specific to black women facing job loss. While such "color blindness" can be understood as a reflection of the social standing that blacks had within society as a whole, it also underscores the narrow conceptions researchers had of the real world. Fortunately, contemporary social research has begun, if inadequately, to be sensitive to problems faced by minority women. For example, in 1982 black teenage women had an unemployment rate of 47 percent; the Department of Labor is exploring possible connections between this type of high unemployment rate and general economic status (Bulletin 2168, 1983). Other important research issues include racial discrimination in employment practices, the complex dependencies of some minority women on the welfare system, and the socioeconomic burdens unique to immigrant third world women.

An additional example of the limited nature and range of unemployment research are the findings of Pruett and Peters (1934). They studied a very select group of women: those over forty, unmarried, with above-average training and education, living in or near New York City, with higher salaries and more work experience than most women, and who belonged to the American Women's Association.

Researchers today have begun to differentiate between unemployed women and men. Findings from this research may help us better understand the full range of complications that unemployment causes in the wage-work and private lives of women. Complementary studies on the full range of occupations within the labor force could provide a lever with which to pry apart the layers of experience that distinguish contemporary women. Marital status was an important variable in categorizing the unemployment experiences of women during the Depression; it continues to remain important, but for different reasons. Fifty years ago it was assumed that married women should not have to enter the wage labor force: today, the majority of women will work in wage labor occupations for most of their lives. Most women now recognize that marriage in no way guarantees financial support. Moreover, as Carolyn Bell reports (1983) the most vulnerable unemployed group in the United States consists of the eight million women supporting their children alone. Solely responsible for their family income, these women's unemployment rates have been the highest of any class of adults. They also have low earnings compared to married women or to men of any marital status and have no savings cushions for hard times.

Large-scale analysis of the labor force in general continues to be the principle information source on women workers—the difficulties particular to very young, inexperienced women workers or to senior women workers have not yet been the focus of direct research attention. Clearly another problem with the traditional research and policy approach has been an association between the "natural" rate of unemployment with the number of women in the labor force. This approach argues that women "naturally" have a high unemployment rate because as wives and mothers their natural place is at home, not in the workplace. As women increasingly enter the paid workforce, total unemployment will rise as women displace men and also experience layoffs themselves.[3]

During cycles of especially high rates of unemployment like the 1980s, the "natural or normal" rate of unemployment is designated to stretch to cover more and more people. The ways that women workers have been discouraged from or excluded from entering the labor force or have been targeted as a "cause" of high unemployment rates all need to be carefully identified and explored.

Let us reemphasize the obvious: unemployment is more than a complex economic issue. Increasingly, the meaning that work has in the lives of individual women determines the consequences of unemployment. Biographical research on women, on their fit into the economy and on the ways that work and unemployment figure into their lives in conjunction with large-scale empirical research on work will enhance our present understanding of the dimensions of the unemployment issue. However, it must be stressed that Western notions of work and unemployment for women, based as they are on experiences within an advanced capitalist economy, do not capture the experiences of most third world women. As research in the area continues, both the women and the work/unemployment situations

149

under study need to be specified. Once the distinct experiences of particular women are identified, we can begin the process of integrating research findings into a comprehensive understanding of the meaning that unemployment has in the lives of women.

AFTERWORD

We began this review on the assumption that comparing unemployment studies from the 1930 Depression with those from the most recent recession would help us better understand both the contributions that women have made and the particular difficulties that women must continually confront during periods of high unemployment. In a very direct way, our research has made clear the fact that economic crises have severe impacts on the lives of all women and that "women's position today is a product of their past" (Tilly and Scott, 1978).

Women today continue to bear the burden of multiple roles. Those contemporary studies that we have reviewed have identified some of the adaptive changes that women have made and continue to make in their lives when unemployment hits. We are also learning about the ways that persistent discrimination against women both in hiring practices and in wage scales precludes any sort of economic stability for women during periods of high unemployment and reinforces financial and health skidding patterns. However, further exploration of the consistencies and differences in women's unemployment experiences and of the immediate and lasting consequences of unemployment for women is necessary as we seek to develop sound social policies that address the needs of contemporary women.

Notes

1. The individual and group experiences characteristic of women workers have rarely been granted specific attention. Furthermore, most traditional Marxist analyses of capitalism have relied on narrow conceptions of

work and of unemployment; both have revolved around wage labor—its specific forms and/or its loss. Increasingly, however, Marxist critiques have incorporated a recognition that investigations of work in general and specifically of women's work and unemployment need to focus on the interrelationships between the spheres of paid labor and of unpaid, domestic labor (Kessler-Harris, 1982; Oakley, 1976).

2. For example, in the 1930 Census, one out of six women workers was black, and further, two out of five black women were counted as workers as compared with one out of five white women. Recognition of the differences between the life situations of black and white women did not prompt any related research during the Depression. Black women today are connected to the wage labor force in vastly different ways than are white women in general: for example, throughout 1980, black women were more likely to be employed full-time year-round than white or Hispanic women. Notwithstanding, the incidence of unemployment for black women is persistently higher; while white women experienced 16 percent unemployment during 1980, the official rate for black women during the same period was 27 percent (Terry, 1982). Such disparities are only slowly being acknowledged as an important topic for serious research.

Reference List

Addams, Jane. 1932. Social consequences of depression. *Survey* 67 (January): 370–371.

Angell, Robert C. 1936. *The family encounters the depression.* New York: Charles Scribner's Sons.

Bakke, E. Wight. 1940. *The Unemployed worker.* New Haven: Yale University Press.

Bell, Carolyn Shaw. 1972. Unemployed women: Do they matter? *Wall Street Journal,* March 15.

Bell, Carolyn Shaw. 1973. Age, sex, marriage, and jobs, *The Public Interest* 30 (Winter): 76–87.

Bluestone, Barry and Harrison, Bennett. 1982. *The deindustrialization of America.* New York: Basic Books.

Brandt, Lillian. 1932. *An impressionistic view of the winter of 1930–31.* New York: Welfare Council of New York City.

Cavan, Ruth S. and Ranck, Katherine H. 1938. *The family and the depression: A study of one hundred Chicago families.* Chicago: University of Chicago Press.

Claque, Ewan and Powell, Webster. 1933. *Ten thousand out of work.* Philadelphia: University of Pennsylvania Press.

Darling, Martha. 1975. The role of women in the economy. Summary of Ten Nation's Reports, Paris: OECD.

Elderdon, Marion, ed. 1931. *Case studies of unemployment.* Compiled by the Unemployment Commission of the National Federation of Settlements, Philadelphia: University of Pennsylvania Press.

Ferber, Marianne, A. 1982. Women and work: A review essay. *Signs* 8 (Winter): 273–295.

Field, Helen. 1932. Are women losing ground? *Survey* 67 (January): 352.

Hartmann, Heidi. 1976. Capitalism, patriarchy, and job segmentation by sex. *Signs* 1, 3 (Spring): 137–169.

Jahoda, Marie; Lazenfeld, Paul F. & Zeisel, Hans. 1971. *Marienthal.* Chicago: Aldine-Atherton, Inc.

Joint Economic Committee, Congress of the United States. 1973. Economic problems of women, Parts 1, 2, 3, 4. Washington, D.C.: U.S. Government Printing Office.

Joint Economic Committee, Congress of the United States. 1977. American women workers in a full employment economy. Washington, D.C.: U.S. Government Printing Office.

Kessler-Harris, Alice. 1982. *Out of work: A history of wage earning women in the United States.* New York, London: Oxford University Press.

Komarovsky, Mira. 1971. *The unemployed man and his family.* New York: Arno Press. (Originally New York: Dryden Press, Inc., 1940).

Kuttner, Bob and Freeman, Phyllis. 1982. Women to the workhouse. *Working Papers,* 9, 6 (Nov.-Dec.):18.

Leventman, Paula Goldman. 1981. *Professionals out of work.* New York: Free Press.

Macdonald, Martha. 1979. Women in the workforce—Meeting of the changing needs of capitalism. Revised version of paper presented in the Political Economy Section of the Canadian Political Science Association Meetings, Saskatoon, June.

Matthaei, Julie. 1982. An economic history of women in America: Women's work, the sexual division of labor, and the development of capitalism. New York: Schocken Books.

Milkman, Ruth. 1976. Women's work and economic crisis: Some lessons of the Great Depression. *Review of Radical Political Economics.* 8, 1 (Spring): 73–97.

Milkman, Ruth. 1987. Female factory labor and industrial structure: Control and conflict over 'women's place' in auto and electrical manufacturing. *Politics and Society,* forthcoming.

Niemi, Beth. 1975. Geographic immobility and labor force mobility: A study of female unemployment, in *Sex, discrimination and the division of labor,* edited by Cynthia Lloyd. New York: Columbia University Press.

Oakley, Ann. 1974. *Women's work.* New York: Vintage Books.

Oppenheimer, Valerie Kincade. 1973. Demographic influence on female employment and the status of women, in *Changing women in a changing society,* edited by Joan Huber. Chicago: University of Chicago Press.

Pruette, Lorine and Peters, Iva Lowtner. 1934. *Women workers through the Depression.* New York: Macmillan.

Rayman, Paula M. 1982. The world of not-working: An evaluation of urban social services response to unemployment. *Journal of Health and Human Services Administration,* 4, 3:319–333.

Rayman, Paula M. 1984. Human and social costs of unemployment, Consortium of Social Science Associations, Occasional Paper No. 2, Washington, D.C.

Rayman, Paula M. and Bluestone, Barry. 1982. *Out of work: The consequences of unemployment in the Hartford aircraft industry.* U.S. Department of Health and Human Services, National Institute of Mental Health Grant No. 5–RO1–MH33251–02, Final Report, October.

Rosen, Ellen I. 1981. Hobson's choice: Employment and unemployment among women factory workers in New England. U.S. Department of Labor Grant No. 21–25–79–19, Final Report, October.

Sarri, Rosemary C. 1983. The response of low-income working women to income loss through AFDC reduction and/or unemployment: A research proposal. Unpublished, Ann Arbor: University of Michigan.

Snyder, Kay A. and Nowak, Thomas C. 1983. Sex differences in the impact of a plant shutdown: The case of Robertshaw Controls. Prepared for ASA Annual Meeting, Detroit, Michigan.

Tentler, Leslie Woodcock. 1980. *Wage earning women: Industrial work and family life in the United States 1900–1930.* London: Oxford University Press.

Terry, Sylvia Lazos. 1982. Unemployment and its effects on family income in 1980. U.S. Department of Labor Bulletin 2148, September.

Tilly, Louise A. and Scott, Joan W. 1978. *Women, work and family.* New York: Holt, Rinehart and Winston.

U.S. Department of Labor. Bureau of Labor Statistics
  1983. Bulletin No. 2168, "Women at work: A chartbook," April.
  1985. Bulletin No. 2222, "Linking employment problems to economic status," March.

U.S. Women's Bureau.
  1932. Bulletin No. 92. "Wage-earning women and the industrial conditions of 1930: A survey of South Bend," by Caroline Manning and Arcadia N. Phillips.
  1933. Bulletin No. 103. "Women workers in the third year of the Depression."
  1933. Bulletin No. 113. "Employment fluctuations and unemployment of women: Certain indications from various sources 1928–31," by Mary Elizabeth Pidgeon.
  1936. Bulletin No. 108. "The effects of the Depression on wage-earner's families: A second survey of South Bend," by Harriet A. Byrne.

153

1936. Bulletin No. 139, "Women unemployed seeking relief in 1933," by Harriet A. Byrne.

1938. Bulletin No. 164, "Women in industry: A series of papers to aid study groups," by Mary E. Pidgeon.

1938. Bulletin No. 165, "The negro woman worker," by Jean Collier Brown.

1939. Bulletin No. 172, "The woman wage-earner: Her situation today," by Elizabeth D. Benham.

Walby, Sylvia, 1983. Women's unemployment: Some spatial and historical variations. Paper presented to Urban Change and Conflict Conference, Clacton, January.

Wandersee, Winifred D., 1981. *Women, work and family values during prosperity and depression,* Cambridge, Mass.: Harvard University Press.

7

Structural Transformation and Minority Families

Maxine Baca Zinn

Social and technological changes now occurring in the United States' economy are altering society in unprecedented ways. Plant closings, industrial exodus, and the rise of the sunbelt are being widely discussed in the media and among academic researchers. Yet, curiously little systematic attention has been focused on the minorities who have been most adversely affected by these developments. This chapter will examine some aspects of the impact of structural transformation on blacks and Chicanos. The purpose of this chapter is to address the relationship between the larger economy and family patterns in the urban underclass. The central thesis is that family structure among minorities has always reflected their material conditions in society. As a result, contemporary family life is undergoing changes in response to new economic constraints.

In the past two decades, the scholarship on minorities has made enormous advances. Racial inequality, subordination, and exclusion have been thoroughly documented. New explanations and models have advanced our understanding of racial ethnic people and their relationships to the dominant society. Despite these changes, much remains to be done for a thorough analysis of class and race. For most Americans, "race" means black people and white people; minority means blacks. Academic social scientists have been extraordinarily blind to Chicanos and other non-blacks (Moore, 1981: 2750), even though the Hispanic population has been expanding rapidly. Hispanic is a catch-all term referring to a variety of categories, including Chicanos or Mexican Americans, Puerto Ricans, Cubans, and other Latins.

In 1980, blacks represented approximately 12 percent of the total population (26 million); Hispanics approximately 6 percent of the total population (14.6 million) of which Chicanos account for 60%. Some researchers have predicted that Hispanics will outnumber blacks in the near future, due to Hispanics' high fertility rates and to the substantial immigration of Hispanics. The Census Bureau has estimated that Hispanics were undercounted in 1980 by about 7.4 percent. Adding this undercount to the census figure of 14.6 million yields an adjusted Hispanic population of 15.8 million in 1980. The claim that Hispanics will soon outnumber blacks is, however, unfounded. Census Bureau projections show that in the year 2000 Hispanics will number 30 million, while black Americans will number 36 million (Exter, 1985:20–23). Nevertheless, Hispanics will constitute a plurality in certain areas. Some states such as California are moving toward populations in which young Hispanics will outnumber other age-race groups (Haues-Baustista, Schinek, and Chapa, 1984). The continuing population dispersion from the Southwest has turned Hispanics into a national population. "The current decade of the 1980's undoubtedly sees nearly half of the Chicano population living outside the five southwestern states" (Maldonado, 1985:157).

Today, the living conditions of blacks and Chicanos are similar in important respects. By the 1970s all were predominantly city dwellers. In 1980, 77 percent of blacks lived in metropolitan areas, compared to 83 percent of the people of Spanish origin. Chicanos were not new to the cities of the Southwest (many of which were founded by Mexican immigrants), but their concentration in urban centers has only recently been revealed. This has occurred at the same time that large numbers of undocumented workers and their families are settling in urban areas. How many such workers there are is the subject of a great debate, but the correct answer would be in the millions (Moore, 1981:279). Moreover, despite the great ethnic diversity between blacks and Chicanos, they share widespread poverty due to unemployment or to the low earnings of workers. Blacks and Chicanos lag behind white Americans in every measure of well-being: jobs, income, educational attainment, housing, and health care. Yet, by the turn of the century the old "minorities" (including blacks, Hispanics, and Asians) will be the new majorities in many areas

(Bennett, 1985:32). The numbers are reasonably clear. Less clear is the fate of the growing ranks of these often poor racial ethnics in an economically shrinking society where technology and political displacement threaten to create new categories of permanently unemployed people.

HISTORICAL OVERVIEW

Because blacks and Chicanos share some important historical features, an overview of these similarities will lay the groundwork for looking at current issues. Blacks and Chicanos were involuntarily incorporated into American society, although in different ways. The involuntary incorporation of Chicanos was by means of the military conquest of a million square miles, an addition that increased the United States by fully one-third its present size (Barrera, 1979, Estrada et al, 1982, Maldonado, 1985). This conquest provided the United States with territory, natural resources, and a Mexican population estimated at 116,000. Unlike those blacks who were conquered on their own land and reduced to landless wage laborers, both blacks and Mexicans "entered" this society against their will and were placed in unfree labor systems. This contrasts with the incorporation of white European immigrants into the nation's industrial labor force. As a result of their voluntary structural placements, white workers could rise to semi-skilled and skilled positions (Blauner, 1972:63). Blacks and Chicanos shared the experience of being put in colonial-type labor systems that varied in form but were structurally similar in their consequences. A colonial labor system exists where the labor force is systematically maintained in a subordinate position; to be "subordinate" means to be disadvantaged with regard to the labor market or labor processes in comparison with other workers (Barrera, 1979:39). Structural, legal, and political constraints made permanent "integration" impossible. Segregation was justified by racist ideologies and enforced through such institutions as slavery, the labor camp, and the corresponding persistence of harsh and unequal treatment of workers. Blacks and Mexicans, therefore, had to deal with coercive labor markets. When

157

Mexicans did begin crossing the border into the United States between 1900 and 1930, a voluntary mode of incorporation was initiated. By then, however, a well-entrenched colonial labor system had structured the presence of Mexicans in this society.

In slavery and in other colonial systems, subsistence or no wages threatened the survival of workers and their families. Survival was accomplished by putting entire families to work. In this way, the structure of colonial labor took a severe toll on family life. Women were workers as well as wives and mothers; their labor was an important means of reproducing the labor power of other family members. Minority women were defined in a different way than the more restricted definition applied to white women of the dominant society. In addition to their labor in the "public" sphere, they were responsible for the domestic care of their own families. In slavery, women were viewed as profitable labor units, regardless of their gender. They were first full-time workers, and then only incidentally wives, mothers, and homemakers (Davis, 1981:5). Their work during slavery and after slavery as wage laborers and agricultural workers has been widely documented. Although Chicanas have a very different work history than black women, new research has revealed clear and consistent work patterns. They were drawn into agricultural labor systems as entire families entered the pattern of seasonal and migratory field work. After 1870, they were incorporated in various types of unskilled labor, subordinated by race and sex. These developments altered traditional patterns of employment and family responsibilities. As they entered the paid labor force, they often assumed multiple responsibilities of mother and wage-earner.

This overgeneralized account of the labor of blacks and Chicanos reveals that families bore the burden of racial labor exploitation. Women's market work resulted from an effort to survive in the face of colonial domination and subsequent poverty. The experiences of racial ethnic women contrast with those of white women of the dominant society, who were excluded from the labor force by a family wage, a wage earned by their husbands that was sufficient to allow women to stay home, raise children, and maintain a family, rather than having all members of the family out at work (Zaretsky, 1978:211). The family wage did not extend to those in colonial labor systems, but families adapted to the lack of external support as women took advantage of society's need for workers.

The more recent patterns of economic life for black and Chicano workers began to crystalize during and after World War II. Blacks followed traditional channels of northern migration and moved to the older northeastern and midwestern cities. Here, metropolitan labor markets were segmented by race. The primary market for white males contained jobs with high wages, good working conditions, fringe benefits, and opportunities for advancement. The secondary labor market for others contained jobs characterized by poor working conditions, low wages, few opportunities for advancement, and little job security. This distinction between labor markets has been crucial for racial ethnics. Only the primary sector offers opportunities in the usual sense, a decent job that offers advancement and a career (Moore, 1981:284). Blacks entered many peripheral manufacturing industries, but for the most part they remained locked in the secondary segment of the labor force. Chicanos who had also been steadily making their way north were also pressed into the dual labor system. In the Southwest, they were concentrated in the lower reaches of the occupational structure, barred from supervisory positions by their ethnic and national origins (Maldonado, 1985:148–149). Despite persistent patterns of labor segregation by race, some blacks and Chicanos did enter better-paying jobs within manufacturing. They used their blue-collar jobs as a main avenue to mobility and security. Movement into higher-level blue-collar jobs was one of the most important components of black occupational advancement in the 1970s (Currie and Skolnick, 1984:182).

Those unable to find work were forced to rely on welfare payments. Support provided by extended family groupings also became increasingly important. Thus, family extension, like women's labor, was a strategy for meeting material family needs. Despite the ethnic diversity in the family lives of blacks and Chicanos, extended family structures have compensated for resources withheld by the larger economic system. MacAdoo (1982:16) has pointed to the presence of the extended family in all minority comunities. Extended family networks that pool resources, share mutual aid, and represent an attempt to cope with the tenuous necessities of survival have been documented in both black and Chicano settings (see, for example, Stack, 1974, and Hoppe and Heller, 1975). While kinship networks are adaptive coping mechanisms, they also extract a large cost. As Rapp has argued:

> These are people essentially living below socially necessary reproduction costs. They therefore reproduce themselves by spreading out the aid and the risks involved in daily life. For the disproportionately high numbers who are prevented from obtaining steady employment, being part of what Marx called the floating surplus population is a perilous endeavor (Rapp, 1982:177).

THE UNDERCLASS PERSPECTIVE ON FAMILY LIFE

A growing body of empirical data suggests that permanent poverty remains a persistent feature of United States society. This poverty conception has subsequently given way to the concept of the urban underclass. Estimates of the size of the underclass vary from 1 percent to 5 percent of the population. The major though not only defining trait of this class is its persistent poverty (Kelly, 1985:161). In its popular usage, the term underclass refers to the concentration, not of undifferentiated poor people, but of poor minorities in America's central cities. Thus, the most severe problems of urban life—unemployment, crime, out-of-wedlock births, female-headed families and welfare dependence—are viewed as problems of race. *Time* magazine's introduction to the underclass read as follows: "Behind the crumbling walls of the ghetto, lives a large group of people, more intractable, more socially alien, and more hostile than almost anyone had imagined. They are the unreachables, the American underclass." The term continues to be popular. But the ubiquitous use of the term disguises sharply different ideas about the nature and causes of urban poverty and underemployment (McGahey, 1981:62–64). While few would disagree that persistent poverty represents a growing American problem, there are varying interpretations of its sources and present dimensions. Data from the Michigan Panel of Income Dynamics indicate that about one percent of the households interviewed between 1968 and 1975 were constantly poor (Duncan, 1984), that poverty is more widespread but much less persistent than is popularly imagined, and that "the persistently poor do not easily fit into the underclass stereotype") (Corcoran, Duncan, and Hill, 1984:243).

The most troublesome assumption within the popular image of the underclass is that economic deprivation in one generation leads to deprivation in future generations due to maladaptive lifestyles in ghettos and barrios. This notion is a throwback to the early "culture of poverty" theories, in which poverty is viewed as "an accepted, ingrained way of life on the part of the poor" (Lowenstein, 1985:40). The feature most responsible for poverty's self-perpetuation in the image of the underclass is the female-headed family. The mother-only family, so common among blacks, is typically assumed to explain poverty. This is usually expressed in the phrase, "the feminization of poverty," a shorthand reference to women living alone being disproportionately represented among the poor. The publicity given to increased marital break-up, births to unmarried women, and to the household patterns that accompany these models suggests that family structure changes *cause* poverty. Despite the growing concentration of poverty among black female-headed households in the past decade, there is no hard evidence that family structure causes poverty.

Female-headed households are not responsible for the growth of the urban underclass. Research conducted by Sarah McLanahan using data from the Michigan Panel Study of Income Dynamics refutes the idea that long-term inequality is due to family structure per se (i.e., the absence of a father), or to other factors such as economics. Her findings emphasize the importance of economic deprivation in one-parent households and suggest that increasing and stabilizing the income of single parents would "eliminate some of the intergenerational disadvantages currently attributed to family structure and single parents" (McLanahan, 1985:898).

In brief, the underclass theory with its emphasis on family patterns diverts attention from the structural causes of poverty. A more fruitful approach lies in understanding how large-scale economic shifts are creating the severe problems of urban life.

ECONOMIC RESTRUCTURING AND MINORITIES

Increasing poverty rates among blacks and Chicanos have complex and interrelated social and economic antecedents. The significant progress against racial inequality made in the late 1960s and early 1970s has slowed since then and even been reversed because of developments in the economy and public policy (Currie and Skolnick, 1984:181). Fundamental transformations in United States society are altering the connections between minorities and the economy. The present causes of the entrapment of blacks and Chicanos can be located in the lack of adequate jobs due to (1) sectoral shifts in which manufacturing is declining, (2) shifts in geographical locations of jobs from central cities toward the sunbelt and rural areas, and to other countries, and (3) the polarization of the labor force into either high-wage or low-wage jobs. The devastating impact of plant shutdowns, corporate relocations, and displaced workers in abandoned communities is well known. Business in general is being affected; municipal budgets are being drained by the rising demands for social services. The mental and physical health of laid-off workers, their families and friends deteriorates; rates of divorce, alcoholism, depression, and suicide climb. Minorities tend to be concentrated in industries that have borne the brunt of recent closings. This is particularly true in the automobile, steel, and rubber industries (Bluestone and Harrison, 1982:54). In addition, they are concentrated within central cities and in those regions of the country where plant closings and economic dislocations have been most pronounced (Bluestone and Harrison, 1982:54). Most Chicanos and blacks live in central cities and the employment bases of these cities are being transformed.

The shift of jobs away from the central cities to the suburbs has created a residence-job opportunity mismatch that literally leaves minorities behind in the inner city. Without adequate training or credentials, they are relegated to low-paying, nonadvancing exploitative service work or they are unemployed. They are becoming superfluous people in cities that are themselves becoming administrative, information, and high-order service centers, rather than centers for producing, and distributing material goods. This change creates changes in the composition and size of their overall employment bases. During the past two decades, most older, larger cities have experienced substantial job growth in occupations associated with knowledge-intensive service industries. However, selective job growth in these high-skill, predominantly white-collar industries has not compensated for the employment decline in manufacturing, wholesale trade, and other predominantly blue-collar industries that once constituted the backbone of urban economic life (Kasarda, 1983:41). Permanent job losses were higher for blacks than whites in 1982, and the percentage of permanent job separations for blacks has worsened over time (Bednarzick, 1983:4).

While cities once sustained large numbers of less-skilled persons, today the newer service industries typically have high educational requisites for entry. Knowlege and information jobs in the central cities are virtually closed to minorities, given the required technological education and skill levels. Commuting between central cities and outlying areas is becoming increasingly common; white-collar workers commute daily from their suburban residences to the central business districts, while streams of inner-city residents are commuting to their blue-collar jobs in outlying areas. But a large portion of minorities cannot afford either the luxury or the employment necessity of owning an automobile. In Chicago, for example, four out of five inner-city blacks do not own a car.

Chicago's loss of manufacturing jobs has greatly affected Hispanics. Nearly two-thirds of the half-million Hispanics in Chicago held blue-collar jobs, both skilled and unskilled. Between 1979 and 1981, 10 percent of the manufacturing jobs disappeared in Chicago. In the same two years, Hispanic unemployment doubled. The largest number of jobs were lost in the steel industry where Hispanics had made strong progress toward better job positions (Moore and Pachon, 1985:47).

The decline in manufacturing jobs has altered the most important role once played by the cities as opportunity ladders for the disadvantaged. Since the start of World War II, well-paying blue-collar jobs in manufacturing have been a main avenue of job security and mobility for blacks and Chicanos. Movement into higher-level blue-collar jobs was one of the most important components of black occupational advancement in the 1970s. The restructuring of these in-

163

dustries creates the threat of downward mobility for the minority middle class (Currie and Skolnick, 1984:182).

Economic restructuring is characterized by an overall pattern of uneven development. Traditional industries have declined in the North and Midwest, while new growth industries are locating in the southern and southwestern part of the nation. To be sure, this regional shift has produced some gains for minorities. Black poverty rates in the South have begun to converge with poverty rates outside of the South. This is related to industrial decline in the North as much as to black employment in the South. Given the large minority populations in the sunbelt, it is conceivable that industrial restructuring could offset these new economic threats to racial equality. But this hope is clouded for several reasons. The sunbelt expansion has been based primarily on low-wage enterprises that use large numbers of underpaid minority workers. For example, the garment industry has moved its concentration from New York City, with its workforce of skilled European trade workers, to the South and Southwest, where more than 80 percent of all apparel workers are women, particularly unskilled, nonwhite women. "Add up these traits, unskilled, female, nonwhite or poor white—and you have the cheapest, most exploited pool of labor to be found in the United States: Chinese women in Los Angeles, Latin and Chinese women in New York, Chicanos in the Southwest, Black and poor white women in the south" (NACLA, 1977:101). The low wage rates that prevail in these regions, low taxes, anti-union right-to-work laws in some of the states, and cheap land are important in encouraging the sunbelt boom (Moore and Pachon, 1985:43). Minorities have been excluded from research and development activities in high-technology areas such as the aerospace and microchip industries. In California's silicon valley, low-wage workers are predominantly women; over half of them women of color (Bernstein, 1977).

POVERTY AND FAMILY STRUCTURE

The rapid growth of poor female-headed households among blacks is a major social trend of the past decade. By 1981, 47 percent of black families with children were headed by women. Among Hispanics, women headed 21 percent of all families, compared to 14 percent of white families with children present. Female-headed households continue to be a larger proportion of black families than any other subgroup. In 1983, 53.8 percent of black families with children were headed by women. The poverty rate for these families was 56.1 percent. Seventy-five percent of the 4.3 million black children that year lived in female-headed households (O'Hare, 1985:32). These facts have resulted in a spate of journalistic articles about "the disintegrating black family." The growth of female-headed households has also posed new questions about the ubiquitous extended minority family.

Is the black multigenerational cooperative family fading from society? Research by Mary Ann Scheirer (1984) on household structures among AFDC recipients in two nationally representative samples found a low overall frequency of people (less than 10 percent) living in extended households. A mother living alone with her children was the predominant structure of all ethnic groups. However, black AFDC mothers were slightly more likely than white mothers to be living with grandparents or elder adults. Furthermore, the study suggested an economic base for the formation of extended families. States with higher levels of monthly AFDC benefits had much lower proportions of families living with the youngest child's grandparents. It appears that in low-paying states, other family members are providing the economic sustenance for many AFDC families that is lacking from welfare payments (Schreir, 1984: 769–770). Gains from modifying household composition by extension or augmentation are revealed by Ronald Angel and Marta Tienda in their study of black, Hispanic, and white households (1982). Adding multiple earners to the household is particularly beneficial for minority female-headed households. Extension does not lift minorities out of poverty, but it does compensate for inadequate earnings (Angel and Tienda, 1982:1377). These studies suggest that minority female-headed households do not preclude family extension.

In general, the rise of black female-headed households is directly related to economic conditions, most specifically to the poor economic status of black men. In 1983, the median income of black men aged fifteen and over ($8,967) was just 58 percent of the median for

165

white men ($15,401). Black men are also less likely than white men to be employed. At the end of 1984, the proportion of working-age black men with a job was 53 percent compared to 61 for white men and the unemployment rate of black men was 13.1 percent versus 5.4 percent for white men. There is also a clear relationship between income and marriage. Men with higher incomes are more likely to be married than men with lower incomes. Many black women leave a marriage or forego marriage altogether because of the shortage of black men with the ability to support a family (O'Hare, 1985:33). According to Noel Cazenave, out-of-wedlock births are sometimes encouraged by families and absorbed into the kinship system because marrying the suspected father would simply be an additional financial burden (Cazenave, 1980:432). High levels of poverty, unemployment, and underemployment also contribute to the disproportionate number of black males killed in wars and criminal homicide (Pearce, 1983:72). These structural conditions leave black women disproportionately separated, divorced, and solely responsible for their children. Female-headed households are an adaptation to structural conditions; they are not the cause of poverty among blacks. While mother-only households fare worse than two-parent households, they are not at the root of the problems currently facing blacks.

Unhappily, a two-parent family is not a guarantee against poverty for minorities. The long-term income of black children in two-parent families throughout the decade of the 1970s was even lower than the long-term income of nonblack children who spent most of the decade in mother-only families. Thus, increasing the proportion of black children growing up in two-parent families would not by itself eliminate very much of the racial gap in the economic well-being of children; changes in the economic circumstances of the parents is needed most to bring the economic status of black children up to the higher status of nonblack children (Hill, 1983:47).

Minority women experience qualitatively more poverty than any other social category in society, no matter what their circumstances or income sources. Even working full-time, year-round, black and Hispanic women have rates of poverty as high as white men who did not work at all (Pearce, 1984:509). Consequently, Heidi Hartmann's contention that recent changes for women have been positive is open

166

to question. Her argument is that increased labor force participation gives women sufficient resources to form their own households and that those changes are largely positive for women because they contribute to women's increased economic independence (this volume). This much is true for both white women and for racial-ethnic women, but for different reasons. Hartmann attributes to the propensity of all women to form their own households a matter of choice. But the generalization that the tendency of women to form households is associated with economic well-being simply does not apply to minorities. Their household formations are caused in large part by the economic vulnerability of men rather than the economic well-being of women. Hartmann, of course, acknowledges that heading families or households means poverty for some women. Nevertheless, conditions associated with female-headed families among racial-ethnics are different and should be interpreted differently. Because white families headed by women have much higher average incomes than minority families in the same situation, we must not confuse an overall improvement with what is in fact an improvement for women in certain social categories, while other women are left at the bottom in even worse conditions. Differentiating women's experiences along racial and class lines forces us to examine the ways in which the structures of class, race, and gender create different sets of social structural constraints.

CULTURAL RESISTANCE OR STRUCTURAL ADAPTATION

Many scholars writing on minority families have argued that families are bastions against racial oppression. The argument was developed by Mina Davis Caulfield in "Imperialism, The Family and Cultures of Resistance" (1974). She contends that the alternative family patterns among racial minorities, especially women's roles, have been the focal points for opposition to forms of imperialism and racial oppression by perpetuating alternative systems of values, customs, and culture that are at the heart of resistance movements. Female-centered kinship networks and elements of traditional culture are ways of "fighting back" under conditions of severe oppression.

This is an important line of thinking that requires searching for connections between family patterns and resistance movements among people of color. Undoubtedly, families can and indeed have provided resistance in particular historical moments. But as Libby Bishop points out, this culture-of-resistance argument ignores the sexual division of labor and the costs extracted from women in protecting their families and culture (Bishop, 1983:24–27). Furthermore, there is a danger of overstating and romanticizing the capabilities of families to oppose racial oppression through alternative family patterns and living arrangements alone. I would argue that "adaptation" is a more generalizable concept than resistance. Families adapt to social and economic constraints by weaving together elements derived from their culture and the limited structural resources available to them. The results may be conceptualized as family strategies. According to Louise Tilly (1978:83) family strategies are influenced by large structural processes, but they take place at the household level. Among blacks and Chicanos, family strategies have included both women's labor force participation and various alternative household and family forms, such as household extension and female-headed households. These are complex phenomena influenced by larger economic and social structures, mediated at the household level.

Women, men, and children in minority communities are not merely the victims of wave after wave of economic exploitation. Clearly, they have fashioned distinctive ways of life that have included alternative household and family patterns. These reflect, in part, the need of minorities to survive within multiple systems of oppression. Yet, family strategies can absorb many of the costs of race, class, and gender inequalities and still undermine family well-being. There may be a limit to what can be achieved by each line of adaptation. Under present economic conditions, female-headed households receive limited gains from economic conditions that the larger society imposes.

Reference List

Angel, Ronald, and Marta Tienda. 1982. Determinants of extended household structure: Cultural pattern or economic need? *American Journal of Sociology* 87(6):1360–1383.

Barrera, Mario. 1979. *Race and class in the Southwest*. Notre Dame: University of Notre Dame Press.

Bednarzik, Robert. 1983. Layoffs and permanent job losses: Workers' traits and cyclical patterns. *Monthly Labor Review* 106,9 (Sept.):3–12.

Bennett, Lerone. 1985. Blacks and the future. *Ebony* (August):29–34.

Bernstein, Alan, Bob DeGrasse, Rachel Grossman, Chris Paine, and Lenny Siegel. 1977. Silicon valley paradise or paradox? In *Mexican women in the United States*, edited by Magdalena Mora, Adelaida R. Del Castillo, 105–112. Chicano Studies Research Center Publications. University of California, Los Angeles and Berkeley.

Bishop, Libby. 1983. The family: Prison, haven, or vanguard? *Berkeley Journal of Sociology* 28:19–37.

Bluestone, Barry, and Bennett Harrison. 1982. *The deindustrialization of America*. New York: Basic Books, Inc.

Blauner, Robert. 1972. *Racial oppression in America*. New York: Harper and Row.

Corcoran, Mary, Greg J. Duncan, and Martha S. Hill. 1984. The economic fortunes of women and children: Lessons from the panel study of income dynamics. *Signs: Journal of Women in Culture and Society* 10(2):232–248.

Caulfield, Mina Davis. 1974. Imperialism, the family, and cultures of resistance. *Socialist Revolution* 20:67–85.

Cazenave, Noel. 1980. Alternate intimacy. Marriage and family lifestyles among low income black Americans. *Alternative Lifestyles* 3(4):425–444.

Currie, Elliot, and Jerome H. Skolnick. 1984. *America's problems: Social issues and public policy*. Boston: Little, Brown and Company.

Davis, Angela. 1981. *Women, race, and class*. New York: Random House.

Davis, Cary, Carl Haub, and JoAnne Willette. 1983. U.S. Hispanics, changing the face of America. *Population Bulletin* 38 (June).

Duncan, Greg J. 1984. *Years of poverty, years of plenty*. Institute for Social Research. Ann Arbor: The University of Michigan.

Estrada, Leobardo, F. Chris Garcia, Reynaldo Flores Macias, and Lionel Maldonado. 1981. Chicanos in the United States: A history of exploitation and resistance. *Daedalus* 110(2):103–131.

Exter, Thomas G. 1985. Focus on Hispanics. *American Demographics* 7(Aug.)29–33.

Hill, Martha. 1983. Trends in the economic situation of U.S. families and children: 1970–1980. In *American families and the economy: The high costs of living,* edited by Richard R. Nelson and Felicity Skidmore, 9–53. Washington, D.C.: The National Academy Press.

Hoppe, Sue Kier, and Peter L. Heller. 1975. Alienation, familism, and the utilization of health services by Mexican Americans. *Journal of Health and Social Behavior,* 16:304–314.

Hayes-Bautista, David E., Werner O. Schinek, and Jorge Chapa. 1984. Young Latinos in an aging American society. *Social Policy* 15 (Summer): 49–52.

Kasarda, John D. 1983. Caught in a web of change. *Society* 21 (Nov./Dec.): 41–47.

Kelly, Robert F. 1985. The family and the urban underclass. *Journal of Family Issues* 6(2):159–184.

Lowenstein, Gaither. 1985. The new underclass: A contemporary sociological dilemma. *The Sociological Quarterly* 26(1):35–48.

McAdoo, Hariette P. 1982. Demographic trends for people of color. *Social Work* 24(1)(Jan.):15–22.

McGahey, Rick. 1981. In search of the undeserving poor. *Working Papers* 8:62–64.

McLanahan, Sara. 1985. Family structure and the reproduction of poverty. *American Journal of Sociology* 90(4):873–901.

Maldonado, Lionel A. 1985. Altered states: Chicanos in the labor force. In *Ethnicity and the work force,* edited by Winston A. VanHorne, 145–166. Madison, Wisconsin: University of Wisconsin System, American Ethnic Studies Coordinating Committee.

Moore, Joan W. 1981. Minorities in the American class system. *Daedalus* 110(2):275–299.

Moore, Joan W. and Harry Pachon. 1985. *Hispanics in the United States.* Englewood Cliffs, New Jersey: Prentice-Hall, Inc.

Moynihan, Daniel P. 1965. *The negro family: The case for national action.* Cambridge, Mass.: M.I.T. Press.

North American Congress on Latin America. 1977. Capital's flight: The apparel industry moves south. In *Latin America and Empire Report* (March) Oakland, California: NACLA.

Norton, Eleanor Holmes. 1985. Restoring the traditional black family. *The New York Times Magazine* (June 2):43–98.

O'Hare, William P. 1985. *Poverty in America: Trends and new patterns.* Population Bulletin 40(June), Population Reference Bureau.

Pearce, Diana M. 1983. The feminization of ghetto poverty. *Society* 21 (Nov./Dec.):70–74.

Pearce, Diana M. 1984. Farewell to alms: Women's fare under welfare. In *Women: A feminist perspective,* edited by Jo Freeman, 502–515. Mayfield Publishing Company.

Rapp, Rayna. 1982. Family and class in contemporary America: Notes toward an understanding of ideology. In *Rethinking the Family: Some Femi-*

nist Questions, edited by Barrie Thorne and Marilyn Yalom, 168–86. New York: Congman.

Scheirer, Mary Ann. 1984. Household structure among welfare families: Correlates and consequences. *Journal of Marriage and the Family* 45 (Nov.)761–771.

Stack, Carol B. 1974. *All our kin: Strategies for survival in a black community.* New York: Harper and Row.

Tilly, Louise A. 1978. *Women and family strategies in French proletarian families.* Ann Arbor: University of Michigan, Michigan Occasional Paper No. 4 (Fall).

U.S. Commission on Civil Rights, Illinois. 1981. Advisory Committee. *Shutdown: Economic dislocation and equal opportunity.* Washington, D.C.: GPO.

Zaretsky, Eli. 1978. The effect of the economic crisis on the family. U.S. Capitalism in Crisis, The Union for Radical Political Economics. *Crisis Reader Editorial Collective.* New York Union of Radical Political Economists, 209–218.

The Farmer Takes a Wife: Women in America's Farming Families

Sarah Elbert

Once upon a time rural America *was* America. Today, although 900 million acres are still classified as farmland in this country, an expert observer claims that "recent years have favored an evolution away from farming as a 'way of life' to farming as a 'business venture'" (Scheuring, 1983). It is, of course, the observer's separation of "way of life" from "business venture" and her use of "evolution" that cues the reader in to her perspective. Rural America's struggles are here being depicted as part of the bittersweet phenomenon known as "modernization" wherein, all too frequently, social conflicts are hidden behind a new social Darwinism—the "natural" environment seemingly selects that species of farmer most competitively adapted to survive in it.

Farming families used to be depicted in texts as active heroes and heroines; not only did they feed the rest of us, but their produce dominated the U.S. export trade throughout the nineteenth century and still amounts to some 33 billion dollars (20 percent of all U.S. exports). Farming families commanded respect from historians and politicians alike, because Euro-Americans were certain that family ownership and operation of commercial farms was the basis of American political democracy. The term "family" or "household," of course, glossed over the question of precisely which family members owned the land and received payments for major cash crops.

Farming as a "business" venture in the twentieth century nevertheless means that farm families are declining in numbers while the total number of acres tilled in the U.S. remains stable. From 1960 to 1970 alone, the farm population diminished from 15.6 million to 8 million. Agricultural production continues to rise and farmers feed urban Americans heartily for a comparatively small share of their paychecks. The definition of a family farm is relatively simple for census purposes: a family-managed farm that uses less than 1.5 (hu)man-years of hired labor is a family-operated farm business (family farm). Family farmers may not be an endangered species yet, but they and consumers are finding themselves in a common vise; the screws are being tightened by agribusiness.

Researchers enter the contested terrain on one side or the other; while Ann Foley Scheuring sees agribusiness as a species naturally evolved from farm families, Ingolf Vogeler bitterly denounces the process as a rapacious social-historical formation. He questions whether the farming family is still an entrepreneurial unit in the traditional sense and argues that instead it is merely occupying an "ecological niche" in which it is allowed to produce (through hard labor and enormous indebtedness) the petty commodities deemed unprofitable for larger corporate investments.

Farm women's participation in agricultural production as well as their responsibility for households and their off-farm work are newly being recognized in the context of the farm crisis. The strategic choices being made by farming families occur within a context of gender hierarchy and, in the most threatened farm households, the struggle for survival may well entail a shift toward more egalitarian gender relations.

After briefly describing the current farm crisis and the historical patterns affecting it discernible in this century, this chapter will discuss systems of labor control and coordination on family farms. As Carolyn Sachs (1985) points out, farm women's "invisible" contributions to farm production and their primary responsibility for the reproduction of households has enabled some family farms to survive the increasing domination of agribusiness. Because farm families do not face the separation of workplace from household, they are more often characterized by interdependence between husbands, wives, and children than are urban families. But "interdependence does not necessarily equal equity. In fact, control of farms has historically been under the male head of the household" (Sachs, 1985). Why men begin in farming from an advantageous position and how they usually maintain their advantage is an important theme that emerges

174

from the long-term studies described in this chapter. Some more egalitarian strategies for farm family survival are also noted.

The farm crisis is a leverage crisis for some 580,000 family farms earning between $40,000 and $200,000 annually from farm produce sales. These are the medium-sized farms that account for 38.5 percent of all U.S. agricultural output. Those farms producing below $40,000 in sales stay in business largely because of their off-farm earnings. The 112,000 largest farms have a cost structure that virtually guarantees their high profitability (*Farm Journal*, 1985).

For medium-sized farms, high interest rates, the farmers' narrow profit margins, and their falling asset values mean cash flow problems and a serious draining of net worth. If a farm's debt-to-asset ratio is over 40 percent the chances of its failure in the next few years are high. The central region of the United States has the worst debt-to-asset ratio, with 42.5 percent of the farms in that region reporting their debt-to-asset ratio exceeding 40 percent. All over the country, young farmers are in the worst trouble and in the central region 63 percent of farm operators under thirty-five years of age are exceeding the safe debt-to-asset ratio (*Farm Journal*, March 1985).

The U.S. Department of Agriculture notes that the value of American farmland fell 12 percent in 1984, the largest one-year decline since the Depression. But land values have been dropping since 1981 and this adds to the financial squeeze on middle-level farmers because much of the money they borrow to operate their farms is backed by their land. The lower the value of the land, the more precarious their financial positions and the less they can borrow. In other words, they have less leverage. Farmers who sell land may well need to rent it back to keep up production and others who need to expand acreage under production by renting land are in trouble because more farm operators have to rent land rather than buy it in a crisis. Younger farmers are being especially hard hit because income flow from farming usually will not cover the principal and interest payments on a farm during the early years of a farm loan and beginning farmers must also support themselves and bear the cost of starting a family from low farm earnings. They are in competition not only with older farmers, who have higher equity in land and equipment and stock, but they are also competing with nonfarming investors who, because of their high income tax liabilities, want to invest in farmland since taxes on capital assets are considerably lower than the tax rate on non-capital gains income.

Experts' advice, rising land prices, rising commodity prices, and liberalized credit all encouraged farmers to risk debt in the 1970s. But by the 1980s the rising prices of oil and gasoline helped to raise farm production costs; high interest rates and falling asset values collided, and the exploding rise of the dollar hurt exports of agricultural products. Farmers "financed up" (refinanced loans) to balance their negative cash flows. Currently they have cut machinery replacements and they face a lowering of the "safety net" the government provides in the form of target prices and loans because of the current administration's proposal to cut big federal deficits at the farmers' expense. David Stockman's infamous remark that farmers in trouble had caused it themselves by overspeculating in land during the 1970s clearly ignores the fact that it is young farmers, the best-educated, most innovative (and least able to speculate), who are facing the worst hardships. Marcia Z. Taylor, an associate editor of *Farm Journal,* recently worried that America could lose its middle-level farm families in this crisis because the average age of the American farmer is fifty-eight and if younger farmers go out of business there may not be any entry level for the next aspiring generation of farmers (Taylor, 1985).

All of this is evidence of a rapid decline from what has been called the golden age of American farming, the period from the Civil War to World War I. That period was marked by a phenomenal growth in the number of farms, and a threefold increase in farm productivity. Family labor and hired help were abundant and cheap and agricultural research by state and private agencies introduced fertilizers, labor-saving machinery, hybrid seeds, disease and pest controls, and artificial insemination. But, as Mann and Dickson (1980) and others have documented, the golden age begins to look more than a little tarnished when one looks at the concentration and centralization of firms supplying farm inputs. Farm machinery manufacturing firms declined in number from 1,943 to 910 in the 1880s alone. And the reduction of risks and uncertainties in producing some commodities led to a greater penetration of those enterprises by agribusiness.

William D. Heffernan describes the transformation of poultry production as one illustration of the concentration of ownership and control of a food production system by agribusiness firms. Diversified family farms commonly kept a flock of chickens and women's control of their "egg money" was proverbial (Jensen, 1981). Hatcheries and feed stores were common in farming communities, providing off-farm jobs. There were many competing firms that would purchase broilers and/or eggs. Poultry flocks produced year-round, production time was short, and the weekly income was a welcome addition to farm families largely dependent upon seasonal enterprises. In the past twenty-five years, over 95 percent of the commercially produced broilers and eggs have become part of an integrated production, processing, and distribution system. The farmer is called a "grower," he/she signs a contract with the integrating firm that supplies him/her with chicks and feed, deducting their cost from the guaranteed price paid to the grower. Broiler firms market under their own brands to supermarkets and some of them market into fast-food outlets and takeout centers (Heffernan, 1984). By 1981 there were only 137 such firms in America and by 1985 each of four firms had 15 to 18 percent of the market. Heffernan describes an international industry in which even these giants are losing to the multi-national conglomerates that dominate the milling and grain trade. Two of the four leading integrated firms are already subsidiaries of conglomerates.

These giants are not interested in limited-resource farmers. They want growers who can supply one family member full-time to poultry production and the growers must supply poultry buildings equipped with feeding systems, ventilation, and watering systems that meet the firm's specifications. To provide full-time work for an adult family member, growers usually need two or three equipped buildings at a total cost of over a quarter of a million dollars. Growers borrow for construction, they mortgage the land, and they must pay off their loans over twenty to thirty years while contract agreements, including prices, are based on each batch of chickens. In other words, the farmer-growers must renegotiate their incomes about five times a year. Growers keep producing in order to pay off their buildings and then they often go out of business rather than face the costs and the loans necessary to modernize or replace buildings and equipment. While they are in business, one or both of the adult family members has an off-farm job to subsidize farming as a "way of life."

177

Fertilizers are supplied to farmers by one of the "largest and most concentrated capitalist industries" (Perelman, 1977). Hybrid seeds produced by two giant companies control 50 percent of the market for seed grains, and while seed production has dramatically increased, the quality of produce has declined. The protein content of corn, oats, and wheat grown from hybrid seeds has declined over the past fifty years (Mann and Dickinson, 1980).

The most serious consequences of the structural transformation in American agriculture from the point of view of surviving farm families, however, has been the recurring cycle of agricultural overproduction, as farmers attempt to compensate for their inability to control costs and markets. Farm families went into debt to increase production for wartime demands between 1917 and 1919. When prices declined over 40 percent after the war, bankruptcies and foreclosures on farms preceded the national Depression. Agricultural surpluses continued to pile up as farmers struggled to stay in business. Finally, the New Deal inaugurated the Agricultural Adjustment Act in 1933 and 1938, hoping to curtail production by using public monies to make payments to farmers who participated in acreage allotments and marketing quotas. Parity payments were authorized to farmers to make up the difference between the prevailing low market prices and the "target" or support prices that might give farmers the same purchasing power they had prior to World War I. The Commodity Credit Corporation was set up to buy, handle, store, and sell surpluses. Farmers received nonrecourse loans for their surpluses. The system has endured with some modifications up to the present time and farmers can place commodities in federal storage and receive loans. If the market price does not go up, farmers can take the government support price. If the market rises, farmers can sell the commodities themselves and pay off their loans.

The problem is that government price supports are distributed in proportion to the share of total production each farmer controls. The largest farms get the most government payments; those farms in the less than $40,000 sales category get virtually no support. Overproduction has not been curtailed because middle-sized and large farmers intensify production with fertilizers, no till corn practices combined with herbicides and, of course, they often cease crop rotation conservation practices in order to maximize cash crops. They also divert their least productive land to meet acreage allotments and land retirement programs. The result is a leverage crisis, great price fluctuations, and unstable farm incomes.

Precisely in the middle of the most recent agricultural history, a small project seeking to document decision making in New York State's farming families began at Cornell University. With help from local agricultural agents, twenty farm families were recruited in 1967 in ten upstate New York counties in which soil resources ranged between marginal and excellent. (Eventually five Iowa farm families producing corn and soybeans were added to the study to explore whether decisions would be made differently where land was worth three or four times the value of New York acreage.) Three other considerations were applied to the selection process: stage in the family life cycle, the type of farming being done (in New York two-thirds of the farms were dairy, one-sixth were poultry, and one-sixth were orchards), and the economic viability of the operations. Thirteen of the original families stayed with the project all the way through until 1982. All the members of these families over seven years of age were interviewed and their responses recorded every other year by a team of two (one man and one woman) or, for two years, by one interviewer (a man) when funding was short. The final collection (thirty-three families) includes taped interviews and typed transcriptions of individual and group interviews, business records, and correspondence between the academic project and the families (Colman and Elbert, 1984).

These interviews, by the end of the first few years, had overflowed the parameters of a decision-making study and had become oral histories of farming families. The real value of long-term, qualitative documentation slowly emerged, gradually setting a new research agenda that involved asking the question, What do the recorded experiences of farm men, women, and children tell us about the persistence of family labor farms in a society dominated by large-scale corporate production? (Buttel, 1982, quoted in Sachs, 1983:65).

The respondents' own depictions of their lives simply did not fit the model of the academic literature of the 1950s and 1960s, which assumed that industrial modernization set a functionalist model for the development of American farms. Ignoring the ever-swelling numbers of women entering the labor force, analysts insisted that men were instrumental in shaping productive forces and women's roles were functionally expressive. In fact, studies agreed that successful male farmers' willingness to adapt to new technologies, to expand operations, and to assume heavier debt loads (to finance the first two adaptations) correlated with their wives' willingness to play supportive roles as homemakers and mothers. If farming was more a business than a way of life, then farming families were advised to emulate social leaders—the families of successful corporate executives (Ross, 1985; Fassinger and Schwarzweller, 1984).

The problem, for interviewers, lay in farm women's reluctance to distinguish between farm and household work. When I, as one of the frequent interviewers, dutifully inquired as to the number of hours spent in farm versus home tasks, one farm woman threw open the lid of her washing machine, revealing a common mixture of barn suits, children's jeans, and furniture slipcovers all tumbling about in the soapy water. Did the laundering of farm apparel constitute a separate chore from the household wash? Telephone calls from equipment salesmen and CB radio communications from tractor operators frequently interrupted household interviews, revealing the constant interpenetration of farm and home duties.

Farm wives seemed amazingly well informed about day-to-day farming operations as they juggled appointments with veterinarians and errands into town for farm machinery with housekeeping chores, child care, and volunteer community activities. Farm recordkeeping and accounting, a growing and integral part of decisions involving both operations and resources, was often a farm wife's job. While researchers found the complexity of modern farm technology eliminating many of the traditional tasks of the farm wife, such as feeding the old-time harvest crews, the same modernization, as it transformed farm account books into computer print-outs, did not render farm wives superfluous to the accounting process. Farm women sought education in the new accounting process, and farm family decision making consequently depended upon the knowledge and skills of these farm wives.

180

SEQUENTIAL PRODUCTION AND FAMILY LABOR

The Cornell farm family interviewers might have remained in a quandry about the discrepancies between their own data and the literature surveyed were it not for a note of caution that emerged when Wilkening and Morrison (1963) astutely noted that husbands and wives often reported differently on their respective roles in farm labor and decision making. It was not only the differences in "his marriage and hers" (Bernard, 1972), however, that finally alerted Cornell investigators to the limitations of many decision-making studies in understanding the farm family's survival. The Cornell case studies reveal a pattern of integration between farm wives', husbands', and children's life cycles, family cycles, and farm cycles. Family labor in farming families remains persistent in the face of gradually intruding industrial farming for several important reasons. First, farm operations take place sequentially in the course of the production cycle, and, as Mann and Dickinson (1980:286) have noted, "for many agricultural commodities there are lengthy periods when the application of labor is almost completely suspended." There is, as they pointed out, a "divorce between total production time and actual labor time." While the factory owner may employ his workers in simultaneous and different stages of production (car engines, bodies, etc., can all be produced at the same time in different parts of the factory, continuously employing a stable workforce on the line), the farmer depends upon a skilled stable workforce who may be inactive for periods within each production cycle. Not only crops but dairy operations also follow this sequential production cycle. Obtaining and managing a farm workforce is further complicated by natural forces such as weather and the risks associated both with crop production and with the maintenance of a healthy, high-producing dairy herd. Farm workers must be available at critical times in farm production, and yet they may be unnecessary to farm operations between the various production stages.

Family labor therefore remains ideally suited to the sequential farm production cycle, because family members can and do sustain periods of intense labor followed by periods of enforced layoff. Farm wives and children fit their off-farm duties such as schooling and housework into the farm cycle. More importantly, farm owners/ operators count on the commitment and discipline of family labor while farm operations are under way. Because family members perceive themselves as a permanent unit bound by ties of affection and kinship, they often submit to a high degree of control during peak production periods without threatening strikes or slowdowns. This consciousness of commitment on the part of family members was best described by one farm wife in an early interview when she firmly observed that "the farm needs everyone." Market constraints are an "externality" that the farmer cannot control, nor can farmers control prices or credit terms essential to making the family farm competitive in the marketplace. But farmers can and do control and coordinate the labor process through their command of family labor power consonant with the integration of the family cycle and the farm cycle.

The categorization of farmers' modes of control and coordination of the labor process (social relations of production) is best understood as similar to the systems identified by Richard Edwards in *Contested Terrain: The Transformation of the Workplace in the Twentieth Century* (1979:19). Edwards posits that "simple control" is usually exercised by a single entrepreneur, often with the help of foremen or managers. The "boss" exercises power personally, often sets the pace himself, hires and fires, and uses "incentives and sanctions in an idiosyncratic and unsystematic mix." As tendencies toward economic resource concentration increase, the scale of production enlarges and production becomes more complex and specialized; "simple control" is then deemed less effective. More formal "structural systems" of control are then devised by large firms. These systems can be "technical," where control is built into the physical structure of the labor process (assembly line), or "bureaucratic," where the control rests in a hierarchical impersonal social strucure ("company policy") marked by precise titles and definitions of each job category.

If a farm prospers economically, it happens generally by increasing its scale of operations and often by moving from simple control to bureaucratic, technical, or even corporate control. In such cases it is not only machines that displace wives and children from their places in a primary, labor-intensive stage of farm operation, but so do new forms of labor control and coordination that are deemed appropriate to the expansion by the owner-operator. The farmer asserts that the "farm" does not "require" the services and, incidentally, the unchallenging authority of a farm wife at her mature life cycle stage, where she may be newly freed from childcare responsibilities. Similarly, various male and female children, maturing and more assertive in their demands for a share in management, encounter a shift from "simple" control, where they might confront their father directly, to "bureaucratic" or "technical" control, where their demands can be rejected through the use of impersonal arguments that turn on what the farm requires at the new stage in its development. The assumption that the "farm" no longer "requires" these family members is an impersonal mechanism of control that is justified by the claim that efficient coordination is needed. An owner may find this assumption useful at any time, but it is an especially striking manifestation at the expanded bureaucratic or corporate stage of farming, when this often coincides with new stages in the family's life cycle.

Farmers, like other owner-managers, also can and often do claim objective or impersonal criteria for determining who shall inherit the ownership and management of the farm and who shall be included in decision making as well. Farmers' needs and their ability to control and coordinate labor power through the dedication of family farming persist despite the competition of industrial farms and their attendant system of wage labor. Family members accede to the farmer's command of their labor resources not solely because of the frequent pattern of male dominance within the family hierarchy—a dominance perpetuated in part because of the assumption of woman's "natural" responsibilities for domestic work and childcare at certain life cycle stages. In questioning the goals of farmers and their families repeatedly throughout the course of the Cornell study, interviewers became convinced that a distinctive feature of farming families is the desire of women, as well as of men, to effect intergenerational transfer of the family farm. Certainly all farming families are concerned about annual income, but net worth and especially the ultimate passing on of the farm to family members have been the clearly stated priorities of all the farm families in both New York and Iowa. These long-term goals make it necessary for analysts to comprehend a specialized form of feminism in farming families and a conflicted aspiration toward autonomy among farm youth. Understanding the persistence of farming families in an advanced capitalist system, furthermore, requires a new categorization of the relationship between distinct stages of the family life cycle and the social relations of production, which include various forms of labor control and coordination. The following discussion of Cornell's panel of farming families only opens the investigation by such new analyses.

FAMILY CYCLE, FARM CYCLE: THE SOCIAL RELATIONS OF PRODUCTION

In the early stages of the farm cycle, which usually correspond to the young married stage of the family cycle, farm wives play both productive and reproductive roles as they bear children and accept the major responsibility for childcare. At the same time, they often have then contributed more heavily to farm operations than at any other time in their lives. Early stages of a farm cycle require women's labor power, though women's work may take different forms depending upon whether the farm is a dairy farm, a cash crop, a fruit operation, or a mixture of these. Women coordinate childcare with farm work by taking children with them into the fields or barns or by calling upon older female members of the extended family for help. Mothers, mothers-in-law, or younger sisters of farm wives may play varying roles in assisting with childcare and household duties. Farm women experienced the burden of a "double day," as do employed urban women, but household tasks and farm work occur on the same terrain, producing a pattern of integrated work processes. Extended kin in the surrounding community find themselves drawn into the farm cycle as helpers, even though they may themselves be occupied with off-farm employment.

In these early, labor-intensive stages of the farm cycle and intermittently throughout the farm's development, women often balance their "double day" and their subordinate roles in owner/manager decisions against their satisfaction at playing an important part in an

184

integrated enterprise where women's labor is visible and rewarded by a marital companionship that is unusual in today's divided world of work and home. Farm women furthermore articulate their feelings of satisfaction in the process of accumulating "family" property and equity that can be passed on to children. Unfortunately, this all-for-one and one-for-all mentality may obscure the question of whether or not farm wives are getting full legal property rights with their husbands in land and enterprise. Whether farm women obtain ownership rights at this stage, when their labor involvement is at its peak, can be crucial to farm women and their children as the farm cycle and the family cycle mature.

TERRAINS OF CONTEST

Farming families in this study did not remain simple unchanging labor forces geared to sequential production during the sixteen years of the study. Systems to control and coordinate the labor process changed as the scale of farming production increased, and increasingly family labor was mixed with hired labor. Moreover, these systems continued to respond to family life cycles. The social relations of production changed several times in the course of each family's development. Farm families went through various stages of gender and age divisions that often created intense conflicts between family members. The fit between the labor requirements perceived by farmers and the needs of other family members became more precarious when the scale of operations enlarged and farmers moved from simple control to technical or bureaucratic control. Farms that "needed everybody" in the early labor-intensive periods of production were finally seen by some owner-operators as not "requiring" the productive labor or the managerial input of various family members as the farms reached a more mature stage of operation. Such a perception was not regarded by male farmers themselves as a personal judgment on the capabilities or desires of family members; rather, farmers reported the change as an "objective" or impersonal decision occasioned by the farm resources and operations themselves.

185

The long-term commitment of Cornell researchers to studying the same farm families over a sixteen-year period was rewarded by insight into the patterns of social relations of production on farms and into stages of labor control and management that may seem familiar to historians of industrial firm development. The similarity between farms and other firms does not, however, lie only in the historical displacement of workers by machines in both forms of enterprise. Rather, it is also that the new forms of labor management control and coordination that are deemed appropriate and necessary to farm expansion by owner-operators aggravate workers in both farm and urban enterprises. In both places a protracted conflict emerges between the desire of the owner-operator to maximize profits and streamline coordination while maintaining his control on the one hand, and the desire of workers on the other to maintain their own varying degrees of control over the production process and to maximize their shares of the profits or avoid an inequitable divison of costs. The family farm becomes a terrain of loving contest. Male farmers themselves have conflicting goals in desiring to maintain their control over farm resources and operations and at the same time to maintain good relations with their wives, who have contributed much to the success of the farm and who wish to maintain their involvement in farming and their place in effecting its intergenerational transfer. In order to ease the psychic burdens of this contradiction, male farmers may resort to the comforting thought that what "father knows best" coincides with the needs of the farm. Farm fathers, furthermore, need to control the labor power of their children and at the same time develop sufficient autonomy in the training of their children to ensure successful intergenerational transfer, a precarious balance of often conflicting goals.

There is nothing inevitable or predetermined about the developmental stages of farm enterprises, because some farms do expand in scale, acquire more acreage, increase production, or diversify for the market and maintain the same simple system of labor control and coordination. If this happens, there is still a serious crisis or contest often occasioned by the larger social relations of production, which are for an indeterminate period in flux. For instance, as a hypothetical dairy farm expands from thirty-five to one hundred plus milking cows, the "simple" control exercised by an owner/husband/

father who has been head worker and pacesetter is rendered ineffective by the fact that he can no longer do most of the milking and supervise the breeding and feeding of his herd himself. He negotiates different degrees of mechanization and a division of labor and elects to purchase services he formerly performed himself or supervised in the utilization of family labor. Adult children on this farm may then contest these decisions made by their father or ally with one another or with their mother or an in-law. If the farm no longer "requires everyone," a farm woman may feel, as one actual respondent bitterly reported at this stage, "We are no longer a farm family," meaning that she perceived the interests of one family member were no longer the interests of all of them. Despite considerable bitterness and family distress, the farm "functions"; indeed, it may have progressed to affluence. The question we must then ask is, who is it functioning for?

INTERGENERATIONAL TRANSFER

There is, of course, an income from a family farm, besides the long-term equity and substantial net worth of the land, equipment, buildings, and machinery. Both the wife and children may receive their shares of the family income in ways that the owner-operator deems commensurate with their value to the "farm"—or, more properly speaking, in ways commensurate with the decisions of the owner-operator to discipline or encourage his workers. A farm wife may then be caught in a redistribution of the "family income" that involves purchasing or refusing to purchase consumer goods as one means of controlling or disciplining the family work force.

A farm wife in the development of the family and farm cycles may find her place taken by her son, first in terms of productive labor and then in terms of managerial and ownership power. She has a genuine stake in this intergenerational transfer and often has worked hard and has "managed" it to this end, but the cost of her success is her own displacement. Researchers must ask why the farm wife is more likely than her husband to be the displaced worker-manager in intergenerational transfers. The answer seems to lie in the long-

187

term pattern of deferment to the farm husband's dominant role, as the farm wife's time and energy have been divided between domestic work and farm operations.

Another pattern discernible in different forms within simple, technical, or bureaucratic control of the farm is an overt decision on the part of male farmers to "keep the women out." In the simple control stage, the male owner-operators in one family partnership assumed that the women were more emotional than men and would tend to disrupt rational decision making if they were genuine partners. The women themselves, both college graduates, often remarked to interviewers that they were fortunate not to have done much outdoor, barn work even in the early, labor-intensive stages of their farms. It was a sign of the farm family's success that they were excluded from productive work. At the same time, one of them was functioning as a highly competent accountant-bookkeeper on the farm, and she resented being kept out of managerial-owner control. Her command of crucial information and her demonstrated competence did not gain her admittance into the male-dominated structure of decision making. She was frustrated but unable to pin the blame for her exclusion on her husband or brother-in-law, because none of the male family members admitted to simple or "personal" control forms. Their partnership was made into a corporation over the course of the study, and impersonal, seemingly "cost-effective" and "scientific" management principles were then invoked in the bureaucratic control stage to exclude not only wives but most of both farm fathers' children from involvement, ownership, or decision making. There was little struggle over the redistribution of the "family income," as profits were so substantial that money and leisure could be used currently or as an inheritance to compensate family members for their exclusion. In this way family responsibilities seemed to have been fulfilled while the family farm remained in the hands of the original brothers/partners and the eldest son of one of them. In this case the "functional" rationale for gender stereotyping (that women are more emotional than men) was invoked as useful and compatible with the consolidation of corporated, bureaucratic control.

The gender hierarchy was gradually reinforced culturally when first one couple and then the second couple joined a local charismatic

Christian church. Husbands and wives in separate and joint Bible study groups confirmed the moral imperative of wifely subordination to the husband's paternal authority and nurturance. The fundamentalist Christian doctrine was not the cause of their business arrangement but rather an accompanying and validating precept. Historically the men sought religious validation for their business decisions in midlife and their wives were converted gradually. The younger farm wife (the bookkeeper) was not comfortable in the new religious-social network, which included marriage encounters, retreats, and regular prayer and study meetings. She returned to the couple's previous neighborhood church and played an increasingly more responsive role there on her own as a vestrywoman and lay reader.

All of the children (eight) who grew up on this family partnership farm were skilled in farm chores and contributed their labor and emotional support to the enterprise. They were all imaginative and independent-minded—burgeoning farm entrepreneurs themselves—as their interviews over the years show. At first there seemed little connection between the bulldozing of the farm's small apple orchard, the growing division of labor, and the building of separate calf and heifer barns, milking parlors, and freestall housing for the milking cows. But gradually the farm became a milk factory, and all but one of the family's children (the eldest son of the eldest male partner) were deemed too "undisciplined" or "disobedient" to work the farm.

The farm operation became an increasingly bureaucratic one—hired men were chosen for expertise, reliability, and obedience. They were rewarded with house lots and access to credit for building their homes; profit-sharing was being considered as well—the brothers' corporation was a most enlightened employer so long as hierarchical control of production was unchallenged. By breaking up the farm labor process into separate tasks, each performed by an "expert," the owner-operators were ensuring that their roles alone were essential to the production process; their "crucialness" and their control was thereby ensured. Farm children seeking to "help out" and thereby maximize their skills and "crucialness" had to negotiate unsuccessfully through hired "experts" who were often hostile or impatient with the young workers' "clumsiness" or "mistakes."

It is important to note, however, that this was a historical process and that it could and did take place in a family business because in all stages of farm and family cycles, labor control is easily and often confused with labor coordination. Unmistakably, male owner-operators often used patriarchal power within the family to control their family workers. Wives and children may work on the farm for many years, hoping that their labor will be rewarded by owner/manager status, only to find themselves "paid off" and "laid off." The fact that family farms report a "family income" can obscure not only very diverse relationships in the social relations of production but also very real "caste" distinctions within families. Some family farms progress from simple coordination and the full utilization of family labor through intergenerational tranfers marked by technical or bureaucratic coordination. If they are fortunate in resources and/or imaginative in devising compatible operations, they can make room for farm women and children who wish to participate fully in the farming operation. Such families, for the most part, are marked by significant participation by women in farm work, decision making, and by joint ownership of both land and enterprise from the beginning of a marital pair's settlement on the farm. One or another spouse may be working off-farm for as much as forty hours a week, but if there is joint ownership and both partners perform seasonal farming work, gender equality is achieved and passed on as a model for the next generation. This kind of equitable coordination is, furthermore, a key factor in enabling middle-level farms to stay in business.

If the farm woman is to remain involved, integrated, and in full possession of her managerial as well as her productive skills, she may have to juggle housework, childrearing, and farm work very precariously for several years. Farm women rarely hire household workers to release them for productive farm work. The hired girl seems to have vanished when household technology "modernized" farmhouses. A family farm with a net worth of several hundred thousand dollars certainly can afford a dishwasher, a microwave oven, a food mixer, and the latest laundry facilities, and they are there. Nevertheless, this consumption is usually to free women for production—although stoves that bear the intriguing logo "Modern Maid" unfortunately do not really shop, prepare the food, and serve it. Farm wives spend less time on housework than they once did, by their own and their mothers' recollections—but they spend their "free time" in accounting, recordkeeping, and, above all, in organizing and coordinating family labor. Sisters, mothers, and female in-laws can be counted on to share some of the domestic burdens, particularly in peak farm seasons, but farm husbands have rarely risked their "crucialness" by fully sharing housework and childcare in the immediate past (Fassenger and Schwarzweller, 1984; Sachs, 1985; Ross, 1985).

FAMILY FARMING AND GENDER EQUALITY

The social interpretation of biological differences between the sexes, or the sex/gender system, is embedded in both family life and economic production. Heidi Hartmann's analysis of the family as a locus of "gender, class, and political struggle" is exemplified in the Cornell case studies of farm families and family farms. As Hartmann puts it in a brilliant alternative to functional analyses of family and gender:

> From an economic perspective, the creation of gender can be thought of as the creation of a division of labor between the sexes, the creation of two categories of workers who need each other. In our society, the division of labor between the sexes involves men primarily in wage labor beyond the household and women primarily in production within the household; men and women, living together in households, pool their resources. The form of family as we know it, with men in a more advantageous position than women in its hierarchy of gender relations, is simply one possible structuring of this human activity that creates gender, many other arrangements have been known. (1981:393)

The significance of Hartmann's analysis to the study of farming families lies in the identification of the sexual division of labor as socially created, a part of the sex/gender system. That fact has been frequently obscured by the dominant functionalist perspective used in social science studies. The family labor farm does not "require" a sexually hierarchical system of ownership, decision making, and labor control, as functional analyses would have it. The observable

191

pattern of male domination and control on family farms is created through the interpenetration of a socially structured family life cycle, with its assumptions about women's primary responsibility for domestic work and childcare, and by the sequential pattern of farm production that allows a male farmer to use his authority as "pater familias" for controlling farm family labor power.

A number of factors in the larger political economy obviously reinforces male farmers' control. As specialized production displaces diversified production, men are better able to gain specialized skills and solidify a pattern of control over decision making during the long period when women's labor is divided between household and farm responsibilities. While agricultural production is becoming increasingly specialized and organized in ways similar to industrial production, childcare and domestic tasks, on the farm and off it, are still private and individual responsibilities, culturally designated "women's work." Furthermore, access to agricultural skills, credit, and political influence is sexually unequal. But as women gain access to these skills through more equal access to farm management, engineering, agronomy, and so forth in agricultural and technical colleges and extension services, farm women can compensate for the loss of traditional resources by their access to new skills. Greater sexual equality in technological training and business management can give women more equity in the social relations of agricultural production. Cornell's panel of farming families yields some evidence of positive relationships between greater sexual equity in ownership, technical and managerial skills, and more equitable arrangements for domestic and childcaring tasks in farm households. Feminists' demands for greater equity in credit arrangements also clearly benefit women seeking full owner-operator status in family farms.

FARMING AS A WAY OF LIFE

In fact, Hartmann's "other relationships" manifest themselves in Cornell's panel of farming families. Some families clearly chose to pool their labor resources in such a way as to provide maximum autonomy for individual family members. In one case, a small poultry farm jointly owned by husband and wife was limited in both land and capital resources yet rich in the cooperative relationships between the husband, wife, and four children. They managed in the early years of their farm by having the wife and older children gather eggs, feed the poultry, and keep accounts, while the farm husband performed the heavy labor involved in producing a small corn crop and managing the poultry houses, in addition driving the bus for the local school district. Although the whole family was devoted to farming as a "way of life," opportunities for work off the farm were much greater than those for expanding the farm operation. As soon as the children were in school for a full day, the farm wife obtained employment as a secretary in a local farm information service, and her salary not only supplemented the farm income for domestic necessities but also helped to put the three older children through college.

When this poultry farmer was asked about his idea of success, he replied, "Well, I figure I'm not a failure. I figure I'm successful when I just make these decisions whether to keep the poultry business or to get out—and I've got a nice wife and family, and they turned out happy and successful, although I don't have much money." By the end of the study, however, this couple was out of the poultry business; they could not risk borrowing a sum large enough to expand and modernize at their stage of life (aged fifty).

Other families on larger and more profitable farming operations can sometimes expand and even incorporate with the express intention of helping sons and daughters buy into the operation. The common pattern of such "buying in" on dairy farms includes young farm family workers assisting their parents in milk, cropping, etc., and receiving wages for their work. They use part of their cash wages to purchase cows, feeding and milking their animals with the larger home herd. Their share of the milk check is used to gradually purchase buildings, equipment, and land from their parents. In this way some families can achieve intergenerational transfers and provide older farming parents with a retirement income at the same time. But this is a precarious business. As the debt load grows, production must be increased, buildings and equipment must constantly be updated and replaced, and usually more land must be rented or bought.

Between 1946 and 1978 there has been a modest increase in female-owned farm holdings in terms of the proportion of total farm-land owned and the average acreage per owner; women do now own about 15 percent of total farmland, averaging 176 acres. However, female-owned land is less valuable per holding and per acre and, more importantly, women tend to gain land ownership as widows when they are past their peak productive years. Over 50 percent of female equity is in the hands of women sixty-five and older, while middle-aged men are the largest category of farmland owners and own the preponderance of acreage. As Waters and Geisler point out (1982) when women do own land it is often controlled in fact by their spouses in partnership or by family corporations or by lending institutions that hold mortgages to the land. Farm widows are frequently custodians of intergenerational transfers more than they are farm operators, as both Sachs (1983) and Scheuring (1983) point out in their case studies of farming families. The pattern of labor control and coordination identified in Cornell's farm family panel may help to explain some of the problems that inhibit farm widows' assertion of themselves as farm operators.

CONCLUSIONS

American farm families, like many peasant families, make choices within the context of the household, and they are influenced by the household's needs and goals as well as by the resources available to the household. These resources included land, water, credit, and family labor. They also include social resources, such as information about agricultural methods or credit and access to them. (Gladwin, 1980) Farm households, however, are part of a larger industrial capitalist system that plays a dominant role in determining who will survive in farming—which family farms can maintain their precarious toehold in the "ecological niche." The battle plan required by farm families, if they hope to survive, must include more egalitarian gender relations. Making housework and childcare more gender-equal within the labor control/coordination pattern would depend ultimately upon changing the gender pattern of farmland ownership and by redefining the intersection between the structure of production and household organization (Sachs, 1985).

The "invisible farmers," farm wives, mothers, daughters, and the small percentage of women who report their principal occupation as farm operators and managers (Jones and Rosenfeld, 1981), play multidimensional roles encompassing activities in the home and on farm and off-farm workplaces (Ross, 1985). Longitudinal studies to document transitions over the time of the life cycles of the family farm are needed in each region of the United States. Furthermore, the relationship between gender hierarchy, household structure, and farm structure needs to be studied within each commodity system (Friedland, 1985). In the current farm crisis, women's work both on and off-farm plus their traditional responsibility for household work often makes the difference between a family's survival or its failure in farming. Whether or not women achieve a greater measure of equity as farmers and farming partners may in turn depend upon the survival of family farms.

Note

THE AUTHOR appreciates the help and encouragement of professors Joan Jensen, Sue Armitage, and Corlann Bush. Portions of this paper have appeared in Colman and Elbert, Harry K. Schwartzweller, *Research in Rural Sociology and Development,* JAI Press, 1984.

Reference List

Bartlett, Peggy F. 1983. Introduction. In *Agricultural decision making: Anthropological contributions to rural development,* edited by Peggy F. Bartlett. New York Academic Press.

Bernard, Jessie. 1972. *The future of marriage.* New York: World Publishing Co.

Bush, Corlann Gee. 1982. The barn is his; the house is mine: Agricultural technology and sex roles. In *Energy and Transport,* edited by George Daniels and Mark Rose. Beverly Hills, Calif.: Sage Publications.

Buttel, Frederick H. and Howard Newby. 1980. *The rural sociology of the advanced societies.* Totowa, N.J.: Allanheld, Osmun & Co.

Colman, Gould, and Sarah Elbert. 1984. Farming families: "The farm needs everyone." In *Research in rural sociology and development,* edited by Harry K. Scharzweller, vol. 1. Greenwich, Conn.: JAI Press.

Edwards, Richard C. 1979. *Contested terrain: The transformation of the workplace in the twentieth century.* New York: Basic Books.

Farm Journal, Eastern Edition, March 1985, 109, 5:13–17.

Fassinger, Polly A. and Harry K. Schwartzweller. 1980. The work of farm women: A midwestern study. In *Research in rural sociology and development,* edited by Harry K. Schwartzweller, vol. 1, 37–60. Greenwich, Conn. JAI Press.

Flora, Cornelia B. 1985. Commodity systems analysis: An approach to the sociology of agriculture. In *Research in rural sociology and development,* edited by Harry K. Schwartzweller, vol. 1, 221—236. Greenwich, Conn.: JAI Press, Inc.

Gladwin, Christina H. 1983. A theory of real-life choice: Applications to agricultural decisions. In *Agricultural decision making: Anthropological contributions to rural development,* edited by Peggy F. Bartlett, 46–47. New York: Academic Press.

Hartmann, Heidi. 1981. The family as the locus of gender, class, and political struggle: The example of housework. *Signs* 6 (Spring):366–394.

Heffernan, William D. 1984. Constraints in the U.S. poultry industry. In *Research in rural sociology and development,* edited by Harry K. Schwartzweller, vol. 1, 237–260. Greenwich, Conn.: JAI Press Inc.

Jensen, Joan M. 1981. *With these hands: Women working on the land.* Old Westbury, NY: Feminist Press; New York: McGraw-Hill.

Jensen, Joan M. 1983. New Mexico farm women, 1900–1940. In *Labor in New Mexico,* edited by Robert Kern, 61–81. Albuquerque: University of New Mexico Press.

Jones, Calvin, and Rachel A. Rosenfeld. 1981. *American farm women: Findings from a national survey.* Chicago: National Opinion Research Center, NORC Report No. 130.

Kalbacher, Judith A. 1983. Women Farm Operators. *Family Economics Review* 4 (October):17–21.

Mann, Susan A., and James A. Dickinson. 1980. State and agriculture in two eras of American capitalism. In *The rural sociology of the advanced societies: Critical perspectives,* edited by Frederick H. Buttel and Howard Newby, 283–325. Montclair, N.J.: Allanheld, Osmun.

Parelman, Michael. 1977. Farming for profit in a hungry world. Montclair, N.J.: Allanheld, Osmun.

Ross, Peggy J. 1985. A commentary on research on American farmwomen. *Agriculture and Human Values,* 2, 1 (Winter):19–30.

Sachs, Carolyn E. 1983. *Invisible farmers: Women in agricultural production.* Totowa, N.J.: Allanheld, Osmun.

196

Sachs, Carolyn E. 1985. Women's work in the U.S. variations by region. *Agriculture and Human Values*, 2, 1:31–39.

Salant, Priscilla. 1983. *Farm women: Contribution to farm and family.* Washington, D.C.: U.S. Department of Agriculture, Agricultural Economics Research Report No. 140.

Sawer, Barbara J. 1973. Predictors of the farm wife's involvement in general management and adoption decisions. *Rural Sociology* 38 (Winter): 412–426.

Scheuring, Ann Foley. 1983. *A guidebook to California agriculture.* Berkeley and Los Angeles, California: University of California Press.

Scheuring, Ann Foley. 1983. *Tillers: An oral history of family farms in California,* New York: Praeger.

Scholl, Kathleen K. 1983. Classifications of women as farmers: Economic implications. *Family Economics Review* 4 (October):8–17.

Vogeler, Ingolf. 1981. *The myth of the family farm: Agri-business dominance of U.S. agriculture.* Boulder, Col.: Westview Press.

Waters, William F., and Charles C. Geisler. 1982. The changing structure of female ownership of agricultural land in the United States, 1946–1978. Paper presented at the Annual Meeting of the Rural Sociology Society, San Francisco.

Wilkening, Eugene A. 1958. Joint decision-making in farm families as a function of status and role. *American Sociological Review* 23 (April): 187–192.

Wilkening, Eugene A. 1981. Farm husbands and wives in Wisconsin: Work roles, decision-making and satisfaction, 1962 and 1979. Madison, Wisc.: University of Wisconsin-Madison, Research Division of the College of Agriculture and Life Sciences, Research Bulletin R3147.

Wilkening, E. A., and Denton E. Morrison. 1963. A comparison of husband and wife responses concerning who makes farm and home decisions. *Marriage and Family Living* 25 (August):349–351.

PART III

Structural Transformation, the Labor Market, and Women

9

Women's Labor in the Office of the Future: A Case Study of the Insurance Industry

Barbara Baran and Suzanne Teegarden

Despite the fact that office automation promises to affect the jobs of millions of women workers, the literature on the impact of technological change—as well as the attention of the unions—remains primarily focused on manufacturing. This unsurprising lacuna unfortunately keeps theory and practice firmly committed to the proposition that men's work is more important than women's and prevents us from making sense of the emerging shape of the labor force.

The intent of our research on the effects of computer-based technologies on the insurance industry is to contribute to a new discussion. Much of what we present here are conclusions from a case study we conducted in a major property/casualty insurance company; at the same time, however, we have broadened those conclusions through more general research on the industry—both our own and the work of others.

This paper is organized into five parts: (1) a review of the existing literature; (2) a brief look at the early applications of computer technology in the insurance industry; (3) an argument that current and future applications will differ significantly because of changes occurring in the competitive environment, in markets, products, and in the technology itself; (4) an analysis of the likely impact of these changes on different categories of women workers; (5) a discussion of the political implications of these changes.

THE EMERGING DEBATE

Glenn and Feldberg (1980), in an influential article, divided the office automation literature into two camps: a dominant "right" camp, which assumes an identity or community of interest between capital and labor, and an oppositional "left" camp, which understands that capitalism necessarily sets capital and labor against one another. Because we believe this simple left-right dichotomy avoids the most interesting and important questions, we want to review the critical literature in terms of three broad theoretical perspectives that seem to us to be more useful in defining the central issues: Bravermanism, postindustrialism, and feminism.

Although the automation of office work is relatively recent, Harry Braverman, in his seminal work on the labor process (1974), argues that the dynamics of the transformation are not new: rationalization and automation of the office are simply part and parcel of the inexorable forward march of scientific management that will ultimately degrade all but the most skilled labor. As such, not only is the dynamic an old one, but the form of labor process being imposed is also familiar: offices are being transformed into factories. In short, the Bravermanists project the generalization of Fordist forms of workplace organization to white-collar settings. As part of this process, they also suggest that we may see the expulsion of labor from the higher-paid capital intensive sectors into low-paid, labor-intensive work.

The postindustrialist challenge to this perspective can be briefly summarized as follows: First, whereas earlier forms of mechanization forced companies to choose between flexibility in production and unit costs—that is, greater flexibility resulted in higher unit costs, computer-based technologies demand no such trade-off, potentially eliminating much of the rigidity in the labor process. This change both fuels and is fuelled by the splintering of the mass market (Sabel, 1982; Gershuny, 1978, 1983). Second, whereas the assembly-line socialized and centralized production, the new technologies offer the possibility of radical decentralization. Production, distribution, and management functions can be fragmented and spatially separated; the various component parts can then be reintegrated electronically (Castells, 1982; Zuboff, 1982). To the extent that decision-making procedures can be largely embedded in computer programs, decentralization is compatible with centralized coordination and control. Third, whereas the Fordist revolution produced ever-increasing numbers of detail workers, the computer revolution promises less functional specialization, especially as the technology becomes more sophisticated (Hirschhorn, 1981; Goldhaber, 1980). In short, the twin advances in microtechnology and telecommunications may "reintegrate" the labor process at the same time that they decentralize and desocialize it. Finally, to the extent that even control functions are shifted increasingly to the machines themselves, human labor may be reserved for "controlling the controls," that is, monitoring and analyzing data, and for functions that involve interpersonal interaction (Hirschhorn, 1981; Sabel, 1982; Zuboff, 1982, 1983).

For Braverman, then, the logic of capitalism leads inevitably to Fordist technical and social relations and therefore to the proletarianization and degradation of labor. The postindustrialists, on the other hand, argue that we are entering an entirely new period of capitalist organization that will be characterized by very different ("neo-Fordist") modes of both production and consumption.

Finally, although most of the feminist literature on office automation remains solidly rooted in the basic assumptions of the Braverman model (e. g., Glenn and Feldberg, 1977, 1980; Gregory and Nussbaum, 1980; West, 1982), the feminists make an important independent contribution in that they insist that it is necessary to make a gender-specific analysis of the impacts of technological change on the workforce. They argue that because of the pervasiveness of occupational sex segregation within the office workforce, women will bear the brunt of the process of "proletarianization" that is underway. Glenn and Feldberg, for example, conclude that the new higher-level technical jobs being created by information technologies are "developing as male provinces," while clerical work is becoming increasingly female (Glenn and Feldberg, 1980:11). According to this argument, then, men may actually benefit from office automation, whereas women's opportunities for upward mobility may decline.

The small number of case studies that have looked at the impact of automation on offices have reported conflicting findings, some more consistent with the Bravermanist model and others more in line with the postindustrialists' predictions. Similarly, they alternatively corroborate and refute the feminist expectation that women will be excluded from any new skilled jobs that are created (see, for example, Faunce et al., 1962; Shepard, 1971; Glenn and Feldberg, 1977; Hoos, 1961; BLS Bulletin #1468; Matteis, 1979; Sirbu, 1982; Murphree, 1982).

Throughout this paper we will argue that some reconciliation between these disparate findings might be reached if we understand that office automation cannot be analyzed as a unitary phenomenon. The effects of the new computer technologies on the workforce vary on the basis of the specific kind of equipment introduced and on the nature of the labor process being automated (originating in the unique characteristics of the product, market, organizational structure, and competitive dynamics of the industry). Even in the case of one industry as diverse and complex as insurance, what this means is that the effect of automation will vary widely across product lines and work procedures. Identical functions will be affected differently depending on the wider work process within which they are embedded. Even more important, as the postindustrialist argument suggests, the process of office automation has to be periodicized. Early and later generations of technology differ dramatically in their impacts.

We are also convinced that one of the problems with much of the literature on office automation is that it has been primarily focused on clerical labor; impacts on higher-level occupational categories have often been ignored. Today, the attention of both users and producers of office automation equipment is firmly fixed on the computerization of professional and managerial functions. Given this focus, the probable outlines of the "office of the future," and the fate of women's labor within it, cannot begin to be assessed without considering the effects of information technologies on all levels of the occupational structure.

Finally, following the feminist tradition, we will argue that the dynamics of this process are being crucially influenced by occupational sex segregation. Not only are women affected differently than men by the introduction of new technologies and the reorganization of the office, but the availability of cheap, educated female labor is playing an important role in shaping the emerging organization of work.

EARLY APPLICATIONS OF COMPUTER-BASED TECHNOLOGY IN THE INSURANCE INDUSTRY

The first applications of computer technology in the insurance industry involved the simple mechanization of extremely structured, high-volume operations. The early mainframes were used primarily as number-crunching machines; they permitted paper-processing industries such as insurance to double and triple their volume of business without corresponding increases in clerical personnel. The automated tasks were fairly discrete, so that the shift from manual to computerized performance had little effect on the organization as a whole; task fragmentation, or Taylorization, had already isolated these routinized functions. Word processors, duplicating machines, PBXs and so on were similarly introduced to mechanize particular tasks without regard for the nature of the overall office procedures.

Both the costs and technical requirements of the early machines and the tendency to automate in conformity with the rationalized structure of traditional administrative bureaucracies resulted in the intensification of the long-term trend toward task fragmentation and functional centralization. Conceptually and in practice, at this stage of development, Taylorization and mechanization were integrated processes.

Routine keyboarding was separated more sharply from other clerical functions and was often spatially isolated from the rest of the firm. This locational flexibility made labor force characteristics an increasingly central criterion in the siting of processing installations. As a result of the heightened fragmentation of work, processing personnel (both DP data processing and WP word processing) typically worked at the machines all day, with only two fifteen-minute breaks and a lunch break. Production standards were usually established for operators, sometimes measuring devices were built directly into the machines, and productivity-linked compensation schemes became more common.

"Industrialization" was not limited to processing functions. Overall, in the last two decades, the labor process in insurance companies has beeen increasingly Taylorized and centralized according to narrow functions. In the company we studied, for example, even the main professional occupation, underwriting, was rationalized in this manner: at the bottom end, certain low-level underwriting functions were given to a newly created clerical position (underwriting technical assistant); at the top end, more specialty underwriting categories were created. Similarly, workers were grouped by function—into sections of underwriters, raters, typists, and so on—each with its own immediate supervisor. Paper flowed from one section of the firm to another, mimicking the assembly line. This spatial segregation by occupation was tantamount to spatial segregation by gender. The professional and managerial categories were overwhelmingly male; the growing clerical workforce solidly and increasingly female. In fact, this form of labor-intensive rationalization of production was largely dependent on the growing supply of cheap female labor that had been liberated by changes in the economic and social relations of the household.

In summary then, in line with the Bravermanist model, the first stage of automation in the insurance industry tended to increase job fragmentation, centralize production by narrow function, heighten occupational sex segregation, and make many routine keyboarding functions spatially "footloose." More recently, however, the greater sophistication of the technologies and transformed market conditions are dictating a new organizational logic that promises to reverse many of these early trends.

THE INSURANCE COMPANY OF THE FUTURE

Changes in Products, Markets, and Technologies

In the last two decades, a combination of influences—inflation, high interest rates, demographic and socioeconomic changes, and heightened competition—has forced the insurance industry to develop radically different products and marketing strategies. Overall, these developments have moved the industry simultaneously in two opposing directions: toward the development of more specialized and/or flexible products on the one hand and toward more standardized products on the other.

At the same time, the technology employed by the industry has been undergoing equally dramatic changes. The miniaturization of electronic circuits, developments in telecommunications, simplification of computer language, and more sophisticated software have increased the flexibility and versatility of office automation systems and greatly expanded the possible range of their applications.

In contrast to many office environments, systems development in the insurance industry has been led by its data processing needs. In the last decade, the most important development in data processing hardware has been the tremendous increase in the capabilities of minicomputers and now microcomputers. Together with the vast improvements in communications technologies, these sophisticated small computers have transformed the insurance industry processing environment by facilitating the development of integrated, decentralized communications systems. Microtechnology makes this not only possible but cheap.

These trends are evident in office automation applications as well as in data processing applications; office automation equipment such as word processing, facsimile transmission, microfilm, and optical character-recognition devices are being linked to the DP-based systems. As a result, both data entry and data processing functions are increasingly being distributed and decentralized.

There are several reasons for this new approach. First, the technology finally permits such decentralization. Secondly, decentralized systems are often cheaper because labor savings resulting from the elimination of redundant data entry more than outweigh the added capital expense. Decentralized and distributed systems also speed up the input and retrieval processes and provide greater flexibility in the spatial location of various operations. Finally, a major advantage of distributed entry is the improved accuracy of the data.

207

Restructuring the Work Process

As the technology has become more sophisticated and as managers have gained experience applying it to their organizations, approaches to the problems of automation have changed as dramatically as the machines. We would characterize this evolution as the gradual movement from functional approaches to systems approaches, that is, from automating discrete tasks (e. g., typing, calculating) to rationalizing an entire procedure (e. g., new business issuance, claims processing) to reorganizing and integrating all the procedures involved in a particular division, product line, or group of product lines.

The transition from automating structured functions to a systems approach to automation began with the simplest procedures—procedures that involved a very small number of discrete tasks, such as payroll, accounting, billing and so on. Over the last decade, more and more complex procedures have been automated and the attention of managers and systems analysts in the industry has turned to the problem of a rational reorganization of the entire firm on the basis of fully integrated computer systems.

What this means is that all the work involved in a particular product line (or series of product lines associated with a particular market segment) is analyzed, the labor process is restructured and, where possible, it is automated. But automation follows the new logic of the organization; older functions may not be automated but simply eliminated as artifacts of an outmoded production process. In these state-of-the-art applications, one totally integrated on-line and batch system handles sales, new business issue, policy updating, renewals, commission calculation and payments, claims adjudication and payments, billing and premium collection, and operations and management reports (Life Office Management Association, 49). Even in less sophisticated systems, functional divisions are being eliminated.

On the basis of these integrated systems, insurers have been able to consolidate all policyholder data into central master records stored in the company's main computer installation. In the past, these records were duplicated in up to a dozen functional units and as a result were often inaccurate and conflicting. Now, users in remote sites can access relevant policies and make all necessary changes; these alterations are then integrated into the master record, often through batch transmissions at night. One individual can therefore handle multiple service transactions; functional units can be eliminated since the individual master record for each policy is a complete database.

As a result, in numbers of product lines, companies are moving to "reintegrate" the work process. First, in many cases, the traditional hierarchical and functionally stratified insurance company is being reorganized into more flexible, multifunctional teams, e. g., of underwriters, raters, clericals, that service a particular subset of customers, often on the basis of geographic location and/or market segment. Symbolically, even the physical environment reflects this new approach; the walls of private offices have been torn down and managers, professionals, and clericals work side by side in shoulder-high cubicles. Second, the range of tasks performed by individual workers is being expanded electronically. As procedures are analyzed and redesigned, new "integrated" job categories are being created.

Most important, companies are creating new kinds of skilled clerical or paraprofessional jobs by combining specific clerical and professional functions. For example, managers and underwriters in the company we studied are predicting that within the next few years a new skilled clerical occupation will perform many of the functions now divided among typists, raters, underwriting technical assistants, and underwriters. This new position will handle all routine underwriting, freeing a greatly reduced number of underwriters for more complex and varied tasks.

Similarly, "mental" and "manual" labor are being somewhat reintegrated as data entry is increasingly done by higher-level originators. For example, it is now possible (although still rare) for insurance salesmen equipped with a terminal that fits into a small suitcase to directly contact their firm's central computer through the telephone lines, eliminating numerous (mostly clerical) intermediaries. The computer is capable of making all the necessary calculations for the issuance of a policy and then it prints it out instantaneously (International Labor Organization, 1981).

In all these ways then the emerging organization of work in the insurance industry differs fundamentally from Ford's assemblyline,

209

although Taylorist logic has not been entirely superceded; that is, higher-level functions are being automated and turned over to cheaper labor. Nonetheless the impetus toward team work, open offices, and multifunctional job categories is new, and more importantly, it is not simply technological in origin. These changes are also responses to the new demands being placed on the organization by flexible products, specialized markets, and even the pace of change itself. All three favor less specialization within the work process, general purpose machines, and modular systems that can be adapted to a variety of different uses, and a polyvalent workforce that is capable of adapting quickly to new conditions.

The Influence of Product and Market Conditions

Ultimately, as we argued earlier, the precise shape that the new labor processes assume will vary across product and market segments despite the fact that a common logic—reintegration of the work flow on the basis of the new technologies—is informing all the various reorganization efforts. The two extreme poles of insurance company product offerings, highly standardized and highly specialized products, best illustrate this proposition.

When a firm (or a division within it) is producing a standardized product for a mass market, the goal is to reduce unit costs to their minimum. The large scale of such production makes it efficient to computerize even fairly complex operations. The nature and size of the customer base lend themselves to mass marketing techniques. As a result, the labor process involved in both production and distribution activities will be highly rationalized and routinized (Sabel, 1982). As much as the sophistication of the technology permits, virtually all routine clerical work, as well as a great many skilled clerical activities and professional and service functions, will be performed entirely by the computer. In the transition from less sophisticated to more sophisticated systems, the labor force will shrink in size; the occupational structure will shift from a more even distribution of skills to a highly bifurcated one (with only a small number of either routine or semi-skilled clerical jobs and more highly skilled professional jobs remaining).

The new personal-lines centers of the property/casualty company we studied are good illustrations of this case. As with most other property/casualty insurers, this company markets its products through a system of independent brokers and agents. These agents interact directly with clients and forward all relevant policy data to underwriters, who have for the most part been located in branch offices. Traditionally, once the underwriter assessed the risk, the policy was given to a rater who calculated the premium charges; the policy was then produced by another clerical worker and returned to the agent or client.

Increasingly the company has been able to computerize this process. As a result, all the personal-lines work previously conducted in over sixty branch offices has been consolidated within three regional centers. The production process in these new centers is roughly as follows: the agent sends the client information to the center, where a clerical worker screens the mail and sends all routine policies directly to data entry operators. These operators code the information in to a terminal that relays it to the company's national computer center. Overnight, the computer underwrites and rates the policies and returns the finished products to the center by morning. Problem policies are processed out by the clerical sorter or returned by the computer. These policies are then handled manually or coded to override the computer's screening process. Either way, the information on the policy is keyed into the computer so that it can maintain a complete file of policyholders. The goal is to have the computer process the underwriting and rating of as many policies as possible.

On the basis of high-volume, standardized production then, the labor process has been centralized, rationalized, and computerized. The few remaining labor functions, both routine and skilled, are those that still defy automation. The occupational structure is bifurcated into data entry clerks and exceptions underwriters (as well as, of course, managers and a small number of other support personnel). Communications networks have made both the clerical and professional aspects of this work highly footloose. The centers are located in small towns; labor force characteristics and the availability of telecommunications hookups figured most prominently in the locations decisions.

At the other extreme, if the product is highly specialized and/or subject to continual changes and if the market is limited, the em-

211

phasis is on innovation and a personalized sales effort. Most of the work is too unstructured and too low-volume to standardize into computerized algorithms. To reduce costs, routine clerical functions will be eliminated to whatever extent possible, perhaps by folding many of them into professional activities. Remaining managerial, professional, sales, service, and clerical personnel will be aided by sophisticated computerized work stations. As much as possible, these functions will be combined and job categories expanded. Overall skill levels should rise and the occupational structure should be less polarized, although, as we will discuss later, there may be important structural barriers to occupational mobility.

Obviously between these two extremes are numerous possible arrangements depending on the ratio of structured to unstructured work processes, external versus internal contact, interpersonal communication versus paper handling, skilled versus unskilled activities, which products and markets dictate (Sirbu, 1982). Most commercial lines products fall into this intermediate category; therefore the commercial lines divisions of the company we studied were less fully automated. Underwriting was computer-assisted, rather than performed entirely by computers; workers were grouped into teams on the basis of product lines and regions serviced; and it was here that the combined clerical/rater/underwriter category described earlier was expected to be created. Finally, however, although the labor process differs among these various cases, everywhere duplication of effort is being reduced or eliminated and structured tasks are being automated.

Recomposition of the Occupational Structure

Overall these trends are likely to transform the existing occupational structure in the following ways: (1) much routine data entry will be eliminated; (2) as many professional functions as possible will be embedded in computer software, either eliminating human labor or transferring the remaining functions to skilled clerical workers; (3) the remaining professional work will be more highly specialized. In combination these changes have significant implications for the size and composition of the workforce.

First, of course, in relation to output, the workforce will be smaller. Whether it shrinks in absolute numbers depends on the rate of growth of the sector relative to these productivity gains. The least-skilled clerical categories will be the most dramatically reduced. Skilled clerical work, on the other hand, may well expand (or at least hold stable), as clerks increasingly take over formerly professional functions.

These trends are already beginning to be visible in aggregate data. Between 1978 and 1981 (the years for which the most reliable aggregate data are available), there was a significant reduction in clerical employment. For most clerical categories, the decline was in relative employment share, although some occupations experienced an absolute drop (see Table 9.1). In this same time period, most professional categories registered relative growth, but underwriters declined relative to other occupational categories and the absolute number of accountants and auditors fell dramatically (see Table 9.1). Managerial and technical employment continued to rise, reflecting the drive to restructuring and automation.

From our case study it was clear that these changes in the occupational structure did indeed vary by product line. In the company we studied, between 1973 and 1979 the number of personal lines underwriters fell by 82.4 percentage points, whereas in commercial lines, underwriting occupations grew by 9.8 percentage points during the same period (see Table 9.2). Similarly in contradiction to aggregate statistics, the number of raters and technical assistants grew dramatically; the difference can probably be explained by the fact that most of this company's work is commercial (where we expect skilled clerical work to grow) whereas the aggregate statistics are dominated by more standardized life and personal property/casualty lines.

Second, occupational mobility, especially for clerical workers, will probably be reduced. Lower-level professional and technical jobs, which have provided clericals with whatever limited access they have had up to now to the upper reaches of the occupational ladder, are also being eliminated. The remaining professional and technical work will be more skilled and complex. As a personnel manager we interviewed explained, a "systems" rater (or underwriter/rater) will

Table 9.1. **Percent Distribution of Insurance Employment by Occupation, 1978, 1981**

Occupations	Insurance carriers		Insurance agents, brokers, and service organizations	
	1978	1981	1978	1981
Total	100.00	100.00	100.00	100.00
Managers/officers	11.64	12.22	19.72	19.97
Professionals	14.83	14.89	11.62	12.35
Systems analyst	.92	1.24	.13	.21
Accountant/auditor	2.74	1.27	1.06	1.03
Claims examiner, P/C	1.21	1.27	1.00	.93
Underwriter	3.76	3.67	6.24	5.19
Special agent	1.40	1.90	.32	2.05
Technical workers	1.77	2.10	.47	.60
Programmers	1.29	1.67	.25	.46
Clerical workers	54.99	53.89	52.83	52.77
Computer operator	.96	.91	.23	.30
Keypunch operator	1.57	1.56	.47	.44
Accounting clerk	2.17	2.16	2.13	1.89
Bookkeeper, hand	.59	.47	2.47	2.37
Claims adjuster	2.92	2.75	3.42	3.22
Claims clerk	2.72	2.63	3.02	2.74
Correspondence clerk	1.23	1.15	.25	.20
File clerk	3.56	2.84	2.80	2.31
General clerk	8.41	7.49	9.34	9.20
Mail clerk	.98	1.02	.34	.34
Policy change clerk	1.23	1.30	2.46	1.73
Rater	2.83	2.63	4.28	4.14
Secretary	4.37	4.41	6.90	7.39
Typist	4.57	4.20	3.75	3.53
Clerical supervisor	3.05	3.13	2.75	2.69
Insurance checker	.82	1.00	.57	2.17
Claims examiner, L/H	2.79	3.36	1.29	1.36
Sales	14.88	15.02	14.24	13.26

SOURCE: Occupational Employment Survey, Insurance, 1978, 1981, unpublished Bureau of Labor Statistics data (Washington, D.C.)
NOTE: For insurance carriers and insurance agents, brokers, and service organizations.

Table 9.2. **Changes in the Occupational Structure in a Major Property/ Casualty Insurance Company: 1977–1983**

Occupational category	% of total employment		% Rate of change 1977–1983
	1977	1983	
Managers	7.1	19.4	+204.7
Professionals	26.3	25.7	= 8.4
Technicians	10.2	11.1	+ 21.3
Sales	0.1	—	
Office/clerical	53.5	42.8	− 11.3

SOURCE: Occupational Employment Survey, Insurance, 1978, 1981, unpublished Bureau of Labor Statistics data, Washington, D.C.)

not acquire the knowledge and skills necessary to qualify her for (exceptions) underwriting. Increasingly, in his words, there will be a "quantum jump" between clerical and professional job categories.

Barriers to mobility are not new, but in the past the barrier between clerical and professional work was simply sex discrimination: for example, men were underwriters, women were raters. Theoretically, a rater could be prepared by her job an on-the-job training for an underwriting position, although in practice this rarely happened because of the gender identification of job categories. The affirmative action victories of the last decade (including many successful suits directed at insurance companies) created new opportunities for women to move up. If "bridge jobs" are eliminated in the manner we just described, a new kind of structural barrier to upward mobility will be created just as the older sexual barrier is being eroded.

Location of Women in the Occupational Structure

This is not to argue, however, that the new occupational hierarchy will be as gender-segregated as in the past. On the contrary, we believe that increasingly occupational stratification will occur along class and race lines rather than gender lines. Perhaps more precisely, as Burris and Wharton (1982) have recently suggested, it is likely that the more middle-class jobs (professional, managerial, technical) will continue to desegregate, whereas clerical jobs will remain solidly female.

215

Table 9.3. **Percent Growth in Selected Professional and Clerical Occupations in the Insurance Industry and Percent of Women in Occupation, 1961, 1966, 1971, 1976, 1980**

Occupation	% women		% change in total occupation				
	1961	1976	1961–1966	1966–1971	1971–1976	1976–1980	1961–1980
Professional							
Actuaries	7.8	11.7	−51.5	8.7	52.1	27.5	2.2
Claims approvers	—	70.5	−15.3	22.5	37.6	53.1	158.2
Computer operators	—	10.9	—	—	5.1	−1.9	—
Programmers	18.2	35.5	122.1	110.6	21.6	18.6	574.5
Systems analysts	8.2	29.2	50.6	229.1	49.4	33.0	885.2
Underwriters	25.9	39.6	0.2	7.0	−0.7	25.7	33.8
Clerical							
Accounting clerk	90.2	100.0	−12.7	25.2	4.2	9.6	21.1
Correspond. clerk	62.8	100.0	−4.2	2.8	4.1	16.3	0.1
File clerk	96.7	100.0	−26.4	−17.7	−4.0	−11.3	−32.9
Policy eval. clerk	90.7	100.0	−130.0	−12.9	−3.7	−1.7	−39.3
Keypunch operator	99.9	100.0	13.8	−0.8	−14.7	−4.8	−8.5
Typists	99.9	99.9	1.9	−18.9	−23.1	−20.7	−49.1

SOURCE: U.S. Department of Labor, Bureau of Labor Statistics, *Industry Wage Survey, Life Insurance,* (Washington, D.C.: GPO) 1961, 1966, 1971, 1976, 1980.

Again the aggregate data seem to confirm this hypothesis. While many already highly feminized clerical categories have clearly become totally segregated female categories, the movement of women into professional and technical categories is quite remarkable (see Table 9.3). Between 1961 and 1976, claims approvers increased from 45 to 71 percent female; computer programmers, from 18 to 36 percent female; systems analysts, from 8 to 29 percent female; and underwriters, from 26 to 40 percent female. According to the Insurance Information Institute, between 1970 and 1979, the number of female managers and officers grew from 11 percent to 24 percent; professionals from 17 percent to 38 percent; and technicians from 38 percent to 65 percent. In the company we investigated, women now comprise 38 percent of all managers, 46 percent of all professionals, and 66 percent of all technicians, as well as of course, 92 percent of all clericals. This bifurcation of the female work force is in accord with gender shifts in the services sectors as a whole.

In fact, on the basis of our research, we began to suspect that rather than expelling women from higher-level jobs, the growing feminization of these occupations may facilitate their transformation into more skilled and responsible jobs without a compensatory increase in pay or status. As Oppenheimer (1968, 1970) has argued, the defining attribute of a female-typed occupation is not that it is unskilled—on the contrary, female-dominated occupations are often quite skilled—but rather that it is low-paid. It seems possible, therefore, that in a restructuring process that actually involves raising the skill levels of much of the workforce, women will function to depress wages. Similarly, to the extent that the new jobs are more routinized and boring, female labor may be preferred.

Changing Social Relations and Forms of Managerial Control

Finally, and somewhat ironically, the "insurance company of the future" may be more superficially egalitarian, despite greater barriers to upward mobility. The rigidity and hierarchy of the traditional insurance company is, as we suggested earlier, antithetical to the logic of the new productive forces and dysfunctional in a period of rapid and ongoing change. For information to move freely in commodity form, as the new production processes require, the "craft mentality" of professionals and managers has to be eroded, that is, the link between information and personal power has to be broken. In addition, patriarchical social relations—which were a central organizing principle of the traditional office—have been undermined by the feminist movement and by the reality that a growing proportion of the professional and mangerial staff is composed of women.

The move to team work, then, represents a new method of managerial control, one that is more compatible with the requirements of the new production process and the changes occurring in the composition of the workforce. Similarly, the move to "open" offices, the elimination of private secretaries, and so on are removing many of the symbols of professional and managerial prestige, although the change is far more than symbolic: the work process is being restructured in preparation for the automation of a number of higher-level functions formerly performed by these professionals and managers.

IMPACTS ON WOMEN WORKERS WILL VARY BY CLASS AND RACE

The effects of all these changes on women's jobs and employment opportunities will vary importantly by class and race. For minority clericals and less educated white working-class women, the threat of redundancy is serious.

Minority women, excluded for years from office employment, have filled in the bottom of the clerical hierarchy; these are precisely the jobs that are now being automated. In addition, many of the routine clerical jobs that do remain, and the more skilled clerical categories being created, are moving out of the central cities into white suburbs and small towns. The three new personal-lines centers described earlier were located in small towns where minorities represented 3.1 percent, 3.3 percent, and 14.3 percent respectively of the populations. The chief administrator of one of these centers, underlining the importance of labor force characteristics in the location decision, described the clerical workforce as well-educated, of German descent, with unemployed husbands. Finally, as Kristin Nelson (1982) has suggested, the move to teams that involve close working relations among high- and lower-level employees may well favor the hiring of "socially compatible" white women. Minority clerks have typically been relegated to the typing and processing pools.

As bulk processing centers are closed and key entry functions are moved to decentralized settings, these minority clericals are in real danger of losing their jobs. In the case of the company we studied, one vice president predicted that within three years the six processing centers located across the country that now employ approximately 1,500 to 1,800 people will have been closed. For women at the bottom of the clerical hierarchy, then, the greatest threat is not degradation or deskilling of their work, but rather its elimination.

The story is different for skilled, and especially, white, clericals. For these women there will probably be jobs but not opportunities. In other words, their situation may essentially remain unchanged, that is, they will continue to be a literate, responsible, low-paid workforce trapped in semi-skilled, dead-end jobs.

218

The only good news is for college-educated professionals and managers; it seems likely that these jobs will continue to be filled by perhaps increasing proportions of women. Nevertheless the positions of these women are potentially threatened in two ways. First, the number of available jobs may contract as their functions are automated and performed by clerks. Second, as discussed earlier, there is a danger that a number of professional and lower managerial categories may be resegregated as female and be implicitly or explicitly reclassified downward as a result.

SOME POLITICAL IMPLICATIONS OF THESE CHANGES

One of the great failings in much of the literature that analyzes the effects of technological change on the workforce is the tendency to fall into some variety of determinism, either technological or the kind of "capital logic" for which Braverman has been criticized. Therefore we want to make clear that although we share the postindustrialists' belief that the emerging productive forces are qualitatively different and are creating a host of new possibilities, we are convinced that the shape of the future will be largely determined through social conflict. For office workers in the private sector, the present picture is fairly gloomy in this regard.

Today only about 5 percent of the insurance workforce is organized into trade unions, and many of the organized workers are industrial life salesmen, a small and dying occupation. Within the finance, insurance, and real estate sector as a whole, less than 2 percent of the workforce is unionized. With the significant exception of the public sector, these figures are representative of levels of union organization among office workers throughout the economy.

Nor is there much hope that the situation will change in the near future. In the old sectors, union busting is rampant; in the new sectors, millions of dollars and much ingenuity is being focused on preventing unionization. The new technologies are aiding employers in this effort. Relocation, for example, is increasingly possible and cheap. Bulk clerical work is being automated and eliminated; clericals working in team environments may be even less open to union

219

appeals and may find it harder to develop ties among themselves than to "pooled" clerical workers. Furthermore, even if unions were to gain a significant foothold among private-sector white-collar workers, historically they have been unwilling to challenge managerial control over the design of technologies and the organization of the labor process. Finally, the recent experience of the farmworkers is a depressing reminder of the contradictions inherent in union organizing efforts; the United Farm Worker victories were followed immediately by greater automation and a dramatic reduction in jobs.

Both of the major feminist efforts to attack discrimination in the labor force—affirmative action and comparable worth—also have serious limitations within the changing context we have just described. Neither, of course, explicitly addresses the number or kinds of jobs that are created; and, to the extent that they raise the cost of female labor, affirmative action and comparable worth victories could fuel employers' biases in favor of low-skilled labor, less labor, or both. In addition, the bifurcation of the female labor force that is already occurring threatens to diminish even further the egalitarianism of affirmative action.

Not all the news is bad however; there are a number of hopeful developments as well. First, although there is no indication that a major redirection of trade union perspectives is occurring, small changes are taking place. A good example is the creation of Service Employees International Union 925, the nationwide clerical local. More important, the new skilled clerical categories being developed place women in precisely the kind of ambiguous and frustrating positions that seems conducive to mobilization, both union and otherwise. Both Working Women and SEIU 925, for example, have had greater success in attracting skilled clerks (such as legal secretaries) than "back office" clericals (such as data processing operators). The new computer-linked jobs contain contradictions similar to those experienced in secretarial work: skills are undervalued and career ladders are virtually nonexistent. In addition, computer-mediated work processes introduce new levels of stress, particularly to the extent to which performances are machine-monitored. In the future, then, issues such as pay equity, access to training programs, and even job design may become increasingly contended. Finally, despite the obvious and increasing hostility of companies to trade union initiatives, there is some indication of a new openness to "working smarter" strategies and other forms of labor process organization that harness the creative intellect of the workforce. It is unlikely, however, that much movement in this direction will occur without pressure from labor and, unfortunately, today the only "revolution" in the office is the one being engineered from above.

Reference List

Barker, Jane, and Hazel Downing. 1980. Word processing and the transformation of the patriarchial relations of control in the office. *Capital and Class* 10 (Spring):64–99.

Bell, Daniel. 1976. *The coming of postindustrial society.* New York: Basic Books, Inc.

Best's Review. 1979. Insurance Office Locations in the 1980's (August): 62–63.

Best's Aggregates and Averages. 1983. Property-Casualty Edition. Special issue.

Block, Fred, and Larry Hirschhorn. 1979. New productive forces and the contradictions of contemporary capitalism. *Theory and Society* 7.

Burris, Val, and Amy Wharton. 1982. Sex segregation in the U.S. labor force. *The Review of Radical Political Economics.* 14, 3 (Fall):43–55.

Braverman, Harry. 1974. *Labor and monopoly capital.* New York: Monthly Review Press.

Castells, Manuel. 1979. The service economy and postindustrial society: A sociological critique. *International Journal of Health Services* 6, 4.

Castells, Manuel. 1982. Crisis, planning and the quality of life: Managing the new historical relationships between space and society. Unpublished paper, Institute of Urban and Regional Development, Berkeley and Los Angeles: University of California.

Cockcroft, David. 1980. New office technology and employment. *International Labor Review* 119, 6 (Nov.–Dec.).

CSE Microelectronics Group. 1980. *Microelectronics: Capitalist technology and the working class.* London: CSE Books.

Cummins, Laird. 1977. *The rationalization and automation of clerical work.* Unpublished Master's thesis, Brooklyn College.

Davies, Margery. 1975. Women's place is at the typewriter: The feminization of the clerical labor force in *Labor market segmentation,* Edwards, Richard C., Michael Reich, David M. Gordon, eds., 279–96. Lexington, Mass.: D.C. Heath and Company.

Driscoll, James W. 1980. Office automation: The dynamics of a technological boondoggle. Unpublished paper presented at the International Office Automation Symposium, Stanford University (March).

Faunce, William, Einar Hardin, and Eugene H. Jacobson. 1962. Automation and the employee. *Annals of the American Academy of Political and Social Science,* 340.

Gershuny, Jonathan. 1978. *After industrial society: The emerging self-service economy.* New Jersey: Humanities Press.

Gershuny, Jonathan. 1983. *Social innovation and the division of labour.* New York: Oxford University Press.

Glenn, Evelyn Nakano, and Roslyn L. Feldberg. 1977. Degraded and deskilled: The proletarianization of clerical work. *Social Problems* 25, (October):52–64.

Glenn, Evelyn Nakano and Roslyn L. Feldberg. 1983. Technology and work degradation: Effects of office automation on women clerical workers. *Machina ex dea,* edited by Joan Rothschild. Elmsford, New York: Pergamon Press.

Goldhaber, Michael. 1980. Politics and technology: Microprocessors and the prospect of a new industrial revolution. *Socialist Review,* (July–August).

Greenbaum, Joan M. 1979. *In the name of efficiency.* Philadelphia: Temple University Press.

Hacker, Sally L. 1979. Sex, stratification, technology and organizational change: A longitudinal case study of AT&T. *Social Problems,* 26:539–57.

Hirschhorn, Larry. 1981. The post-industrial labor process. *New Political Science* (Fall).

Hoos, Ida. 1961. *Automation in the office.* Washington, D.C.: Public Affairs Press.

Insurance Information Institute. 1983. *Life insurance fact book.*

International Labour Organization. 1981. Advisory Committee on Salaried Employees and Professional Workers. *The effects of technological and structural changes on the employment and working conditions of non-manual workers.* Geneva: 8th Session, Report 2.

Life Office Management Association, Reports No. 43, 44, 47, 52, 53, 54, 57, 62, 63, 66, 67, 73, and numerous internal documents

Matteis, Richard J. 1979. The new back office focuses on customer service. *Harvard Business Review,* (March–April).

Mintzberg, Henry. 1972. The myth of MIS. *California Management Review* (Fall).

Murphree, Mary. 1982. Impact of office automation on secretaries and word processing operators. Presented at the International Conference of Office Work and New Technology, Boston.

Nelson, Kristin. 1982. Labor supply characteristics and trends in the location of routine offices in the San Francisco Bay Area. Unpublished paper presented at the 78th Annual Meeting of the Association of American Geographers, San Antonio, Texas (April).

Noble, David F. 1979. Social choice in machine design: The case of automatically controlled machine tools. In *Case studies in the labor process.* Monthly Review Press: New York.

Noble, David F. 1977. *America by design: Science, technology, and the rise of corporate capitalism.* New York: Alfred A. Knopf.

Nussbaum, Karen, and Judith Gregory. 1980. Race against time: Automation of the office. Cleveland: Working Women Education Fund.

Oppenheimer, Valerie. 1968. The sex labeling of jobs. *Industrial Relations,* 7, 3 (May).

Sabel, Charles F. 1982. *Work and politics: The division of labor in industry.* Cambridge: Cambridge University Press.

Shepherd, J. 1971. *Automation and alienation, A study of office and factory workers.* Cambridge, Mass: The MIT Press.

Sirbu, Marvin A. 1982. Understanding the social and economic impacts of office automation. Unpublished paper, MIT (November).

Sirbu, Marvin A., and Michael Hammer. 1980. What is office automation. Unpublished paper, MIT (January).

Strassman, Paul. 1980. The office of the future: Information management for the new age. *Technology Review* (December–January).

Teegarden, Suzanne, Barbara Baran, and Barbara Facher. 1983. Women's labor and changes in the occupational structure in the office industry: A case study of an insurance company. Unpublished Master's thesis, Department of City and Regional Planning, University of California, Berkeley.

U.S. Department of Labor. 1965. Bureau of Labor Statistics Bulletin No. 1468, Impact of office automation in the insurance industry. Washington, D.C.

U.S. Department of Labor. 1969. BLS, National trends and outlook: Industry employment and occupational structure. *Tomorrow's manpower needs,* vol. 2, Bulletin 1606. Washington, D.C.

U.S. Department of Labor. 1981. BLS, *Employment and unemployment: A Report on 1980,* Special Labor Force Report 244, April, A–22 to A–34. Washington, D.C.

U.S. Department of Labor. *Employment and Earnings,* Table B–3, March issue various years.

U.S. Department of Labor. *Employment and Earnings, United States, 1909–1978.*

U.S. Department of Labor. 1981. BLS, *The national industry-occupation employment matrix, 1970, 1978, and projected 1990,* vol. 2, Bulletin 2086. Washington, D.C.

U.S. Department of Labor. 1980. BLS, *Handbook of labor statistics,* Bulletin 2070, December. Washington, D.C.

U.S. Department of Labor. 1978. 1981. BLS, *Occupational employment survey of insurance,* unpublished data. Washington, D.C.

Werkneke, Diane. 1983. *Microelectronics and office jobs: The impact of the chip on women's employment.* Geneva: International Labour Office.

West, Jackie. 1982. New technology and women's office work. In *Work, women, and the labour market,* edited by Jackie West. London: Routledge and Kegan Paul.

Zisman, Michael D., 1978. Office automation: Revolution or evolution. *Sloan Management Review* 7 (Spring):1–15.

Zuboff, Shoshana. 1982. Problems of symbolic toil. *Dissent* (Winter):51–61.

Zuboff, Shoshana. 1983. Some implications of information systems power for the role of the middle manager. Harvard Business School Working Paper, May. Cambridge.

10

The Mythology of Part-time Work: Empirical Evidence from a Study of Working Mothers

Sheila Kishler Bennett and Leslie B. Alexander

Among the variety of alternative work patterns available in this country today, part-time work is the predominant alternative work schedule for women. Between 1970 and 1985, the voluntary, part-time labor force of workers, aged twenty and older, increased 48 percent. During this time, women comprised almost three-fourths of the part-time labor force each year (U.S. Dept. of Labor, 1986).

The availability of part-time employment is of particular importance in allowing women to remain active in the labor force during the years of heaviest parental responsibilities. In recent years, approximately 30 percent of all employed women have worked part-time, primarily at permanent, full-year jobs, and the majority of all women with children will likely do so at some time during their childbearing years (see Leon and Bednarzik, 1978; Moen, 1983; Moen and Smith, 1983; U.S. Dept. of Labor, 1984). For some, the income represented is essential. For others, maintaining employment is critical to establishing themselves in a career or line of work. Employment doubtless also fulfills personal needs in these years.

Part-time jobs typically held by women are not, however, generally very desirable when placed against otherwise comparable but full-time work with respect to pay, benefits, prestige, promotional opportunities, and the probability of developing stable, supportive relationships with co-workers and supervisors (see Bosworth and Dawkins, 1982; Deuterman and Brown, 1978; Association of Part-Time Professionals, 1984; and Rothberg and Cook, 1985). Part-time

jobs are often either routine or unskilled (Nollen, et al., 1978), offering minimum salaries and benefits. Even part-time employed professional and semi-professional women are likely to find themselves
placed in lower and less desirable positions in the organizations in
which they are employed, receiving salaries below those commanded by full-time workers of similar education and competence.
The decision to work part-time generally means, therefore, restricted entry and advancement prospects and lower pay, despite
comparable training and qualifications (see Theodore, 1971:26;
Owen, 1978:13; Appelbaum, 1981; Rothberg and Cook, 1985).

The devaluation of women's part-time work, like "women's work"
generally, receives support from a number of untested assumptions
employers make about part-time workers as women. These include
the notions that part-time working women are casual workers who
move rapidly in and out of jobs and the labor force, that they are not
psychologically committed to their jobs, and that their behavior reflects a traditional attitude toward women's social roles in which
home and family life take precedence over work commitments. In
short, the needs of part-time working women for such things as
higher pay, job security, control over scheduling, enhanced on-the-
job training, and promotional opportunities are readily overlooked
by employers who believe that female part-time workers are less
serious and concerned about their work than full-time workers. We
refer to these beliefs as myths in order to underscore the unexamined
nature of these assumptions and the legitimization they provide for
discriminatory practices and procedures, however indirectly.

In this chapter we will evaluate these beliefs against the evidence
provided by a study of part-time and full-time employed mothers
working in the health services industry. We chose hospital employment because the range of occupations it represents is typical of the
kinds of jobs that many women perform, and because hospitals provide a useful example of the highly "feminized" organizational settings within which many women work. The health service industry
is also the single service industry that accounts nationally for the
largest proportion of women's full-time and part-time employment,
and is the largest sector of feminized employment that continues to
grow and is projected to continue to do so (Nollen, 1979; Sekscenski,
1981; Waldman and McEaddy, 1974). The experience of women in

226

hospital settings is therefore relevant to a large number of women, but especially to those working in traditionally "feminine" lines of work. Health service organizations also provide the opportunity to observe women of diverse social, educational, and ethnic backrounds in one of the few organizational settings that employs women both full-time and part-time in a broad range of occupations. Consequently, full-time and part-time workers can be compared directly within occupational strata doing comparable work.

We begin with a brief description of the study group. We then use the extensive work histories and attitudinal data available for these women to examine three beliefs employers hold about such part-time workers when compared to full-time workers: that part-time employed women with children are casual workers, disinterested workers, and "traditionalists."

THE STUDY GROUP: WOMEN WORKING FULL-TIME AND PART-TIME IN THE HEALTH SERVICES INDUSTRY

Two hundred and fifteen women, aged twenty-five to forty-five and with at least one child in the home under age eighteen, participated in intensive individual interviews. All were employed in one of two large metropolitan hospitals. These women include nurses and other professional staff (ninety women), administrators (thirty-one), technicians and technologists (thirty-one), clerical workers (forty-nine), and service workers (fourteen). Because female physicians have been extensively studied, they were not included in our sample. As the elite among employees in hospital settings, physicians are also not always subject to the same employment practices as other, less credentialed, employees.

To the extent permitted by the actual distribution of women working in the two hospitals, these women were selected to balance the pool of participants with respect to race (white, black), occupational levels (adminstrative, professional, technical, clerical, service), and work status (full-time, part-time). The participants do not form, therefore, a statistically representative sample, but rather they were strategically recruited to permit meaningful comparisons by

227

work status and race within and across occupational levels. Approximately a third are black, employed largely in lower-status clerical, technical, and service jobs. Approximately half were employed part-time when interviewed, working fewer than 37.5 hours a week (the number of hours considered "full-time" with the case institutions) and averaging twenty hours a week. Although all participants had dependent children when interviewed, somewhat fewer than a third were not married at that time, including a high proportion of the black women.[1]

Part-time employed participants were slightly younger than full-time employed participants (31.8 years compared to 34.2) and had spent correspondingly fewer years in the labor force (11.6 years compared to 14.2). Part-time employed participants were much more likely than full-time workers to have younger, preschool children in the home, the average age of the youngest child being approximately four years for part-time workers and eight years for those employed full-time. Finally, part-time workers were much more likely to have been married at the time of interview (86 percent married, compared to 62 percent for full-time workers). With respect to race, part-time workers were twice as likely as full-time workers to be white. Since participants were not a statistically representative sample of the women working in these two hospitals, these comparisons do not necessarily describe the actual differences between the two groups in the case institutions. However, it is clear that single parents and minority women of limited income experience greater financial pressures to work full-time, as observed among our participants, and that women with younger children are less likely than women with older children to work full-time.

THE MYTHOLOGY OF PART-TIME EMPLOYMENT

This study permits the critical assessment of a number of beliefs about part-time female workers, and specifically those with children. We examine three: that part-time employed women with children are more likely to be casual workers, disinterested workers, and "traditionalists" than are full-time workers.

Are Part-time Workers Casual Workers?

The belief that women who work part-time have shorter job tenures and are more intermittent in their employment than full-time workers—like the belief generally that women are more "casual" workers than men in these respects—represents one assumption that logically legitimates employers' treatment of part-time work and part-time workers. An employer who believes that workers in a particular type of job are likely to leave that job will seek to minimize the cost of rapid turnover among these employees. From a "human capital" perspective, the employer is less likely to invest training, compensation, and opportunity in the part-time employee, because the employer does not expect her or him to remain with the organization long enough for the employer to realize a return on this investment. Evidence on length of job tenure, when part-time employed women are compared to full-time employed women (and men), allows us to evaluate this key element in supporting or refuting this myth.

Among study participants, part-time workers do not, as a group, evidence shorter job tenures (with respect to their then-current jobs) or a greater number of job changes than full-time workers. With respect to the number of months each group had been employed in the case institutions, part-time workers had actually been employed somewhat longer than full-time workers (47 months compared to 44 months), although the difference is not statistically significant. Neither were there differences between full-time and part-time employees in the number of times they had changed jobs since entering the labor force (approximately 3.5 times), when the slightly younger age of part-time employees is taken into consideration.

Observing more closely, we found that the kind of work done, however, does make a difference in the length of time participants had been employed in the case institutions (job tenure). Part-time employees in the lowest status jobs requiring the least credentialization and offering the greatest ease of entry and reentry (clerical and service work) did demonstrate fewer months with the employer than full-time workers in the same jobs, although the average for both groups indicates "stable," long-term employment (29 months compared to 46 months, a statistically meaningful difference). Since many of the part-time workers at this level anticipated moving into full-time work in the future, we might hypothesize that their relatively shorter job tenures reflected a tendency to assume more hours at a certain point in their job histories rather than a tendency toward job shifting. No differences in the number of jobs previously held were observed between part-time and full-time workers in lower-status jobs, when years in the labor force is statistically controlled.

The opposite relationship is found for the higher status, credentialed administrative, professional, and technical workers. At this level, part-time workers averaged 53 months employed by the case institutions, compared to 43 months for full-time participants (a statistically meaningful difference). Therefore, it is among exactly those workers representing the greatest "human capital" investment in education and training that assumptions regarding rapid turnover hold least rather than most true. Yet in the case institutions, the discrepancy between part-time and full-time workers in hourly wage levels and prospects for advancement was greatest at this level.[2]

Because black women are concentrated in the lower-status group and tend also to be younger, they have less job tenure generally than whites. However, when months employed in the case institutions are statistically adjusted to take into consideration differences in job levels and age, blacks are no longer different than whites.

With respect to patterns of employment across time, there is no evidence that women employed part-time when interviewed had less continuous work histories than full-time employees. In fact, again the tendency is in the opposite direction. Although equal proportions of each group had been continuously employed since leaving school or entering the labor force (23 percent), women employed full-time when interviewed included a somewhat higher proportion of women who had withdrawn from paid employment for a year or more for the birth of children or had been unemployed during the childbearing years (39 percent compared to 26 percent). That is, women in the part-time employed group were somewhat more likely to have maintained employment through the years of most demanding parental responsibility, and as a consequence they were also somewhat less likely to exhibit a disorderly pattern of movement among jobs (40 percent vs. 33 percent; see Wilensky, 1961).

230

These observations are not based upon a sample of women statistically representative of their institutions, and therefore we must be cautious in overly elaborating and generalizing these findings. Nevertheless, we believe it is clear that suppositions based upon employment status at one point in time may be misleading, and that in these two organizations there is no evidence that part-time employed mothers are more casual in taking and leaving employment than those working full-time, at least among those employed in higher-status positions. In fact, as a group, the part-time workers of this study, typically women with preschool children, demonstrated a higher level of labor force attachment over time, if indexed by continuity of employment, than full-time employees as a group, because the latter group included a larger proportion of those who had chosen not to work when they had children of similar ages. From an employer's point of view, one might argue that the best way to ensure that a woman who will not leave her job during the childbearing years is to hire a woman in her childbearing years, full or part-time.[3]

Are Part-time Workers More Uninterested in Their Work?

The belief that part-time women workers are less interested in and psychologically invested in their work and in this sense less "work committed" than full-time employees leads to the supposition that part-time employed women don't "care" as much about the job—or, by inference, about how they are treated in the job and rewarded for it. That is, the committed worker is allegedly a full-time worker, while a woman who doesn't work at all isn't really interested in doing so. Assumptions based upon the relative disinterest of part-time and full-time workers are logically injurious in their effects upon employer practices.

These beliefs are not restricted to employer mythology. Social scientists as well have tended to confuse psychological commitment with hours worked and continuity of employment. For example, one well-known sociologist has written that "the conceptualization of work commitment as uninterrupted work participation, even when the children are young and when financial needs do not dictate the

231

married woman's gainful employment, is well suited to the particular case of married women" (Safilios-Rothschild, 1971). Such a view ignores the very real constraints on employment many women face, and it confuses the psychological meaning women attach to employment with employment itself.

To test this assumption of the relative disinterest of part-time workers among study participants, we compared part-time and full-time workers on a number of items used in national surveys to judge labor force commitment, satisfaction with current work, and the type of general satisfactions sought in a job. Although we found differences with respect to occupational levels and education (as one would expect), we did not observe differences between part-time and full-time workers among women of comparable education or those employed in similar work. Neither were racial differences observed.

For example, a part-time worker was just as likely as a full-time worker to report that she would choose to continue to work even if she "were to get enough money to live as comfortably as you'd like for the rest of your life." Part-time workers were also equally as satisfied with their jobs as full-time employees. Differences between the two groups in specific satisfactions sought also failed to indicate that part-time workers cared less about their work. Both groups rated "self-fulfillment" as equally important, while part-time workers were especially likely to indicate the desire to "keep my hand in the labor force" as a reason for working. Full-time workers as a group were more likely to cite financial reasons for working full-time, but financial pressures existed and operated independently of personal orientations.

On these established measures of commitment and interest, then, part-time workers were fully as involved as full-time workers at comparable levels of education and occupational position. For participants in this study, that means that both groups evidenced very high levels of commitment to their work.

Are Part-time Workers More "Traditional"?

The third assumption we examined is that part-time employed women are more traditional in their attitudes toward gender roles in general. From this point of view, a woman's place is in the home, and a woman who works less than full-time is expressing a preference for homemaking and the care of children over investment in a job.

The implications of this belief are several. Like the assumption that part-time employed women are more disinterested and simply care less about job conditions and rewards, the "traditionalist" assumption leads employers to expect the part-time worker to be less committed to her work and less caring about its conditions and rewards. Furthermore, the "traditionalist" assumption posits a basic conservatism in gender and general social attitudes with respect to the legitimacy of female employment and female employment demands, and encourages a paternalism on the part of the employer that limits the responsibility and self-determination the worker is expected to evidence on the job.

To test this belief, we administered to all participants the Attitudes Toward Women Scale (Spence, et al., 1973). This instrument is designed to measure attitudes concerning the rights, roles, obligations, and privileges that women should have in modern society. Because we found that both higher education and being white predict higher, more liberal or "modern" responses, we statistically controlled these two variables in comparing part-time and full-time employees in order to avoid the confounding influence of differences between these two groups with respect to race and educational attainment.

When this is done, both groups of women rate equally high on this measure (62.4 for part-time workers, compared to 60.6 for full-time workers). Neither were any differences found on specific items. Most significantly, this means that part-time and full-time workers agreed on issues of economic equity, women's abilities, conjugal relations, and maternal responsibilities, and on questions of legal rights, social prerogatives, and sexual freedom.

In sum, on these and many other measures, we observed no evidence that part-time employed mothers are more traditional or conservative in their basic role orientations and beliefs, or that they attached greater importance to home and family life than full-time employed mothers. In fact, part-time employees are somewhat more likely than full-time employees to report that they feel work and family life promote and generally benefit one another.

233

PART-TIME WORK AS WOMEN'S WORK:
SOME INTERPRETATIONS AND CONCLUSIONS

In this chapter we have tested three assumptions concerning part-time working mothers, using data available from a study of women working in a variety of occupations within two large metropolitan hospitals. These assumptions are of two sorts. The belief that part-time working mothers are likely to move in and out of jobs more quickly is a belief about behavior, while the beliefs that part-time working mothers are less committed to their work and are more traditional in orientation toward women's social roles are beliefs about attitudes and personal orientations.

The first belief is important because it underlies a "strictly economic" explanation for the lower wages and mobility prospects that characterize part-time work. Our results indicate that such "strictly economic," human capital theory-based explanations must be critically assessed. Part-time workers in low-status clerical and service jobs may be somewhat less likely to stick with their jobs, at least as part-time work. However, these are jobs for which the "strictly economic" argument makes least sense, for these are jobs characterized by great substitutability, ease of entry, and low levels of job-specific training. The fact that our lower-status part-time workers evidenced as long and continuous histories of work as full-time employees (when part-time workers' younger ages are taken into account) indicates that these workers are as attached to the labor force as are full-time workers, even though they may shift among jobs as marginal conditions of work change, or shift into full-time work as that becomes possible. Among our participants, many of these women are black or single parents, for whom we find that the choice lies not between part-time and full-time work, but between finding any job at all that fits parental responsibilities and involuntary unemployment. This is evidenced by the larger proportion among lower-status than higher-status workers of those who would prefer to be employed full-time. Among women employed in the higher-status and better paid jobs requiring credentialization and training—those jobs for which the "strictly economic" argument might more nearly apply—part-time employed women in this study were fully as "stable" in their patterns of work as full-time employed women, if not more so.

The belief that part-time employed women do not share the same attitudinal orientations and commitments as full-time employed women is important less because this belief is adduced to account for the lower wages and other prospects that characterize part-time work than because it becomes an excuse for such devaluation. The employee is hypothesized not to care. In examining the validity of these attitudinal assumptions, we statistically controlled for differences in educational level and race. We did so because lower educational attainment is related to a more instrumental orientation toward work and to holding more conventional beliefs and attitudes, and because minority women—who are much more likely than white women among our participants to be employed in lower-status positions and to live on severely limited economic resources—face as a group very different job prospects and conditions. Taking these statistical controls into account, we found no evidence for our participants that the part-time employed were any less committed to their work or were more traditional in attitudinal orientations than full-time employed women. To employers who use the argument that part-time employed mothers "don't care" to excuse discriminatory practices, we reply that our participants clearly *do* care. Many of our part-time employees were quite explicit on this point, expressing anger and resentment at policies with respect to pay, benefit, promotion (including the opportunity to move into full-time work) that they believe discriminate against them as part-time employees.

The overwhelming majority of our participants working part-time in higher-status positions are voluntarily employed part-time. That is, these workers did not when interviewed wish to be working full-time. However, preference for part-time work at a particular point in time does not excuse discriminatory practices any more than the belief that part-time workers "don't care." Nor did we find voluntary part-time workers any less committed to and invested in their jobs than full-time workers. Significantly, most of these women anticipated working full-time when their children were older. Furthermore, many voluntary part-time workers worked despite significant cost to themselves, when the expenses of childcare, transportation, and other incidentals are taken into account.

Why do part-time jobs typically offer such limited prospects? How

235

do beliefs about women's employment behavior relate to the nature of part-time work?

In thinking about these questions, we have found it useful to follow the distinction between "primary sector" and "secondary sector" labor markets proposed by some economists. "Jobs in the primary market possess several of the following characteristics: high wages, good working conditions, employment stability, chances of advancement, equity and due process in the administration of work rules. Jobs in the secondary market, in contrast, tend to have low turnover, little chance of advancement, and often arbitrary and capricious supervision" (Doeringer and Piore, 1971:165).

Within many organizations and industries, the recruitment of workers to the jobs of increasing responsibility and rewards that are found in the primary sector occurs primarily through the promotion of workers from within, from an "internal" labor market. In contrast, workers within the secondary sector are generally recruited or assigned to jobs from the much larger "external" labor market of individuals offering a given set of generalized skills. Jobs in the secondary sector provide limited access to internal labor markets, but are likely to meet the needs of women in their childbearing years— for example, ease of entry and reentry, generalized or undifferentiated qualifications, substitutability. Employers enjoy much greater latitude for the play of tastes and preferences—and generalized assumptions—in recruiting from this external labor pool (see Blau and Jusenius, 1976: Doeringer and Piore, 1971; Gordon, 1972; Wolf and Rosenfeld, 1978).

Part-time employment is highly characteristic of the secondary sector. Drawing upon Owen, Appelbaum concludes that "in almost direct contrast to the neoclassical (economic) vision, in which the wage a worker can command is related only to his or her productivity characteristics (and hence is independent of hours worked), it is evident that the labor market is segmented and that part-time workers are unable to compete for jobs on an equal basis with similarly qualified full-time workers" (Appelbaum, 1981:104; Owen, 1978). In our own case institutions, many participants employed part-time in higher-status jobs requiring formal training, credentialization, and experience (and equally as qualified as full-time employees doing the identical work) reported that their hours were restricted in such a way as to prevent their working full-time and therefore from obtaining the benefits and mobility prospects of full-time employees. Others reported that in order to work full-time, they would have to leave their part-time jobs and look elsewhere for full-time positions.

The limited prospects offered by part-time work cannot simply be described either as a form of discrimination against part-time employees or fully explained by the nature of the work itself. However, when a particular worker is allocated to such a secondary sector job—part-time or full-time—on the basis of characteristics ascribed to some general group, the effect is discriminatory for that worker. (This is referred to by economists as "statistical discrimination" [see Piore, 1971].) And, we would argue, when the characteristics ascribed to that group represent unexamined assumptions of questionable empirical validity, the effect is discriminatory for both the individual worker and that group.

In this chapter we have examined three such assumptions concerning part-time working mothers, using data available from a study of women working in one employment sector. Further studies of this sort are necessary to confirm our conclusions, and are vitally important to the interests of women as earners and workers, if we are to challenge employment policies that discriminate against women, both as employees and as the caretakers of children and homes.[4]

Notes

---

1. This study is designed to meet two criticisms of earlier research on women's employment and family life. First, available studies have been largely restricted to dual-career or dual-professional couples. Dual-professional couples, however, constitute a minority of all dual-earner families (12 percent in Moen's national sample), and they are hardly representative of employed mothers with respect to such characteristics as race, socioeconomic background, or even marital status. (For well-known studies of dual career couples, see Bird, 1979; Holmstrom, 1973; Pepitone-Rockwell, 1980; Rapoport and Rapoport, 1969, 1971, 1977. For a recent comprehensive review, see Gilbert, 1987, Gilbert and Rachlin, 1987.) For recent work on

dual-earner families, see Pleck, 1987; O'Donnell, 1984; Hood, 1983; Lein, 1983; Piotrkowski, 1979; Walshok, 1979.) Second, available research has tended as well to provide limited insight into the temporal dimension of the ways decisions regarding childbearing and movement in and out of marriage, education, and employment are mutually contingent and structured across the life cycles course (see Bennett and Elder, 1979; Elder and Rockwell, 1976; Hogan, 1978). The study reported here includes women in a wide variety of occupations and provides a variety of information on the temporal components of the life cycle course.

2. All participants were employed as "permanent employees" by the case institutions. Therefore, the participant pool did not include temporary and short-term workers, such as "contract nurses" hired to supplement the permanent nursing staff. The case hospitals were not unionized, and have in recent years sought to decrease the attraction of unionization by upgrading their benefit packages. Less than full-time employees working more than twenty hours a week may qualify for partial benefits. Although significant discrepancies existed between full-time and part-time workers within each job level in terms of pay, benefits, and promotion opportunities, the two hospitals from which participants were recruited probably experienced somewhat less turnover among permanent employees (including nursing staff) than some other types of hospitals in some other metropolitan areas.

3. As Hayghe (1986) reports, the proportion of job-seeking or job-holding wives with infant children rose from less than one-third to almost one half between 1975 and 1985. The labor force participation of married mothers of children under eighteen rose from 44.9 percent to 61 percent during those same years.

4. In March 1987 a mail questionnaire follow-up was completed on this study group resulting in a 95 percent response. The objectives of this phase are: to update employment and family event histories; to probe employment decisions, including movement into and out of paid employment and between part-time and full-time work; to update information on childcare arrangements, including those for older children; and to provide indicators of health status, with particular attention to areas of health behavior known to be related to stress responses. Data analysis of this phase is in progress.

Reference List

Aldous, J. (ed.) 1982. *Two paychecks: Life in dual-earner families.* Beverly Hills, Ca: Sage Publications.

Appelbaum, Eileen. 1981. *Back to work: Determinants of women's successful reentry.* Boston, Mass.: Auburn House.

Association of Part-Time Professionals. 1984. Part-Time Employment in

America: Highlights of the First National Conference on Part-Time Employment. McLean,, Va.: Association of Part-Time Professionals.

Bennett, Sheila K., and Glen H. Elder, Jr. 1979. Women's work in the family economy: A study of Depression hardship in women's lives. *Journal of Family History* 4:153–176.

Bird Carolyn. 1979. *The two-paycheck marriage.* New York: Rawson, Wade.

Blau Francine D., and L. Jusenius. 1976. Economists' approaches to sex segregation in the labor market: An appraisal. *Signs* 1:181–200.

Bosworth, Derek, and Peter Dawkins. 1982. Women and part-time work. *Industrial Relations Journal* 13:32–39.

Deutermann, William U., and Scott Campbell Brown. 1978. Voluntary part-time work: A growing part of the labor force. *Monthly Labor Review* 101 (June):3–10.

Doeringer, Peter B., and Michael J. Piore. 1971. *Internal labor markets and manpower analysis.* Lexington, Mass.: Lexington Books.

Elder, Glen H., Jr., and Richard C. Rockwell. 1976. Marital timing in women's life patterns. *Journal of Family History* 1:34–54.

Gilbert, Lucia Albino, ed. 1987. *The counseling psychologist* 15 (January): entire issue devoted to Dual-Career Families in Perspective.

Gilbert, Lucia Albino, and Vicki Rachlin. 1987. Mental health and psychological functioning of dual-career families. *The Counseling Psychologist* 15 (January):3–49.

Gordon, David M. 1972. *Theories of poverty and underemployment.* Lexington Mass.: Lexington Books.

Hayghe, Howard. 1986. Rise in mothers' labor force activity includes those with infants. *Monthly Labor Review* 2 (February):43–45.

Hogan, Dennis P. 1978. The variable order of events in the life course. *American Sociological Review* 43:573–586.

Hood, J. A., 1983. *Becoming a two-job family.* New York: Praeger.

Holmstrom, Lynda Lytle. 1973. *The two-career family.* Cambridge, Mass.: Schenkman.

Lein, Laura. 1983. *Families without villains: American families in an era of change.* Lexington, Mass.: Lexington Books.

Leon, Carol, and Robert W. Bednarzik. 1978. A profile of women on part-time schedules. *Monthly Labor Review* 101 (October):3–12.

Moen, Phyllis. 1985. Continuities and discontinuities in women's labor force activity. In *Life course dynamics: 1960's to 1980's,* edited by Glen H. Elder. New York: Academic Press.

Moen, Phyllis, and Ken R. Smith. 1983. Women's work commitment and labor force behavior over the life course. Paper presented at the Annual Meeting of the American Sociological Association, Detroit, Michigan, (September).

Nollen, Stanley D. 1979. *New patterns of work.* Scarsdale, N.Y.: Work in America Institute, Inc.

Nollen, Stanley D., Brenda B. Eddy, and Virginia H. Martin. 1976. *Perma-*

nent part-time employment: An interpretive review. Springfield, Va.: National Technical Information Service.

O'Donnell, L. N. 1984. *The unheralded majority: Contemporary women as mothers.* Lexington, Mass.: Lexington Books.

Owen, John D. 1978. Why part-time workers tend to be in low wage jobs. *Monthly Labor Review* 101 (June):11–14.

Pepitone-Rockwell, Fran (ed.). 1980. *Dual-career couples.* Beverly Hills, Calif.: Sage.

Piore, Michael J. 1971. The dual labor market: Theory and implications. In *Problems in political economy: An urban perspective,* edited by David M. Gordon. Lexington, Mass.: D.C. Heath Co.

Piotrkowski, Chaya S. 1979. *Work and the family system.* New York: The Free Press.

Pleck, Joseph H. 1987. Dual-career families: A comment. *The Counseling Psychologist.* 15 (January):131–133.

Rapoport, Robert N., and Rhona Rapoport. 1969. The dual-career family: A variant pattern and social change. *Human Relations,* 22:3–30.

Rapoport, Robert N., and Rhona Rapoport. 1971. *Dual-career families.* Baltimore, Md.: Penguin Books.

Rapoport, Robert N., and Rhona Rapoport. 1977. *Dual-career families re-examined: New integrations of work and family.* New York: Harper and Row.

Rothberg, Diane S. and Barbara Ensor Cook. 1985. *Part-time professional.* Washington, D.C.: Acropolis Books, Inc.

Safilios-Rothschild, Constantina. 1971. Towards the conceptualization and measurement of work commitment. *Human Relations* 24:489–493.

Sekscenski, Edward S. 1981. The health service industry: A decade of expansion. *Monthly Labor Review* 104 (May):9–16.

Spence, Janet T., R. Helmreich, and J. Stapp. 1973. A short version of the Attitudes Toward Women scale (AWS). *Bulletin of the Psychometric Society* 2:219–220.

Theodore, A. 1971. The professional woman: Trends and prospects. In *The professional woman,* edited by A. Theodore. Cambridge, Mass.: Schenkman.

U.S. Department of Labor, Bureau of Labor Statistics. 1984. *Employment in perspective: Working women.* Report 716, Fourth Quarter/Annual Summary. Washington, D.C.: U.S. Government Printing Office.

U.S. Department of Labor, Women's Bureau. August 1986. *Facts on U.S. working women: Alternative work patterns.* Fact Sheet No. 86, 3. Washington D.C.: U.S. Government Printing Office.

Waldman, Elizabeth, and Beverly J. McEaddy. 1974. Where women work—an analysis by industry and occupation. *Monthly Labor Review* 97 (May): 3–13.

Walshok, Mary. 1982. *Blue collar women.* Berryville, Va.: Doubleday and Company.

Wilensky, Harold L. 1961. Orderly careers and social participation: The impact of work history on social integration in the middle mass. *American Sociological Review* 26:521–539.

Wolf, Wendy C., and Rachel A. Rosenfeld. 1978. Sex structure of occupations in job mobility. *Social Forces* 56:823–844.

11

Women Workers and the Changing International Division of Labor in Microelectronics

David C. O'Connor

S tudies on women workers in the microelectronics or
semiconductor industry proliferated in the late 1970s
and the early 1980s.[1] Such studies were part of a broader corpus of
research on the increasing internationalization of production in the
late 1960s through the 1970s of certain labor-intensive light manu-
factures, most notably garments, consumer electronics, and electronic components. Certain third world countries were achieving
the status of major exporters of garments and textiles as well as
being major assembly bases for certain electronics products. Those
products and production processes where the shift to third world
countries was most dramatic were characterized by a high proportion of female workers. This high proportion is explainable largely
in terms of the perceived "suitability" to the detail work involved in
electronics or garment assembly. Male/female wage differentials are
at best only a secondary explanation. The most dramatic wage differentials are those between the United States and other advanced
capitalist countries on the one hand and the third world "export
platforms" on the other. Indeed, low labor costs are generally recognized as the principal rationale for the siting of labor-intensive assembly activities in third world countries.

In the garment industry the process of internationalization frequently involved the loss of market shares by domestic manufacturers in the developed countries to imports from indigenous manufacturers in Asian countries like Hong Kong, Taiwan, and the People's
Republic of China. By contrast, transnational corporations (TNCs)

243

were the principal agents of internationalization in the electronics industry. In the consumer electronics industry this process assumed the form of the classic "runaway shop," with major TV producers like RCA and Zenith shutting down their U.S. factories and transferring production to Taiwan, Mexico, and elsewhere. General Electric produces its clockradios in Malaysia and its TV receivers there and in Singapore.

In the case of semiconductors, however, the process of internationalization has until recently not involved the elimination of U.S. jobs. Rather, it has assumed the form of a shift in the relative growth rates of different types of jobs. The internationalization of semiconductor production has been almost exclusively a function of intrafirm specialization. The separability of the "back-end" assembly and testing processes from "front-end" wafer processing has made possible the transfer of relatively labor-intensive assembly operations to "offshore" locations where labor is cheap and relatively abundant. This expansion of offshore assembly activity in the semiconductor industry began in the early 1960s with the introduction of the integrated circuit (IC). With the emergence in the middle to late 1960s of a number of start-up firms committed to the mass production of ICs for sale on the open market the growth in offshore assembly subsidiaries in the third world rapidly accelerated.

Since assembly is the most labor-intensive subprocess of semiconductor production, this trend occasioned a steep decline through the 1970s in the relative importance of production workers in the total U.S. semiconductor labor force. In turn since women make up a sizeable percentage of the semiconductor assembly labor force, the relative decline of production jobs has had implications for their participation in the industry. In short, women's share in domestic U.S. semiconductor employment has remained roughly constant or declined slightly (depending on the base year), in contrast to the steady increase in the ratio of women workers to all employees in manufacturing as a whole (from 28.6 percent in 1972 to 31.9 percent in 1982).

The changing characteristics of the U.S. semiconductor labor force can by no means be explained fully by the shift to offshore assembly from the late 1960s onward. Rather, certain fundamental changes in the international competitive environment as well as in the eco-

244

nomic and technological prerequisites for effective competition in the industry have contributed substantially to its changing labor force characteristics. The bulk of this chapter will be devoted to a description of those changes and to an analysis of their likely implications for women workers in the U.S. microelectronics industry. The chapter attempts as well to explore the likely impacts of the current global restructuring of the industry on women semiconductor assemblers in the third world. It is argued that the transformation presently occurring in the international technological areas and in the broader competitive environment may well have comparable sets of implications for women workers in the U.S. and those in the third world.

The ensuing discussion proceeds in four steps. The next section presents some empirical evidence to illustrate the trends mentioned in the structure of the U.S. semiconductor labor force. There follows an analysis of the major economic and technological factors that serve to explain these observed trends. Next, there is a discussion of the most recent period of industry restructuring, which has not been fully reflected in presently available data. A final section summarizes these trends and provides a tentative assessment of their probable implications for women workers in the United States as well as in third world countries.

EMPIRICAL EVIDENCE ON EMPLOYMENT TRENDS IN THE SEMICONDUCTOR INDUSTRY

The semiconductor industry accounts for a relatively minor share (1.7 percent) of total female employment in manufacturing. In 1982 there were just over one hundred thousand women employed in semiconductor manufacture as compared with a total female workforce in manufacturing of slightly over six million. (The electronics sector as a whole, on the other hand, was a substantial employer of women, accounting for 11.6 percent of female manufacturing employment in 1982, second only to garments.)[2] Yet, despite the small proportion of the female labor force nationwide employed in semiconductors, semiconductor employment is far more significant

245

Table 11.1. **High-Tech Employment by Race, Ethnicity, and Sex: Mass Production Only—Santa Clara County (Percentage)**

	Male-Female		White - Black - Span. - Asian - Indian				
Total	57	43	70	5	12	12	1
Managers (14)	85	15	88	2	4	5	<1
Professionals (20)	82	19	83	2	3	12	<1
Technicians (15)	75	25	71	4	10	15	<1
Sales workers (2)	67	33	91	2	3	3	<1
Clerical (15)	19	81	77	6	10	6	<1
Craft workers (7)	56	44	63	6	17	14	1
Operatives (24)	31	69	49	9	23	19	1
Laborers (2)	38	61	41	8	34	17	1
Service workers (1)	86	14	49	12	26	13	1

SOURCE: Lenny Siegel and Herb Borock, Pacific Studies Center, "Background Report on Silicon Valley," prepared for the U.S. Commission on Civil Rights (Mountain View, California) September 1982.

NOTE: This and subsequent tables covering mass production high-tech industries include SIC codes 357, 366, 367, 381, 382, and 383. Due to reporting peculiarities, the Santa Clara County figures may include 2 percent from SIC 376 (guided missiles and space vehicles). Lockheed, the large 376 company in the area, actually files its EEOC data under SIC 739 as a research and development firm.

a share of total female employment in those regions and localities where the industry happens to be heavily concentrated. These areas include primarily Santa Clara County, California, (otherwise known as Silicon Valley), San Diego County in southern California, and parts of Arizona, Oregon, and Texas. In Silicon Valley, for example, in early 1983 electronics firms—principally semiconductor manufacturers and their suppliers—employed some ninety thousand people, approximately one out of every three local workers. Of all Silicon Valley high-tech workers, 43 percent are women, while 69 percent of operatives are women (see Table 11.1).

Additionally, the semiconductor and related industries are a particularly important employment source for minority women, most especially for recent immigrants. In the electronics factories of Silicon Valley, a significant percentage of the production workers are of Hispanic or Asian origin (23 percent and 19 percent of operatives respectively). The same holds true of semiconductor factories located in the Southwest and in Texas, with the Hispanic portion of the labor force relatively more significant in those locations. A recent study conducted by the Pacific Studies Center for the U.S. Civil Rights Commission shows two areas of concentration of Asian workers within the electronics labor force in the United States (Pacific Studies Center, 1982). On the one hand, there is a heavy concentration of Asian women—principally Filipino, Indochinese, and Korean —in low-paid semi-skilled production jobs. On the other, there is a concentration of well-paid Asian and Asian/American males— mostly Chinese, Japanese, and Korean—filling skilled engineering and technical jobs.

More significant than absolute numbers of women employed in the industry has been the growth of female employment in the industry over time. (See Table 11.2). Between 1972 and 1982, for example, when total female employment in manufacturing grew by less than one percent per year, female employment in the semicon-

Table 11.2. **Employment Trends in the U.S. Semiconductor Industry, 1967–1982 (thousands)**

	Total employment (1)	Female employment (2)	(2) as % of (1)	Prod. worker employment (4)	(4) as % of (1)
1967	85.4			57.9	68.0
1968	87.4			60.5	69.0
1969	98.8			69.3	70.0
1970	88.5			60.3	68.0
1971	74.7			45.5	61.0
1972	115.2	54.8	47.6	58.5	50.8
1973	139.9	70.3	50.3	73.8	52.8
1974	148.3	73.5	49.6	76.1	51.3
1975	121.7	55.6	45.7	56.4	46.3
1976	129.8	61.6	47.5	61.5	47.4
1977	147.5	70.5	47.8	69.6	47.2
1978	168.9	81.3	48.1	79.2	46.9
1979	201.1	95.9	47.7	94.3	46.9
1980	223.4	105.8	47.4	99.1	44.4
1981	223.7	102.6	45.9	91.9	41.1
1982	226.7	103.5	45.7	90.0	39.7

SOURCES: 1967–1971: U.S. Department of Commerce (1979); 1972–1976: *Predicasts' Basebook,* 1982 Edition; 1977–1982: U.S. Department of Labor, Bureau of Labor Statistics, Employment and Earnings Supplement.
NOTE: The 1967–1971 data on total employment in semiconductors do not appear to be comparable with those for the later period; hence, the break in the table.

ductor industry increased by 6.6 percent annually. While female employment grew more slowly than total semiconductor employment during this period, it rose slightly more rapidly than production worker employment. This presumably reflects the fact that while female production jobs were affected by the shift of assembly offshore and by the automation of various phases of the production process, the expansion of secretarial and clerical jobs partially offset the effects of declining growth in predominantly female production jobs.

The impact of offshore expansion on the composition of the domestic labor force is seen most clearly from the relative growth rates of total employees and production workers in the semiconductor industry over the last two decades. The rapid overseas expansion of IC assembly by U.S. semiconductor firms began around 1967, though a few firms had set up offshore assembly plants before that year. From 1960 to 1967, total semiconductor employment rose by 7.2 percent annually, while production jobs increased by 6.5 percent per year. From 1967 to 1982, by contrast, while overall employment continued to grow at a 7.2 percent annual rate, production job growth slowed to only 3.2 percent a year. As a result, the ratio of production workers to all semiconductor employees has declined over time, from .68 in 1967 to only .40 by 1982. While production jobs declined relative to all manufacturing jobs during the last decade, the decline in the semiconductor industry has been considerably steeper than that for all manufacturing.

The trend to offshore assembly and later testing of ICs can explain only part of this decline. Additionally, the technology-intensive nature of the industry has been an important contributory factor. Over time the demand for skilled scientists, engineers, programmers, and technicians has outpaced the demand for semi-skilled production workers. Whereas in 1964 technical personnel accounted for 16 percent of the semiconductor industry labor force, by 1971 they accounted for 27 percent (U.S. Department of Commerce, 1979). In 1980 the figure stood at 39 percent for all high-tech industries, including the 11 percent of the labor force who were managers.

Data are difficult to obtain on changes in the degree of capital intensity of the U.S. semiconductor industry over time. Yet, the available evidence suggests that rising capital intensity may also have contributed in recent years to the slow rate of growth of production worker employment. From 1970 to 1972, net expenditures on plant and equipment amounted to $2,215.5 per production worker; between 1973 and 1976 net capital expenditures averaged $5,448.1 per worker; from 1977 to 1980 annual net investment totaled $10,162.9 per production worker (Predicasts' *Basebook,* 1982). Clearly, data on capital stock per worker would be a more accurate measure than new capital expenditures, since a high value for the latter might reflect a high rate of obsolescence for existing plants and equipment. Such data, however, were not available to this author at the time of writing.

In the first seven years of rapid overseas expansion from 1967 to 1974 offshore employment grew at an average annual rate of 35.8 percent, while domestic employment rose at an annual rate of 6.6 percent (U.S. Department of Commerce, 1979). Offshore employment continued to outpace domestic employment growth in the next several years, with the result that by 1978 the number of persons employed in producing semiconductors in foreign subsidiaries of U.S. firms was almost exactly equal to the number employed domestically in such production (89,300)[3] (U.S. International Trade Commission, 1979). More recent trends in offshore employment are not known with any certainty, but one estimate puts the total employment for offshore assembly plants as of 1982 at roughly 180,000, three-quarters of domestic semiconductor employment. Of that total, more than 80 percent were production workers; the overwhelming majority, women (U.S. Congress, OTA, 1983).

THE INCORPORATION OF CERTAIN THIRD WORLD COUNTRIES WITHIN THE INTERNATIONAL SEMICONDUCTOR INDUSTRY DIVISION OF LABOR

The first offshore assembly plant for integrated circuits was established by Fairchild Camera and Instrument (one of the first to mass produce ICs) in Hong Kong in 1962. That initial move was followed by every major IC manufacturer in the United States (see Table 11.3 for a listing of the offshore investments of the major U.S.-based semiconductor firms). As previously noted, the principal mo-

Table 11.3. **Offshore Assembly Subsidiaries of Major United States Semiconductor Transnational Corporations**

Parent company	Name of subsidiary, if different	Year established	Country	Current employment
Texas Instruments			Taiwan	
		1969	Singapore	
			Curaçao	
		1972	Malaysia	
		1980	Philippines	3,000 (est.)
			El Salvador	1,000
Motorola		1967	Rep. of Korea	3,600 (1982)
		1972	Mexico	
		1973	Malaysia	8,000 (1982)
		1979	Philippines	1,706 (1979)
		1984	Taiwan	
National Semiconductor			Hong Kong	
		1969	Singapore	8,000 (1980)
		1972	Malaysia	8,000 (1980)
		1973	Thailand	5,000 (1979)
		1974	Indonesia	
		1976	Philippines	3,000 (1980)
Intel		1973	Malaysia	
		1974	Philippines	1,500 (1980)
		1977	Barbados	
		1982	Mexico	
Fairchild		1962	Hong Kong	
		1966	Rep. of Korea	4,300 (1980)
		1968	Singapore	
		1974	Indonesia	5,000
		1980	Philippines	3,000
			Brazil	
			Mexico	
Signetics		1966	Rep. of Korea	2,500 (1982)
		1974	Thailand	1,500 (1979)
		1978	Philippines	1,386 (1979)[a]
Mostek		1973	Malaysia	
		1982	Malaysia	1,200
AMD		1972	Malaysia	
		1976	Philippines	2,459 (1979)[a]
		1984	Thailand	

Type of device assembled	Testing (Yes/No)	Annual capacity (mill.)	Square footage	Estimated investment ($ mill.)	Comments
IC, d	Yes				Wafer fab planned plant closed
	Yes				
	Yes				
IC, d				4.95	
d					
IC, d					
IC, d		227.5			
IC					
	Yes				
	Yes				
	Yes				
IC, d	Yes	364			
IC					
IC	Yes	72	160,000		
IC	Yes		123,000		Progressive automation of assembly lines underway
IC	Yes	65	109,000		
IC			60,000		
IC				20	Under construction
IC, opto					
IC, d, opto			82,000	4.6	
IC	Yes				Large number of Beta bonding machines
IC		450	114,000	12	
IC, d	Yes		100,000		
			12,000		
IC, d			28,500		
IC				3.6	
IC	Yes	200			
IC	Yes	63			Plant closed
IC					
		16.3			
IC	Yes		111,000		
IC	Yes	200	81,000		

Table 11.3. *(continued)*

Parent company	Name of subsidiary, if different	Year established	Country	Current employment
RCA		1974	Malaysia	
		1975	Brazil	
			Taiwan	
GI Micro-electronics		1971	Taiwan	
		1979	Malaysia	3,000
Harris Corporation		1974	Malaysia	
			Philippines	
			Sri Lanka	
AMI	Korean Microsystems	1970	Rep. of Korea	1,200 (1982)
		1982	Philippines	600 (1982)

tive for such investments was the attempt to cut labor costs by performing the labor-intensive assembly operations in low-wage countries. The initial wave of overseas investments by U.S. semiconductor firms flowed into Hong Kong, South Korea, Singapore, Taiwan, and Mexico. With rising labor costs and worsening labor scarcities in some of those locations, firms expanded into new countries, first Malaysia, then the Philippines and, more recently, Thailand. Thailand's industry is still relatively small as compared with those in Malaysia, the Philippines, and Singapore, the three countries that have come to dominate the offshore assembly business of U.S. semiconductor firms. (See Table 11.4 for data on U.S. semiconductor imports from offshore locations.)

The economics of the integrated circuit business explain in large measure the rationale for offshore assembly. The introduction of techniques for mass producing large numbers of electronic components on a single chip of silicon led to dramatic savings in the unit cost of computing power. A mass market for computer chips (ICs) rapidly developed as such costs fell exponentially. Declining costs were matched by dramatic price reductions, as each of the growing number of IC manufacturers sought to increase the volume of its shipments as rapidly as possible to realize the substantial learning

Type of device assembled	Testing (Yes/No)	Annual capacity (mill.)	Square footage	Estimated investment ($ mill.)	Comments
IC, d					
d					Includes wafer fab
opto					
IC					
IC					Planned
				5.6	Planned
IC					Joint venture in wafer fab
IC	Yes			0.53	

SOURCE: United Nations Center on Transnational Corporations.
aFull capacity employment.

economies and yield improvements that occur in the wafer fabrication process with large-scale production. As costs fell with cumulative output in front-end processing, the costs of assembly came increasingly to pose a barrier to further price reductions. In order to economize, therefore, on assembly costs, U.S. firms began to shift assembly offshore.

Table 11.4A. **Semiconductors and Parts: U.S. Imports for Consumption by Principal Sources, 1977–81 (In thousands of dollars)**

Source	1977	1978	1979	1980	1981
Malaysia	286,297	465,560	591,257	817,195	880,284
Singapore	257,379	302,026	414,280	564,204	593,075
Phil R	71,476	126,515	204,811	357,039	470,724
Japan	86,925	136,788	246,270	405,965	397,598
Kor Rep	223,494	224,676	255,898	238,014	237,649
Canada	7,075	11,490	74,421	127,003	159,333
Mexico	78,423	83,486	108,873	120,945	148,889
China t	93,346	91,601	96,548	137,833	131,327
All other	253,094	333,344	434,945	557,510	563,148
Total	1,357,509	1,775,487	2,427,302	3,325,709	3,582,026

SOURCE: Compiled from official statistics of the U.S. Department of Commerce.

253

Table 11.4B.   **Discrete Semiconductors and Parts: U.S. Imports for Consumption by Principal Sources, 1977–81 (In thousands of dollars)**

Source	1977	1978	1979	1980	1981
Mexico	34,146	39,680	60,455	69,169	84,173
Malaysia	31,811	43,550	44,634	65,482	75,254
Japan	39,821	45,010	53,546	59,175	67,794
Hong Kong	43,341	42,111	49,252	50,835	52,909
Kor Rep	51,750	40,283	50,156	37,648	32,378
Singapore	23,405	29,279	26,649	25,543	28,770
China t	10,210	14,466	20,967	17,237	26,004
Fr Germ	8,432	11,111	19,690	23,322	21,651
All other	48,003	63,596	71,089	80,293	94,804
Total	290,118	329,086	396,437	428,704	483,735

SOURCE: Compiled from official statistics of the U.S. Department of Commerce.

Table 11.4C.   **Integrated Circuits and Parts: U.S. Imports for Consumption by Principal Sources, 1977–81 (In thousands of dollars)**

Source	1977	1978	1979	1980	1981
Malaysia	255,286	422,010	546,623	751,714	804,786
Singapore	233,974	272,748	387,631	538,662	564,296
Phil R	68,429	123,175	200,785	344,554	448,088
Japan	47,104	91,778	192,724	346,790	321,330
Kor Rep	171,745	184,393	205,742	200,365	203,656
Canada	3,789	4,714	66,863	119,285	149,654
Thailand	20,832	54,966	50,587	83,374	108,253
China t	83,136	77,135	75,581	120,596	104,841
All other	183,096	215,483	304,330	391,666	376,556
Total	1,067,391	1,446,400	2,030,865	2,897,005	3,081,462

SOURCE: Compiled from official statistics of the U.S. Department of Commerce.

An alternative not pursued vigorously at the time by U.S. firms was assembly automation. The reason for this may have been that, given the costs of automated assembly equipment, it was not perceived as cost effective. Japanese firms, however, tended to adopt more automated assembly techniques from the outset. While the reasons for this preference are not clear, it may have had to do with the structure of the Japanese semiconductor industry as well as with the captive nature of the Japanese semiconductor market. With respect to the former, Japanese semiconductor manufacturers are vertically integrated into large, diversified electronics giants, which may have been able to support an automation program more readily than the U.S. merchant IC houses. The performance of employment in the Japanese electronics industry over the last two decades reflects to a considerable degree the effects of progressive assembly automation, not only in semiconductors but in other electronic products as well. After 1970, for instance, employment within the fifteen largest Japanese electronics firms leveled off, and from 1973 on, employment actually began a steady decline (see Figure 11.1). At the same time, sales of Japanese electronics products enjoyed unprecedented growth. How much of the decline in employment, if any, occurred within the semiconductor sector, and, in particular, within semiconductor assembly, cannot be ascertained from the data. Nevertheless, the figures are suggestive, since, as will be discussed below, U.S. semiconductor manufacturers are under growing pressure to imitate the automated assembly techniques adopted first by the Japanese.

To an extent the Japanese semiconductor TNCs have followed the lead of U.S. firms in establishing foreign assembly subsidiaries in

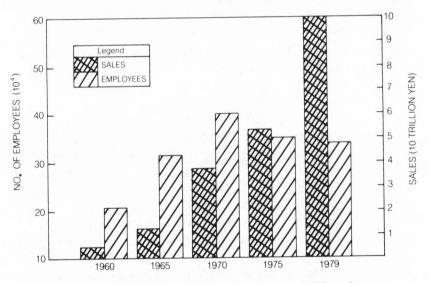

Figure 11.1. Employment and Sales Trends in Japan's Fifteen Largest Electronics Firms
SOURCE: Nikkei Electronics, Jan. 7, 1980

255

recent years. The Japanese subsidiaries, however, tend to be of a somewhat different character than their U.S. counterparts. Frequently they are integrated with the foreign consumer electronics assembly operations of the parent company. Moreover, the Japanese firms tend to focus their foreign assembly activities more heavily toward the major markets they seek to penetrate. Historically, their foreign assembly operations have been more highly automated than those of U.S. firms as well.

Since the mid-1970s, U.S. semiconductor firms have invested heavily in assembly automation within their offshore plants. The move toward higher levels of assembly automation has been a consequence of several factors. First, the increasing complexity of ICs, as the technology has moved from small-scale integration through medium-scale integration to large-scale integration and now very-large-scale integration (VLSI) has made manual assembly more time-consuming as well as more difficult. The likelihood of error in manual assembly has increased with chip complexity at the same time that customer tolerance of defective devices is diminishing. Manual asssembly also contains a relatively high risk of damage during handling or of contamination. The more valuable the chips are when they leave the front-end wafer processing—and the value added in wafer processing has been increasing with VLSI—the more costly is any damage to the chips sustained during assembly. Assembly automation offers the advantages of (1) minimizing operator contact with the chips and (2) enhancing process control and defect detection. With respect to the latter, defects tend to occur randomly with manual assembly, whereas with automated equipment they tend to be serially correlated. Furthermore, automation greatly reduces the amount of operator time required to assemble an IC of given complexity into a given package type. In view of the rather steep increase in wage costs in many offshore assembly locations in recent years, the time element is particularly important. Nevertheless, considerations of quality control rather than cost per se would appear to provide the principal motivation for increased levels of assembly automation.

Thus far, assembly automation has not meant the wholesale transfer of semiconductor assembly activity back from the third

256

Table 11.5.   **Employment of U.S. Semiconductor Firms in Malaysia,
by Category**

Year	Total employees	Semi-skilled employees		Technical, supervisory, and managerial employees	
		#	% of total	#	% of total
1981	34,900	27,800	79.7	7,100	20.3
1982	36,300	28,700	79.1	7,600	20.9
1983	39,900	31,300	78.4	8,600	21.6
1984	42,300	32,600	77.1	9,700	22.9

SOURCE: Electronics Industry Segment, American Business Council *U.S. Based Semi-Conductor Companies Operations and Futures Development in Malaysia*, Malaysia, December 1984.

world to the advanced capitalist countries. It has, however, resulted in a change in the skill composition of the labor forces in offshore assembly plants. The introduction of automated assembly equipment has resulted in the deskilling of such operations as wire bonding. Whereas previously this operation had required manual skills that could take several months to perfect, with microprocessor-controlled pattern recognition systems, the operator does not utilize her hands any longer, except intermittently when the machine malfunctions. As a result, little training is required. At the same time, it has increased the need for line maintenance technicians to keep the automated equipment in working order, since uptime is crucial to the economic utilization of that equipment. Since the latter tend to be predominantly male, one would expect the sex composition of the offshore assembly labor force to have shifted over time, although no statistics are available on trends in that composition. Some data from Malaysia on employment in U.S.-owned semiconductor plants confirm the trend toward a higher proportion of skilled labor in total employment (see Table 11.5). Meanwhile, the growth rate in employment for semi-skilled assembly operators is apt to slow markedly as a result of widespread automation. A single assembly operator using a fully automated wire bonder fitted with a pattern recognition system can operate as many as four machines simultaneously, each machine having a productivity five times greater than that of manual assembly. Thus, with higher levels of automation, fewer workers will be needed for a given assembly capacity.

Because of the fact that automated assembly is likely to be economically justifiable only for ICs assembled in large lots so that the equipment can be operated virtually nonstop, automation may well result in a consolidation by semiconductor TNCs of their offshore operations. It is conceivable that in the future they will operate fewer larger-scale assembly facilities in a smaller number of countries. Moreover, given the higher levels of capital investment involved in automated assembly plants, the TNCs are likely to weigh political risk factors more heavily in deciding where to maintain their offshore assembly plants. Already a major U.S.-based (but Dutch-owned) semiconductor TNC, Signetics, has phased out one of its three offshore assembly plants—the one in the Philippines—consolidating the equipment employed at that plant within its South Korean and Thai operations. The reason cited for the shutdown was that assembly automation rendered the Philippine plant superfluous. It was widely understood that labor strife was a principal consideration behind the closure. More recently, National Semiconductor closed down one of its three plants in Malaysia, allegedly because the facility was too small to operate efficiently on an integrated basis, i.e., with assembly, testing, and direct shipping consolidated within a single facility.[4] It is not yet certain whether these two are isolated instances or represent the beginning of a trend.

It remains to be explained why automation has not been accompanied by the wholesale transfer of TNC assembly operations back to the advanced capitalist countries. There are several reasons. First, such firms have substantial sunken investments in offshore assembly facilities that they are not inclined simply to write off before their useful life has expired. As long as they are able to run those facilities at a profit, they are likely to do so. Moreover, there is no evidence that U.S. TNCs are simply running their existing plants into the ground, "milking" them for the last dollar of profit they can yield before discarding them. Rather, there has been considerable upgrading of existing facilities, although some capital investment projects have been postponed during the current industry slump.

Additionally, while the costs of unskilled labor are a diminishing share of overall manufacturing costs, the costs of skilled labor are an increasing share. Moreover, certain more economically advanced third world countries have fairly abundant supplies of engineering, technician, and computer programming graduates eager to work at wages a small fraction of what comparable workers would be paid in the United States. Even more importantly, there exist already in locations like Malaysia, Singapore, and the Philippines, large pools of workers skilled and experienced in operating semiconductor assembly operations. Since mass assembly has been all but phased out of the United States, no comparable skills can be found in the U.S. workforce any longer. Thus, the transfer of assembly back onshore would be a major technical risk, at least in the near future.

Furthermore, the large and growing number of consumer electronics, minicomputer and microcomputer, telecomunications equipment, and computer peripheral manufacturers that are manufacturing or assembling their products in Asia's newly industrializing countries (or NICs)—Hong Kong, Republic of Korea, Singapore, and Taiwan—provides a growing market for the semiconductor assembly plants' output. For this reason, many of the semiconductor TNCs have integrated their back-end operations like final test, mark and pack, inventory, and shipping with their Asian assembly operations so as to be able to ship directly from their Asian plants to the growing "Asian" semiconductor market. In this respect as well U.S. semiconductor firms are coming to resemble more closely their Japanese counterparts, which have for some time practiced a degree of vertical integration within their foreign subsidiaries; the difference has been that in the latter case, the integration has occurred within firms, while in the former case, it is generally occurring across firms (exceptions being AT&T, Hewlett-Packard, and Texas Instruments, which assemble both components and end products in Asia).

A final reason why semiconductor assembly is not likely to return completely to the advanced capitalist countries is that for certain types of devices that are produced in relatively small batches, the economics of assembly may not justify complete automation. To the extent that firms need to continue to produce such devices to fill out their product lines, they may choose to continue assembling them with semiautomatic or manual techniques in offshore assembly plants. In other instances, assembly continues to be relatively labor-intensive because of technical difficulties in automating the assembly of particular package types (e.g., hermetic packages). Relatively low volume is also a deterrent to the full automation of hermetic assembly. In general, onshore assembly is most likely to occur for those devices whose transport costs from offshore assembly plants are relatively high (i.e., those assembled into bulky, heavy packages) and those requiring quick "turnaround" times (the time from order to delivery).

A final consideration is that a number of the electronic equipment manufacturers in the Asian NICs are indigenously owned firms that have integrated backward into semiconductor manufacture. They are seeking to become major world producers of certain types of semiconductor devices, in particular, memory products. Assuming that their efforts succeed, they should provide growing employment in the semiconductor sector in the future. As part of their semiconductor strategies, several of those electronics firms (especially those from South Korea) have begun to invest in the Silicon Valley area, principally as a method of acquiring access to technology and to highly skilled scientists, circuit designers, engineers and software specialists, for use in the development of their own product and process capabilities. In this respect they resemble the Western European firms, which went on a buying spree in the United States in the mid-1970s, acquiring equity stakes in a number of independent U.S. semiconductor firms. In other respects, however, the strategies of the new Asian electronics giants resemble more closely those of their Japanese counterparts. In consumer electronics—like black-and-white TVs, radios, and cassette recorders—they have initially succeeded in penetrating the United States and other developed countries' markets with their exports. Already a few of the large firms (e.g., the Korean Gold Star and the Taiwanese Sampo and Tatung) have invested directly in manufacturing facilities in the United States. To the extent that they replicate their consumer electronics success in semiconductors, they may eventually decide to establish point-of-sale assembly facilities in the United States and other major markets, as the Japanese semiconductor firms have done in recent years.

SHIFTING INVESTMENT PATTERNS AND PATTERNS OF INTERNATIONAL COMPETITIVENESS

Virtually every major Japanese semiconductor TNC has established a foreign subsidiary in either the Western European or the U.S. market or both. In the majority of cases, the subsidiaries were for assembly rather than for complete manufacture of the ICs. The high levels of assembly automation in those plants have meant relatively little employment generation. Their principal motivation was to allay increasing trade frictions with the United States over the growing Japanese semiconductor trade surplus (approximately $200 million in 1980) and the rising protectionist sentiments within the U.S. industry. Both U.S. and Japanese firms have been investing heavily in the EEC market (the third largest), which has been growing rapidly, especially the industrial and telecommunications segments. Indigenous producers, moreover, have in many instances suffered eroding market positions in the face of U.S. and Japanese competition. The bulk of new investments by both Japanese and U.S. semiconductor firms in Western Europe have occurred in Ireland and Scotland, which can export duty-free to the EEC market, and which at the same time have relatively abundant supplies of low-paid engineering, technical, design, and production labor. (Spain has also attracted sizeable investments in recent years.) Additionally, a growing number of U.S. and Japanese electronic equipment manufacturers have been establishing production facilities in those locations, not only providing a ready market for the IC plants' output but also fostering the development of a local infrastructure to support and service electronics-related industries in general. (Most recently, Digital Equipment Corporation [U.S.] has decided to build a new wafer processing plant in Scotland, part of whose output will be used in DEC minicomputers also being made in the U.K.)[5]

In general, semiconductor TNCs have established more extensive international linkages in recent years, designed to counter the effects of intensifying competition and the escalating costs of research and development and capital equipment. Cross licensing, technology exchange agreements, and second sourcing arrangements have proliferated with little regard for the nationality of the technology partner. There continues to be an inherent tension in such cooperation arrangements among competitors, but at the same time, semiconductor firms perceive a mutual advantage to be derived from economizing on scarce research and development personnel and financial capital for investment in even more costly processing equipment. Another source of friction is the reluctance on the part of some developed country governments or private sector firms to allow foreign firms to participate fully in joint research and development projects at the national level.

The predominant trend in recent years has been toward greater interpenetration by semiconductor TNCs in one another's home markets, combined with greater integration of foreign semiconductor operations with electronic equipment manufacture. While TNCs have not pulled back from the third world, new investments in off-shore assembly subsidiaries have slowed. In the future there may well be a consolidation of offshore operations within a smaller number of more politically stable and more technologically advanced third world countries. It is in those countries where semiconductors as well as other electronics TNCs are apt to find the most favorable conditions for investment, because of rising levels of automation and the increased demand for skilled technical and engineeering labor that they generate. Other third world countries have little prospect of riding a boom in offshore assembly comparable to the one that was ridden by countries like Malaysia and the Philippines in the 1970s and early 1980s. With advances in chip technology and process technology, the emphasis in overseas investment by semiconductor TNCs has shifted away from a singleminded pursuit of cheap, unskilled assembly labor.

IMPLICATIONS OF GLOBAL RESTRUCTURING FOR WOMEN WORKERS IN THE UNITED STATES AND THE THIRD WORLD

The current period of global restructuring in the semiconductor industry differs in certain important respects from that which occurred in the 1960s and early 1970s. In that earlier period U.S.-based semiconductor firms were the uncontested technological leaders, and competition among U.S. firms themselves tended to dominate their strategic planning. Offshore production became the most widely employed method of reducing production costs. Assembly methods during this period remained highly labor-intensive, relying on the "manual dexterity" of low-paid Asian and, to a lesser extent, Latin American women. The rapid expansion of offshore assembly by U.S. semiconductor firms, while it generally did not occur at the expense of already existing jobs in the United States, clearly meant a slower rate of production employment growth here. Since minority women were heavily represented in such jobs in the U.S. industry, the shift to offshore assembly had a significant impact on their prospects for employment.[6]

By the middle to late 1970s the international competitive and technological conditions facing the U.S. industry had changed considerably. Perhaps the single most significant development competitively was the emergence of the Japanese industry as a major challenger to U.S. dominance of world markets. The significant inroads made by Japanese exports into the U.S. memory chip market caused a defensive reaction by U.S. manufacturers, who moved increasingly in the direction of the more automated production methods employed by the Japanese firms. At the same time, changes in product technology were accelerating the rate of diffusion of automated techniques in design, front-end wafer processing, assembly, and testing. In particular, increasing levels of circuit integration required increasingly sophisticated capital equipment and ever stricter process and quality control procedures to maintain high production yields. The general trend in recent years, therefore, has been to rely more heavily on automated equipment (a) to minimize operator contact with wafers and chips, thereby reducing the likelihood of damage or contamination; (b) to achieve better process control and defect detection; (c) to boost productivity. Automation has been diffused widely throughout the offshore assembly operations of the semiconductor TNCs, with a resultant dramatic reduction in the number of operators needed to assemble a given volume of chips. Skill levels of assemblers have been downgraded, while demand has increased for skilled technicians and engineers. While some companies have begun to retrain women workers to perform the new tasks required by automated assembly, the sex composition of the offshore assembly labor forces is apt to shift perceptibly in the direction of male workers. While those women workers already employed may be reabsorbed through the expansion of capacity, the prospects for future growth in female production worker employment in such facilities seem quite limited. Moreover, it is possible that, at least for the most complex VLSI memory and microprocessor chips, the bulk of future assembly capacity will be added in the advanced industrialized countries rather than in third world countries. Employment may expand for third world women workers in certain countries like Hong Kong, Singapore, South Korea, and Taiwan in other areas of electronics production, but those areas are also being affected by increased automation. Those countries in any case are already plagued by relative labor shortages and thus employment generation is not a pressing concern, at least for unskilled categories of workers. For those countries, however, with large surpluses of unskilled labor that had planned to capitalize on the next offshore electronics assembly boom, that boom may never materialize.

The employment situation facing women workers in the semiconductor industries of developed countries may be only marginally brighter than that for women workers in third world countries. The growth in semiconductor employment in the United States has occurred principally in the predominantly male technical occupations—scientists, engineers, circuit designers, production technicians, and so forth. While some growth occurred in female employment over this period, much of the increment in that employment was in administrative occupations—principally secretarial and clerical—which tend to be filled primarily by nonminority women. Thus, while the changes in the skill requirements and sexual composition of the microelectronics labor force have been generally detrimental to women workers, minority women are the segment of the semiconductor labor force most vulnerable to the effects of technological innovations occurring in the production process. (Nonminority office workers within the electronics companies as well as within a broad spectrum of other industries may of course be affected by the introduction of office automation systems based on the components produced in the semiconductor industry.) It would clearly be premature

264

to make any predictions regarding the net effect on female employment within the U.S. semiconductor industry of the restructuring process underway at present. Much depends on the growth of overall demand for semiconductors, which is expected to remain particularly strong, with periodic slumps, for at least the next decade. One can only generalize confidently that growth in production levels of workers, and, in particular female production workers, is not likely to return to historic levels. This is very different from predicting a net reduction in the numbers of production workers and of women workers as a group, something that has already occurred for example in the radio and TV manufacturing sectors of the U.S. electronics industry. One area of electronics production in which female employment is growing rapidly is the manufacture of electronic computing equipment (from 65,400 in 1976 to 151,300 in 1982). Overall female employment in electronics has increased by roughly half in the last decade.

This chapter has had the objectives of tracing some of the critical changes in the technological and international competitive environment of a single industry that has been characterized by a largely female production labor force; to analyze the impact those changes have had on women working for semiconductor firms both in the United States and in the third world; to highlight the similarities in the ways those changes have affected women workers in both locations; and to indicate why third world women workers in the U.S. semiconductor industry have cause for greatest concern about the consequences of technological changes and structural transformation for their work lives.

Notes

1. June Nash and Maria Patricia Fernández-Kelly, eds., *Women, Men and the International Division of Labor* (New York: State University of New York Press, 1983.)

2. Electronics and garments combined accounted for roughly one-third of total female employment in manufacturing. (International Labor Organization, *Yearbook of Labour Statistics,* Washington, D.C. 1982).

3. This figure is generally regarded to be an underestimate of the magnitude of offshore employment in 1978.

4. *The Asian Wall Street Journal,* 26 June 1985.

5. *Financial Times,* 1 August 1985.

6. At the same time, female employment in the garment industry, a sector traditionally employing large numbers of third world immigrant women, stagnated after 1966, then began to decline.

Reference List

Electronic Industries Association. 1982. *Electronic market databook 1982.* Washington, D.C.

Integrated Circuit Engineering Corporation. 1982. *Status 1982: A report on the integrated circuit industry.* Scottsdale, Arizona.

Nash, June, and Maria Patricia Fernández-Kelly, eds. 1983. *Women, men and the international division of labor.* Albany: State University of New York Press.

O'Connor David C. 1983. Changing patterns of international production in the semiconductor industry: The role of transnational corporations. Paper presented at Conference on Microelectronics in Transition, University of California-Santa Cruz. 12–15 May.

Pacific Studies Center. 1982. Background report on Silicon Valley. Prepared for the U.S. Commission on Civil Rights. (September), Mountain View, California.

Predicasts' Basebook. 1982 edition.

Snow, Robert T. 1980. The new international division of labor and the U.S. workforce: The case of the electronics industry. Working Papers of the East-West Cultural Learning Institute. East-West Center. Honolulu, Hawaii.

United Nations Center on Transnational Corporations. *Transnational corporations in the international semiconductor industry.* ST/CTC/39— forthcoming (available in draft form). New York: United Nations.

United Nations International Labor Organization. 1982. *Yearbook of labour statistics.* New York: United Nations.

United States Congress. Office of Technology Assessment. 1983. *International competitiveness in electronics.* Washington, D.C.: GPO.

United States Department of Labor. 1982. 1983. Bureau of Labor Statistics. *Supplement to employment and earnings.* Revised Establishment Data. Washington, D.C.: GPO.

United States Department of Commerce. 1979. Industry and Trade Administration. *A report on the U.S. semiconductor industry.* September. Washington, D.C.: GPO.

United States International Trade Commission. 1979. *Competitive factors influencing world trade in integrated circuits.* USITC Publications 1013. November. Washington, D.C.: GPO.

United States International Trade Commission. 1982. Summary of trade and tariff information: Semiconductors. USITC Publication 841. Control No. 6-5-22. July. Washington, D.C.: GPO.

PART IV

Institutional Responses
and Initiatives

The Impact of Federal Policy Change on Low-Income Working Women

Rosemary C. Sarri

The standard of living of low-income families has been declining for many years due to the effects of high and persistent unemployment, stagnating wages, and reduced work benefits. This change has paralleled the rise of the numbers of women who have become single parents and the increased participation of women in the labor force. As of September 1985, the Bureau of Labor Statistics reported that 54.5 percent of all women were working outside the home, but among women with children six to seventeen years 70 percent were in the labor force and 60 percent of those with children under three years were in the labor force (U.S. Department of Labor, 1985). It is probable that these rates of participation were accelerated by federal policy changes in 1981, particularly for low-income working women. This paper examines the impact of selected aspects of these changes implemented under the Omnibus Budget Reconciliation Act of 1981 (OBRA) on certain working women who were single parents and their children. These were families receiving supplementary assistance because the women's earnings were below the state level for eligibility to receive Aid to Families with Dependent Children (AFDC) prior to the passage of this legislation.

FEDERAL AFDC POLICY CHANGES

In 1981 at the request of the Reagan administration the Congress passed and the president signed into law legislation that terminated benefits for AFDC recipients who were working. These benefits included cash supplements, Food Stamps, Medicaid insurance, and eligibility for numerous other programs in childcare, housing, emergency assistance, and so forth. In this study we have examined the impact of provisions in the law that restricted eligibility and benefits for the working poor. These included: (1) establishing a cap on eligibility for gross income at 150 percent of the state need standard; (2) eliminating the earned income disregard after four months; (3) creating a cap on childcare and other work-related expenses; (4) counting in advance earned income tax credit and income of all minor children; and, (5) requiring that all presumed or actual stepfathers' income be included in determining eligibility and benefits for all minor children.[1]

From the several evaluations that have been made of the impact of OBRA on working welfare women and their children it is quite clear that the federal government and many state governments have realized a savings in social welfare expenditures from the programs affected, despite the fact that AFDC is a minuscule program when compared with Social Security benefits for retirees. Between 1981 and 1984 programs serving needy families sustained 30 percent of all budget cuts although they constitute less than 10 percent of all federal expenditures (U.S. Congress, 1985a; 1983:78–79). The General Accounting Office estimated that as of June 1984, the monthly caseload had been dropped by 442,000 cases or 1.3 million individuals (of whom 70 percent were minor children) with savings of nearly $100 million per month, or approximately 6 billion over five years (U.S. General Accounting Office, 1985:115–124).

As a result of these program cuts, thousands of families were plunged into poverty in 1982 in the midst of one of the most serious economic recessions experienced in the United States. The number of people living in poverty grew by nine million—an increase of 35 percent in four years. Research by congressional committees indicates that over 550,000 persons fell into poverty because of the OBRA policies and that these persons were disproportionately single-parent females and their children (U.S. Congress, 1983:83–85, 1985b). Despite the economic recovery that occurred in 1984–85, this population of working poor women and children has remained in poverty. Poverty statistics in 1985 indicate that the poverty rate declined for white males and for two-parent families but not for minorities or for female single parents with children. In fact, in 1984, the gap widened between high- and low-income families (U.S. Department of Commerce, 1985).

Why, then, was this population of working single parents and their children targeted for benefit reductions? Resistance to welfare support for low-income women and children is longstanding in the United States. Pearce points out that differentiating the "deserving" from the "undeserving" poor was the most consistent theme of the many policy and program changes that occurred in federal and state legislation in this century (Pearce, 1982). Moreover, the Reagan administration espoused philosophies that were antithetical to support for these families.

The writings of Martin Anderson and George Gilder provided the ideological underpinnings for the changes that were implemented in the OBRA legislation.[2] Anderson argued that poverty in the United States had been virtually eliminated and that existing social programs were more than adequate for those truly in need—that the best welfare reform was work because guaranteed income would only reduce work efforts (1978:87–132). In turn, Gilder asserted that working-age, ablebodied poor people (especially women) should be weaned away from the welfare programs, because of the "moral hazard of liberalism" (1981:67–74). He further argued that welfare programs "promote the value of being 'poor' and perpetuate poverty."

Despite the compelling data to the contrary and perhaps because of ideologies, policymakers in the Reagan administration accepted the thesis of the dangers of welfare dependency and implemented changes whereby working-age, ablebodied, poor women were terminated from AFDC and other income supports. No consideration was given to environmental factors such as economic recessions, double-digit unemployment, sex discrimination in employment—all factors that make it impossible for many women to earn the income needed for the basic survival of their families. Also ignored was the fact that 40 percent of all AFDC recipients who left AFDC had incomes below the poverty level in the years following receipt of AFDC support (Bane and Ellwood, 1983).

OBRA, a radical redirection of federal welfare policy, has sparked an intense debate, particularly since the publication of a major critique of welfare programs for the poor done by Charles Murray

(1984). Federal officials claim that the Reagan reforms preserved the AFDC safety net by targeting resources toward those who genuinely needed assistance, and that those beneficiaries who were cut as a result of the reforms were "families with enough income to support themselves." Critics contend that the cutbacks in federal benefits between 1981 and 1983 disproportionately affected households with annual incomes below $10,000 and especially have hurt poor working families whose work efforts were thereby being undermined rather than supported by public policy (U.S. Commission on Civil Rights, 1983:5–7; Dear, 1982; Duncan, 1984). Not yet heard in these debates have been the voices of the families themselves, working mothers and their children, whose present and future economic well-being and quality of life have been dramatically changed. Our research provided the opportunity to hear directly from those who experienced the impacts of federal policy changes.

Conceptual Framework

This study examined the impact of OBRA policies on working women and sought to determine how these women coped with the cuts and attempted to maintain individual and family well-being when confronted with the losses of AFDC benefits, cash income, Food Stamps, and/or Medicaid insurance, as well as housing, energy, childcare or school lunch allowances in some special circumstances. Our guiding hypothesis was that both objective factors (e.g., economic need) and subjective factors (e.g., perceived stress) would influence the respondent's coping behavior, but that responses would be mediated by informal social networks (e.g., kin, friends, and neighbors) and formal social networks (e.g., social agencies) and by the availability of resources such as health insurance that is associated with employment. We hypothesized that coping behavior might be either adaptive or maladaptive in terms of the family's subsequent well-being.

Crisis and stress theories have long recognized that the same objective event may have different functional effects depending upon: (1) how it is perceived; (2) the decision-making and problem-solving strategies subsequently implemented; and (3) the response of the family, work environment, and community to those strategies (Catalano and Dooley, 1977; Cobb, 1974; Gore, 1978; Hill, 1974; Kessler, 1979). The perception of an event as a crisis is further conditioned by both individual sociopsychological factors and by the situational context within which it occurs (Dill et al., 1980). Thus, when confronted by changes in AFDC policy that reduced incentives to work, how did women conceive their options? What steps, if any, did they take to overcome the impact of their loss of income so as to restore their family's well-being? How important in a woman's decision making was her need for Medicaid protection? Until now most research has focused on economic rather than social and psychological factors. Thus, much attention was paid to whether women did or did not receive benefits and for how long, but almost no attention was paid to the qualities of these families' lives.

Following a woman's initial decision to work, it is important to detail the various strategies that a woman employs to master her problems in balancing work, income, and family needs. As Belle, Dill, and their colleagues observed in the Boston study of AFDC families and stress, the social environment of low-income women frequently opposes their efforts to master problematic situations, that is, the lack of availability of childcare, housing or transportation (Belle, 1982; Dill et al., 1980). Strategies that would be effective in more hospitable social contexts may fail to produce the desired results for this sample of working AFDC recipients.

Methodology

We selected six counties in Michigan in 1982 with unemployment rates ranging from 9 percent to 20 percent. Three of these counties had low rates of unemployment, three had rates at the upper end of the range. Variation in unemployment rate was selected as a critical sampling variable because of the wide range among Michigan counties and because it was an important indicator of relative opportunities for employment. Counties were selected as a critical unit for analysis because the social services programs in Michigan are administered through county government, and some discretion remains at that level in making decisions about services. With the cooperation and assistance of the Michigan Department of Social Services, 3,200 eligible recipients, terminated from AFDC because of the OBRA policies during the period 1 September 1981 to 1 April 1982 were identified and a sample was randomly chosen.

Respondents were contacted by mail to obtain their consent for participation in the study. All of the interviews were completed in the respondents' homes. Each interviewer obtained information on welfare experiences and attitudes, health, household composition, income and expenses, employment, education, marital experience and family background, parenting and childcare, formal and informal social supports, and on coping behavior. A total of 356 complete interviews were obtained, but this chapter reports on the sample of 316 whose welfare benefits were clearly terminated only because of the OBRA policy changes. The remaining forty cases included persons who did not experience termination or were persons who were unqualified for other reasons.

FINDINGS

Personal and Social Characteristics

The median age of the respondents was thirty-three years; 37 percent were nonwhite and more than nine in ten were urban residents. Eighty percent had completed high school or its equivalent; 27 percent had some post–secondary education, and 12 percent were enrolled in school at the time of the interview.

Seventy-seven percent identified themselves as single parents, but there were other adults or children not belonging to the respondent residing in more than half of the households. There were 2.1 children in the average household, but only 1.8 children had been included in the formal AFDC unit at the time of termination. Most of the other children were stepchildren, nieces, or nephews. Among the other adults 31 percent were female; 80 percent reported that most of these adults made some contribution to the household income. However, that contribution was often small, variable, and sporadic. Few reported that child support was ever received from the children's fathers.

Fifty percent of the respondents had been married only once; 25 percent had been married two or three times and an equal number

Table 12.1. **Personal and Social Characteristics of Working Former AFDC Recipients (N = 279)**

Median Age	33 years
% Non-white	37%
Education:	
Less than grade 12	22%
High school grad or GED	78%
Some post-secondary	27%
Currently enrolled	12%
Average no. of children:	
In household	2.1
In AFDC unit	1.8
Marital status:	
Age at first marriage	19 years
% Currently married	23%
% Married 1+ times	24%
% Married once	49%
% Never married	26%
AFDC Experience:	
Age at first grant	24 years
No. of times on AFDC	2.21
Respondent's Family Background:	
% Reared in two-parent family	76%
% Father employed full-time	90%
% Mother employed half-time or more	46%
Household Mobility in 1982:	
% Moved 1 or more times	23%
% Households with persons moving out	23%
% Households with persons moving in	29%
% Households with 1 or more mobility indicators	53%

NOTE: Only single-parent family households were included in this table.

had never been married. Two-thirds grew up in traditional two-parent households with blood relatives. Although our data do not permit us to conclude that they were reared in low-income families, most of their fathers had working-class occupations—95 percent had been employed full-time. Forty-seven percent of their mothers were employed more than 50 percent of the time while they were growing up and they also were employed in working-class operations.

Given the difficulties that had been encountered in attempting to locate and contact these respondents, it was not surprising to learn that they reported high levels of mobility. Twenty-three percent had moved one or more times in 1982. Twenty-four percent of the household had had one or more person move in with them and 29 percent had had someone move out. Overall, 53 percent had moved in with their parents or siblings, or had someone move in or out as a way of stretching meager resources.

Intrafamilial conflict was overwhelmingly the major factor that led to marital disruptions, separations, and/or divorces and then to applications for AFDC. No one stated that the availability of welfare was a factor in his/her decision. For many the marital conflict was serious and longstanding; 45 percent reported that their spouses had been repeatedly violent toward them or their children or both; and 55 percent reported that there was serious general conflict in the family. Several respondents reported still being in fear of battering, but few had access to or had ever received any services from a domestic violence program. At some point in the cycle of violence, each of these women decided to leave home with their children and applied for AFDC.

Bane and Ellwood reported that the single largest cause of movement into poverty was decline in the household head's income— overall 37 percent, but 60 percent for male heads and 14 percent for female heads indicating that for female-headed households it is not a strong predictor of poverty (1983:14–18). Instead, the poverty "spells" begin when a woman becomes a female head, especially if she has young children, and they last far longer for her. In this Michigan survey 74 percent of respondents reported that they applied for AFDC when their marriage or partnership broke up, clearly similar to the findings of Bane and Ellwood.

Welfare Use and Experience

Some researchers and policymakers argued that AFDC– earner families would not attempt to return to the rolls once they were terminated, although others argued just the opposite.[3] The former state that women would obtain adequate incomes through full-time employment and seemed unaware that they would encounter any problems in meeting the costs of childcare or health insurance because many were employed in uncovered industries. They also failed to note that many AFDC recipients eligible for termination were already employed full-time, but that they could not earn suffi-

Table 12.2. **Welfare Support after Termination (N = 279)**

	AFDC	Medicaid only	Food stamps only	One or more programs
Received assistance for at least one month between termination and interview	24.0	31.9	43.0	55.9
Percent on Medicaid or Food stamps at interview	—	21.9	12.0	27.7
Percent returned to AFDC after termination and following reapplication	24.0	10.0	33.0	39.8

NOTE: This sample includes only those cases fully meeting all OBRA criteria for termination in 1982—but excluding those terminated because of the stepfather rule since their situations tended to vary substantially from this sample.

cient income given the types of jobs and compensation typically available to low-income working women.

The overall return rate for women to AFDC, Medicaid, and/or Food Stamps in this Michigan sample was 55.9 percent over an eighteen-month period, as the results in Table 12.2 indicate. County differences were pronounced, with higher rates in the counties with high unemployment, as had been predicted.

Higher numbers of women received Food Stamps after having been terminated (43 percent); and Medicaid (31.9 percent). The terminations were implemented beginning 1 October 1981 and by December 1981, 70 percent of this sample had been terminated—primarily because of having too high incomes rather than other criteria applicable in OBRA. Among the 24 percent who reapplied and were successful in their reapplications, their average benefits at the time of the interview was $116 higher than it had been when they were terminated. State benefits had not been increased, but these women who returned were not working and therefore became eligible for the larger amount. Thus, the state experienced a greater cost when the women had to return to AFDC.

Less than 10 percent of the respondents understood the details of the policy decision, knew how much income they would have, or how much property they could have before they would be terminated.

Only 7 percent ever appealed a decision of the Department of Social Services, but among those who did 61 percent were successful with their grievances. Only 1,367 reported that they had been informed that they might continue to be eligible for Food Stamps after termination.

Forty-four percent reapplied for welfare after being terminated, and an addditional 37 percent said that they wanted or needed to reapply—for an overall total of 73 percent. More than half of these people visited the local social services office an average of three times to inquire about or to reapply for benefits. Among the 41 percent who did not reapply 69 percent said that they did not do so because they thought that they were ineligible. The need for health insurance was the most frequently stated need (39 percent), and that was not surprising because 37 percent did not have health insurance coverage for their children.

Ten percent of the sample were terminated because of the application of the "stepfather" rule. Among that group many initially had had far higher household incomes than those headed by females, but several returned to AFDC after their husbands deserted as a result of the increased unwanted burdens. This group was terminated more rapidly and received fewer benefits of all types, regardless of their income levels. Many of these families then ended up receiving far higher AFDC benefits than they had received prior to termination when the stepfather had lived with the family. Undoubtedly, the social costs of another family disruption were significant for these women and children.

Economic Well-Being

When OBRA took effect, all of the women in this survey had their AFDC benefits terminated, and most also lost Food Stamps and Medicaid, as we have noted. What did that mean in terms of income? At the time of the OBRA cut, the average grant for this sample was $173.00 per month; the average Food Stamp grant was $40.00; and the average earned monthly income was $609.00. Therefore, 74 percent of total income was being received through the respondent's employment. Employment earnings were of overriding importance in determining economic well-being. However, an irony

Table 12.3. **Occupation of AFDC Sample Women Compared with Women Workers in the United States (1982)**

Occupation	Respondents (N = 279) (percent)	U.S. (female) (N = 43, 256,000)[a] (percent)
Professional	2.5	17.7
Managerial	1.8	7.4
Sales	7.2	6.9
Clerical	32.6	34.4
Crafts	0.7	2.0
Operatives	10.8	8.9
Transportation operatives	1.8	0.7
Laborers	1.4	1.2
Service	41.4	19.7
cleaning service	4.7	[b]
food service	14.7	[b]
health service	11.5	[b]
personal service	9.0	[b]
protective service	1.1	[b]
private household	0.4	[b]
Farm workers	0	1.1

NOTE: Question: "What type of work do (did) you do?"
[a] Source: Table No. 693, *Statistical Abstract of the United States: 1984,* (104th ed.). Washington, D.C., 1983.
[b] Detailed data not available for 1982.

in OBRA as well as in other welfare-related legislation is that when women who are working get a small portion of their income from AFDC, their overarching or predominating role becomes that of "welfare recipient." They are no longer considered as employees, even though they work full-time, nor are they considered among the "deserving" poor.

The type of employment that the women had explains why they depended upon welfare to support their low earnings (Fox and Biber, 1984; U.S. Department of Labor, 1980). Their jobs were located in two main sectors: (1) clerical jobs (33 percent); (2) service jobs (41 percent). Only 11 percent were in manufacturing despite Michigan's being an industrial state. Their average gross wage was $5.13 per hour. These women had very stable employment patterns. Ninety percent of the women working at the time of the interview had held the same job that they had had at termination 12–15 months earlier.

When earned income is as low as it was for these women, even a small amount of additional income can be a high proportion of total income and make a substantial contribution to well-being. On the average, when these women lost their AFDC benefits, they lost 21 percent of their income with one month's or less notice. In addition, the loss of Medicaid, Food Stamps, and childcare transfers took on great importance for the many who had few or no benefits in their employment.

Expenses for these families did not fall when their incomes plummeted. In fact, expenses continued to rise because of inflation, especially expenses for utilities and housing costs. Respondents reported that expenses for housing, utilities, food, childcare, transportation, medical care, and clothing consumed 105 percent of their total household income, leaving almost nothing for school and other necessary expenses.

Those shaping OBRA determined that working women should be independent of the welfare system. They argued that receiving supplementary welfare benefits was disruptive of families and/or psychologically damaging (Anderson, 1978:148–150). No consideration was given to the fundamental problems being experienced in this deindustrializing society by female single heads of household who had limited access to high-paying positions or even to jobs that had social benefits that middle-class people take for granted as basic job provisions. As Sandra Danzinger has noted (1985), the rate of employment for welfare mothers rose more steeply between 1965 and 1978 than for all other groups of single mothers. Thus, clearly these women evidenced high levels of commitment to labor force participation, contrary to the assertions of Anderson, Gilder, Murray, and Stockman.

If we compare the incomes of these families with those for white married two-parent families in the United States in 1982 the differences are pronounced. The median income of the latter was $26,443, and the average income of the women in this survey was $9,250— about one-third of that received by married two-parent families. It was even below the poverty level for a nonfarm family of four, which was $9,862 in 1982 (Joe et al., 1984:9).

Regardless of the rationale offered by federal policymakers in 1981, the fact is that many mothers who were in questionable income statuses suffered a substantial loss of income as a result of the policy changes included in OBRA. At the time of the OBRA cuts, 18 percent of these families had incomes below the poverty level, but by the end of 1982 42 percent had fallen below the poverty level. Clearly federal policies substantially contributed to their increased poverty—whether they were intended to do so or not.

Constraints on Well-Being

Health. Perhaps the most serious problem for families who were cut by OBRA was illness and lack of adequate health insur-

Table 12.4. **Morbidity: Comparison of AFDC and National Health Interview Survey**

	% Women		% Children	
Health Measures	AFDC Sample	NHIS[a]	AFDC Sample	NHIS[a]
Arthritis/rheumatism	13.7	5.81	1.0	.74[b]
Asthma/hay fever/allergies	15.0	2.65	32.7	7.61
Blood circulation problem/Hardening of arteries	5.4		.3	
Cancer	2.9		.3	
Diabetes	5.1	.90	1.0	.23[b]
Epilepsy	1.3	.32[b]	2.9	.73[b]
Gynecology problem	15.9	3.50	.9	.27[b]
Heart problem/angina	3.8	4.12	2.3	3.55
Hypertension/high blood pressure	14.0	5.71	.6	.38[b]
Kidney problem	4.5	4.24	3.2	1.64[b]
Liver problem	.3	.13	.3	—
Repeated chest colds/strep throat	12.1		27.9	
Repeated ear infections	1.9		19.1	
Sickle cell anemia	0.6		1.2	
Tonsillitis/enlargement of tonsils	2.5		11.7	
Ulcers/frequent stomach pains	10.8		3.2	

[a] SOURCE: L. Verbrugge, 1982, National Health Interview Survey Analysis. Washington, D.C.: U.S. Department of HHS, National Center for Health Statistics, 1979 Survey.
[b] Unreliable rate (high sampling error).

ance. As Table 12.4 indicates the rates of incidence of several serious chronic diseases was far higher for both mothers and children in this study sample than was observed in the National Health Interview Survey in 1979 with a comparable sample of women and children. Moreover, 37 percent of these women had no health insurance for their children and 27 percent had none for themselves. Even those with insurance often had such poor benefits that their coverage was almost meaningless for the types of care that they required.

Poor health and illness was associated with an inability to remain employed as the findings in Table 12.5 indicate. Families with higher incidences of illness, with more bed and hospital days, and who received more prescription drugs were less likely to be employed. When they were not employed, they were forced back on AFDC at higher costs and for more extended periods. Many respondents reported that the loss of Medicaid insurance was their most serious problem.

Crises. Having to cope with serious crises, with having no money, with having no food, a serious illness, death, job loss, family violence, and problems of their children were almost routine for these families, as Table 12.6 indicates. Nearly nine out of ten ran out of money at least once and 62 percent reported that they were without money seven or more times. Half were without food at least once and a quarter ran out of food more than seven times. Several interviewers visited households in which there was no food available and where respondents were extremely anxious because of their children. Many reported that they always ran out of food at the end of the month when wages were gone and emergency food was unavailable.

Respondents replied that the following were the most serious problems they experienced in 1982: lack of money (28 percent); lack of food (10 percent); having something bad happen to their children (14 percent); having someone close die (9 percent); and their own illnesses (7 percent). Women with lower incomes experienced somewhat more crises, particularly those involving crime and lack of money, but the correlation was not strong—probably because the income range for the entire sample was limited relative to overall need and because nearly all of the respondents experienced several serious crises during the year. Several reported suicides within the family, serious fires, rapes, and other crises.

284

Table 12.5. **Morbidity by Employment**

Number of Incidences	Employed (N = 232)	Not employed (N = 82)	Total (N = 314)
Mother's morbidity			
(# of incidences)			
None	44.8	34.1	42.0
1	29.6	24.4	28.0
2–7	25.6	41.5	29.9
Total	100.0%	100.0%	99.9%
Children's morbidity			
(# of incidences)			
None	44.8	32.9	41.7
1	29.3	26.8	28.3
2–6	25.8	40.2	29.9
Total	99.9%	99.9%	99.9%
Mother's/children's morbidity			
(# of incidences)			
None	23.7	17.1	22.0
1	24.1	17.1	22.3
2	21.6	19.5	21.0
3–13	30.6	46.3	34.7
Total	100.0%	100.0%	100.0%
Bed days			
None	34.8	39.5	35.8
1–4	34.1	25.9	31.9
5–90	31.5	34.6	32.3
Total	100.4%	100.0%	100.0%
Hospital nights			
None	85.8	72.8	82.4
1–4	8.6	7.4	8.3
5–96	5.6	19.8	9.3
Total	100.0%	100.0%	100.0%
Prescription drugs			
(# of incidences)			
None	67.7	52.4	63.7
1	24.6	36.6	27.7
2–3	7.8	11.0	8.6
Total	100.1%	100.0%	100.0%

The mean number of crises per respondent was 12.59 for the twelve-to-fifteen-month time period. Only 3 percent reported not having had one or more of the crises we asked them about. In a similar survey of low-income women in Boston, Dill reported that in a two-year period they experienced an average of fourteen serious crises that required change and adjustment by the women (Dill et al., 1980:507). The Boston study reported that the lack of money took the greatest toll on mental and physical health; that one-third did not have enough money for food; 48 percent had at least one child with a serious school problem; and 23 percent rated their own health as poor. These results from Boston are quite similar to the crises observed in the Michigan survey, again pointing to the fact that low-income women disproportionately experience serious crises and stress. The General Mills survey of a random sample of all United States' families in 1979 reported that in order to cope with inflation, 75 percent of single-parent families reduced health-related expenses. This sample of single-parent families showed responses to their

Table 12.6. **Crises Following Termination (N = 316)**

	% Responding one or more times	Mean number of times
Run out of money	88.6	5.3
Run out of food	49.1	2.4
Become seriously ill at least once	39.9	.7
Borrowed over $300	36.8	.6
Had someone important die	34.6	.5
Had problems with partner	37.1	1.3
Had furnace or major appliance break	32.6	.4
Had something bad happen to child	29.4	.5
Been a victim of crime	11.1	.1
Been to court or was arrested	12.9	.2
Had gas turned off	8.6	.1
Had electricity turned off	7.3	.1
Had something repossessed	3.1	.0
Had some other crisis	24.4	.4
Mean no. per family		12.6

NOTE: Since January 1982, how many times, if at all, have you _____? The time interval covered 12–18 months from the month of termination.

Table 12.7.   **Crises by Post–OBRA Welfare Status**
(**Selected crises in percentages**)

Status	Mean no. of crises	Money	Food[a]	Illness[b]	N = 316
No welfare	11.899	69.4	24.9	32.1	209
Food stamps	12.060	78.0	32.0	30.0	50
AFDC only	15.167	83.4	33.4	50.0	6
AFDC and food stamps	15.667	80.4	49.1	52.4	51

[a] Percentages indicated for food and money crises are for families reporting 5 or more of their crises in the 15-month period.
[b] Percentages indicated are for families reporting that the mother had one or more serious illnesses in the 15-month time period.

crises similar to the ones our respondents associated with reduced income.

One might expect that families experiencing a large number of crises, especially frequent crises associated with lack of money or food, with illness, or with housing problems, would reapply for AFDC and would be relatively successful in being reinstated. Support for that proposition is contained in Table 12.7 which reports on the number of crises evaluated by welfare status. Sixty-six percent of the sample did not receive AFDC or Food Stamps after their initial termination in 1981–82. That group had the smallest mean number of crises (11.90). Those who subsequently received only Food Stamps had a mean of 12.06 crises, while those who returned to AFDC had 15.17 and the highest mean number (15.67) of crises occurred for those who were back on both AFDC and Food Stamps.

All of the families had serious financial and other problems. How, then, did they cope and survive? They tried many alternatives but ultimately they had to rely primarily on informal supports, such as those from family and friends, rather than on support from formal sectors such as social agencies.

Social Support and Networks

Many recent studies have shown that family, neighborhood, and mutual self-help groups mediate the impact of economic stress.

Most investigators concur that social support has emotional, cognitive, and material elements; that is, it has positive health benefits for individuals and that it reduces the negative effects of strain (Jones, 1981). It has the potential for moderating the effects of unexpected crises by acting as a buffer to ameliorate the effects of stressful changes such as those experienced by the women and children surveyed in this study.

What has not been fully understood in terms of the research presently available is the form and frequency of assistance provided through social networks in which an individual is embedded or to which she has access. The findings from this research provide some information about the sources and nature of social supports for poor women and children in crises. Moreover, it is possible to determine in a general manner the relative effectiveness of the different forms of social support. Information was obtained about informal social support provided by family and friends, but also about that provided by formal help-giving agencies, and about that which is available because of social structures in the welfare state, e.g., social insurance.

A family can cope with crises more successfully if it is embedded in one or more social networks that can provide social support when it is needed. The data in Table 12.8 indicate that both relatives and friends were contacted and utilized extensively by these families when they were terminated from AFDC and also when they dealt with serious problems throughout 1982, the year after their termination. The size of their friendship networks was considerable— only 4 percent reported not having close friends with whom they could visit and nearly three-fourths had between one and ten close friends. Because the size of these friendship networks is more under the control of the woman than is her network of relatives, these findings suggest that the large majority of these participants were not socially isolated. However, many reported that their friends were in circumstances similar to their own.

Only 5 percent reported that they never visited relatives, but 15 percent responded that they had no relatives with whom they felt free to talk about problems or whom they could count on for advice or help. A similar percentage (4 percent) reported that they never visited friends, but 9 percent reported having no friends with whom they could talk about problems of concern to them. Nonetheless, it is

Table 12.8. Coping Behavior: Help Received from Social Network at Time of Most Serious Problem

| | | Type of Help Received | | |
Helper	% Contacted	Counsel/ reassurance/ referral	Money/ material goods	Services
Partner	50	73%	31%	12%
Children	52	83	6	3
Other relatives	75	78	35	10
Friends	56	91	14	7
Minister	9	96	8	4
Social worker	13	64	—	23
Medical personnel	23	68	—	65
Community	7	37	63	10
agency	8	70	—	35
Lawyer	10	53	—	53
Police	13	46	23	29
Other				

clear that kin and children provided the greatest amount of social support of all types and that formal caregivers assisted only in specialized areas. In turn, most of these women also reported providing social support for families and friends when they encountered crises. Some of these women, in fact, suffered because of the amount of support they had to provide, particularly to elderly parents with whom they resided. These women became caregivers in return for having a place to live.

Coping Behavior

How did women cope when they were terminated from AFDC? Most sought immediately to improve their employment situation; 38 percent asked employers for increased hours or a better job; 31 percent searched for a new or better job; 18 percent sought help from their children's father; 12 percent returned to school. Unfortunately, most were unable to effect any real changes. Sixty-nine percent reported no job changes except that 14 percent were able to increase the number of hours that they worked. In contrast to the myth that welfare recipients give up jobs to remain on welfare, only

.7 percent voluntarily reduced their hours or quit working. When asked why they continued working rather than attempt to receive a full AFDC benefit, more than one-third said that they had no choice except to work. However, 22 percent reported that they did not like being on AFDC, and 18 percent said that they felt women should work. Only 22 percent reported that they continued working because they enjoyed their jobs, but given the types of jobs most held and the level of their remuneration, their responses were not surprising.

Because these respondents were employed mothers, childcare was a serious problem, particularly after they were terminated from AFDC. They lost childcare allowances and they found that public childcare programs were terminated in 1981 and 1982 because of cutbacks in Title XX and Title IV-A (Children's Defense Fund, 1983). Half of the respondents had children under twelve; 87 percent of these women reported that they needed childcare in order to work. The childcare providers that they were able to obtain included: relatives (48 percent); private sitters (32 percent); and other siblings (10 percent). Nonwhite mothers were more likely to use relatives, while white mothers more often used private sitters and older children, sometimes keeping them out of school for that purpose. The average cost of child care was $106 per month.

Women with older children appear to have encountered at least as serious problems with them as those with younger children. More than one-third had been called to school for special conferences. Twenty-two percent reported that their children had been suspended at least once. A small number of these children had been expelled, referred to juvenile court, sent to special schools, committed to institutions, or victimized by a crime. The numbers, although small, were disproportionately greater than would be expected in a random sample of families with children of these ages.

These women also coped by "stretching" their incomes through a variety of survival tactics. Forty-nine percent obtained old produce; 72 percent obtained used clothes; 19 percent obtained emergency goods; and 21 percent sold bottles and cans that were redeemable in Michigan. Working with neighbors and bartering were also frequently employed. Few women reported illegal behavior other than paying by check without funds in the bank. Other forms of credit were typically denied to these families because of their low and precarious incomes.

Despite their financial difficulties, most of these women were unaware of benefits for which they might have been eligible, and apparently welfare staff did not inform them of their entitlements. However, 93 percent reported filing an income tax return but only 56 percent applied for an earned income tax credit, and only 15 percent claimed a childcare tax credit. In most instances, lack of information about eligibility appeared to have been the deterrent against their taking action, because those who did appeal were usually successful. Although it is not commonly recognized, the average working AFDC family of four in 1982 paid $956 in income and payroll taxes, but only received $900 in Food Stamps—the principal nonincome transfer available to these families (Smeeding, 1983). The net effect of taxes and Food Stamps was to reduce the average family of four's income by $46. Clearly, this nonincome transfer does not have the results suggested by some federal policymakers, namely that the poor are better off than is realized because of the nonincome transfers. The data, however, refute another myth about AFDC recipients as noncontributing members of society. The federal government continues, however, to attempt to include estimates of nonincome transfers in poverty statistics so as to "reduce" the number of persons who are reported to be below the poverty level. In 1985, they have attempted to calculate an average benefit for Medicaid and to assign that statistic as income to recipients so as to raise their supposed income levels. This assignment would be made regardless of whether or not the individual actually received a benefit.

Discussion and Implications

Overall, both subjective and objective indicators point to greater hardships for these families in the post-OBRA period. The findings correspond to those observed in several other state surveys. These women, all of whom had been terminated from AFDC at least once, perceived that their economic and social situations had declined substantially after 1982, and many reported being in almost continual crises. They felt themselves to be worse off than similar women in prior years in terms of their increased indebtedness, problems of childcare, and health. Their lives were negatively affected by the OBRA cuts despite their wholehearted and continuing work efforts. Clearly this population is at high risk for extended periods of income below the poverty level, and the problem will be exacerbated as the number of mother-only families below the poverty level increases.

Poverty is a painful reality for millions of American women and children—just as it is for millions throughout the world. The United States stands apart from other industrialized countries of the world in that it has only reluctantly extended income supports to its needy citizens—even when those in need are children, disabled, or ill—unable to care for themselves. Rather than the "Great Society," it might be more appropriate to refer to us as the "Mean Society," because we have the resources to eliminate poverty, but not the will to do so (Harrington, 1984; Ozawa, 1982). Moreover, any income support programs are gender-marked in that they are far more punitive toward women than toward men. They have explicit and implicit requirements controlling the roles and behavior of women who are recipients of income support. On the other hand, women are assigned primary responsibility for socialization of the children but they are expected to fulfill these responsibilities without long-term assistance with those costs.

Whether the OBRA changes were intended to increase poverty or not will be long debated, but one is inevitably drawn to the conclusion that the basic motivating force for the changes was far more ideology than economics, and that ideological factors overrode empirical reality. There is little doubt that the states and Congress now recognize the need for change. Society cannot tolerate the rate of increase in the feminization of poverty that is presently occurring, nor will it tolerate the profound negative effects that are being felt by children. But, whether recognition of these problems will produce ad hoc legislation or a sound reassessment and the establishment of a more viable income security policy is highly uncertain. For example, passage of child support legislation in 1985 was a positive step, but quite insufficient relative to the need. It does nothing to alleviate wage and employment discrimination nor does it address the problems of health care.

Our industrialized peer countries view income support for women and children as a priority, in contrast to social policy in the United States.[4] In addition, legislation to ensure comparable worth in salaries paid to women is essential. Finally, publicly funded health care must again become a high priority if future generations are not to be jeopardized.

After several decades of more or less steady economic growth, smooth social and political development, and improved general welfare in industrialized countries, we now have experienced serious structural crises in the welfare state. Poverty, unemployment, and insecurity threaten large segments of the population, especially women, minorities, youth, and the handicapped. The recovery of 1984, while beneficial to the middle and upper classes, has not relieved the poverty of female-headed single parent families, nor that of minorities. In fact, the gap between rich and poor increased in 1984 (U.S. Department of Commerce, 1985). The 1978–1983 recession pushed eleven million Americans into poverty, but the economic recovery of 1984 was only able to help two million move above the poverty level. Additionally, the ecological and social limits of growth and the bureaucratization of the human services are aggravated by more rather than fewer problems. Thus, at least nine million people remain in poverty from the 1982–83 recession, and these persons are disproportionately children and their single mothers. These families find themselves less able to obtain health care and social services because so many are now provided on a profit basis or at a higher cost than they can afford. Moreover, if the women become unemployed or are otherwise further impoverished, they then must seek AFDC again. If they are successful in obtaining assistance, they will be required to work, but often at the minimum wage and without adequate support for childcare and work-related expenses. Little wonder that most feel that their overall status continues to deteriorate, as Danziger (1985) notes.

The most serious victims of impoverishment are children—at least in long-term costs to the society—and they are innocent victims of these conservative policy initiatives. Increasing numbers of children are being reared in families with scarce resources. Resources available to families do determine to a considerable extent the opportunities and life chances of youth, especially with respect

293

to health and education (Greenberg, 1982). If present trends continue whereby mother-only families have less than half of the incomes of their male counterparts, despite working full-time, the number of women and children in poverty will continue to increase. Moreover, that poverty will not be relieved by AFDC programs unless present policies are changed. The levels of AFDC benefits in 1985 in all of the states are below those of 1965 in constant dollars. Lastly, the proposed tax reforms will also not benefit these families, as the analysis of the Children's Defense Fund indicates (1985).

It is impossible to design a new welfare state by slight modifications of selected features of social policy and not produce disastrous results. What is now required is a thoroughgoing analysis of the basic elements of the social structure, of societal ideologies regarding family policy, and of the traditions that led to the development of the modern welfare state. Such an analysis will then enable us to discuss alternative solutions for preservation of the structures that are necessary and desirable for the entire society, while avoiding the emergence of new problems and inequalities.

In late 1986 a series of proposals for welfare reform were announced by a variety of individuals and groups in Washington. These included senators Evans, Durenberger, and Moynihan, Governor Cuomo, former governor Babbitt, and Arthur Fleming, the American Public Welfare Association, and several proposals from the Reagan administration. Although there are vast differences among these proposals, it is clear that all acknowledge that fundamental changes are required in income-support programs for poor families with children. It is likely that several years of debate will ensue before legislative changes are effected. Hopefully, the proposals for change will be informed by the negative experiences of families following the passage of the Omnibus Budget Reconciliation Act of 1981, so that the errors of that legislation will not be repeated.

Notes

THE RESEARCH reported here was funded in part by grants from the Ford and Shiffman Foundations and the Ruth Mott Fund. The author is indebted to other members of the research staff on the working welfare women project: Nicky Beisel, William Barton, Jacques Boulet, Amy Butler, Deborah Eddy, Sue Lambert, Aisha Ray, Carol Russell, Joan Weber, and Deborah Zinn. Our appreciation is also expressed to Agnes Mansour, Mark Murray, and Joseph La Rosa of the Michigan Department of Social Services, and last but not least, to the women who gave us freely of their time and knowledge without which this study would not have been possible.

1. A comprehensive description and analysis of OBRA is presented in John Palmer and Isabel Sawhill, *The Reagan Experiment* (Washington, D.C.: Urban Institute, 1982). This was one of the most complex statutes in recent U.S. history. It incorporates changes in more than two hundred categorical and block grant programs. Implementation by the states has seen substantial variability, so that the law's consequences for recipients have differed within and among the states.

2. Two of the more thoroughgoing critiques of welfare support to working women and their children are contained in Anderson, 1978 and, Gilder, 1981.

3. D. Stockman in "Poverty in America." Statement before the House Ways and Means Subcommittees on Oversight and Public Assistance and Unemployment, 3 November 1983, argued that they would not return, whereas T. Joe and F. Farrow argued the opposite. See *Profiles of Families in Poverty: Effects of the FY 1983 Budget Proposals on the Poor*. Washington, D.C.: Center for the Study of Social Policy, February 1982.

4. Kamerman and Kahn, 1983. Kamerman and Kahn compare the income transfer programs of eight industrialized countries in terms of bringing the income of poor families up to their respective nation's "average production worker's wage." Even if the United States is characterized by a fairly high AFDC benefit state (Pennsylvania), it still ranks last among its industrialized peers in the relative income provided. See also Kamerman, 1985.

Reference List

Anderson, Martin. 1978. *Welfare: The political economy of welfare reform in the U.S.* Stanford: Hoover Institute Press.

Bane, Mary Jo, and Daniel Ellwood. 1983. *The dynamics of dependence: The route to self-sufficiency.* Cambridge, Mass.: Urban Systems Research, Inc.

Belle, Deborah, ed. 1982. *Lives in stress.* Beverly Hills: Sage.

Catalano, R., and C. D. Dooley. 1977. Economic predictors of depressed mood and stressful life events in a metropolitan community. *Journal of Health and Social Behavior* 18:292–307.

Children's Defense Fund. 1983. *A children's defense fund budget: An analysis of the 1984 budget.* Washington, D.C.: Children's Defense Fund.

Children's Defense Fund. 1985. *Tax reform proposals and their impact on children.* Washington, D.C.: Children's Defense Fund.

Cobb, S. 1974. A model for life events and their consequences. In *Stressful life events,* ed. B. S. Dohrenwend and B. P. Dohrenwend. New York: Wiley.

Danziger, Sandra. 1985. *The impact of the Reagan budget cuts on working welfare women in Wisconsin.* Madison: Institute for Research on Poverty, University of Wisconsin.

Dear, R. B. 1982. No more poverty in America? A critique of Martin Anderson's theory of welfare. *Children and Youth Services Review* 4 (1/2):5–34.

Dill, Diana, E. Feld, J. Martin, S. Burkeman, and D. Belle. 1980. The impact of the environment on the coping efforts of low income mothers. *Family Relations* 3(October):503–509.

Duncan, G., et al. 1984. *Years of poverty, years of plenty.* Ann Arbor: Institute for Social Research, University of Michigan.

Fox, M. F., and S. Biber. 1984. *Women at work.* Boulder, Col.: Westview Publishing.

General Mills. 1979. *The American family report 1978–1979: Family health in an era of stress.* Minneapolis: General Mills.

Gilder, George. 1981. *Wealth and poverty.* New York: Basic Books.

Greenberg, David. 1982. Education and life chances of children of maritally disrupted families. *Children and Youth Services Review* 4 (12):167–168.

Gore, S. 1978. The effect of social support in moderating the health consequences of unemployment. *Journal of Health and Social Behavior* 19: 157–165.

Harrington, M. 1984. *The persistence of poverty: New American poverty.* New York: Holt, Rinehart, and Winston.

Hill, R. 1974. *Families under stress.* New York: Harper.

Joe, Tom, Mitchell Ginsberg, Steve Kulis, and Rosemary Sarri. 1984. *Working female-headed families in poverty.* Washington, D.C.: Center For the Study of Social Policy.

Jones, Betty. 1981. Mental health and the structure of support. Ph.D. dissertation, University of Michigan.

Kamerman, S. B., and A. J. Kahn. 1983. Income transfers and mother only families in eight countries. *Social Service Review* 57 (September): 448–464.

Kamerman, S. 1985. Young, poor, and a mother alone: Problems and possible solutions. In *Services to young families,* ed. H. McAdoo and J. Parham, 238. Washington, D.C.: American Public Welfare Assn.

Kessler, R. C. 1979. A strategy for studying differential vulnerability to the psychological consequences of stress. *Journal of Health and Social Behavior* 20 (June):100–108.

Murray, Charles. 1984. *Losing ground.* New York: Basic Books.

Ozawa, M. N. 1982. *Income maintenance and work incentives.* New York: Praeger.

Pearce, Diane. 1982. Farewell to alms: Women and welfare policy in the eighties. Paper presented to the Annual Meeting of the American Sociological Association, San Francisco.

Smeeding, Timothy. 1983. Recent increases in poverty in the U.S.: What the official estimates fail to show. Testimony before the House Ways and Means Committee Subcommittee on Oversight, Public Assistance, and Unemployment Compensation, U.S. House of Representatives, Washington, D.C., 18 October.

U.S. Commission on Civil Rights. 1983. *A growing crisis: Disadvantaged women and their children.* Washington, D.C.: GPO.

U.S. Congress. House. 1983. Committee on Ways and Means. Subcommittee on Oversight and Subcommittee on Public Assistance. *Background material on poverty.* (17 October). Washington, D.C.: GPO.

U.S. Congress. House. 1985a. Committee on Ways and Means. *Children in poverty.* (22 May). Washington, D.C.: GPO.

U.S. Congress. House. 1985b. Committee on Ways and Means. Subcommittee on Oversight and Subcommittee on Public Assistance and Unemployment. *Effects of the omnibus budget reconciliation act on welfare changes and recession of poverty.* (25 July). Washington, D.C.: GPO.

U.S. Departmment of Commerce. Bureau of the Census. 1985. *Money, income, and poverty status of families and persons in the U.S.: 1984.* Current Population Series P–60, No. 142 (28 August). Washington, D.C.: GPO.

U.S. Department of Labor. Bureau of Labor Statistics. 1985. Labor force activity of mothers of young children continues at record pace. *News* USDL 85–381 (19 September).

U.S. Department of Labor. Bureau of Labor Statistics. 1980. *Perspectives on working women: A databook.* Bulletin 2080 (October). Washington, D.C.: GPO.

U.S. General Accounting Office. 1985. *An evaluation of the 1981 AFDC changes: Final report.* (2 July). Washington, D.C.: GPO.

13

Women and the Economy: Issues for the States

Joan L. Wills, Barbara Beelar, Martha Warren, and Robert Friedman

For fifty years, U.S. policymakers have relied on macro-economic strategies to maintain the health of the main-stream economy—largely the domain of white men—and social service/income maintenance policies to assist people unable to support themselves in that economy—largely women and minorities.

The limits of this bifurcated policy are becoming increasingly clear: social progress is being blocked by an erratic economy while economic progress is limited by our inability to bring new people and products into the marketplace. Neither set of policies has successfully integrated women and minorities into the mainstream economy. The entire reduction of poverty during the last two decades has been the result of an expanding, publicly financed income maintenance system.

The social service and income maintenance programs have mitigated a portion of the adverse impacts of extreme poverty and economic dislocation. Yet they have not offered an escape from dependency for those who are dependent because they are involuntarily unemployed or underemployed. Most income maintenance programs, particularly the means-tested programs, are structured to reduce or eliminate benefits for recipients who enroll in training programs, who work, or who try to create their own jobs. They have become a form of economic methadone that dulls the pain of dependency but offers no cure. Social service programs meanwhile attempt to correct the deficiencies of individuals—real and imagined—which prevent them from entering the labor market, but these programs do little to create employment opportunities.

Public policy is not the sole, or perhaps even the major, cause of this situation. The decline of high-wage industrial employment and the expansion of lower-wage service jobs are both key factors. The effectiveness of macroeconomic policies in opening up productive opportunities for women and the disadvantaged has been limited by structural and institutional microeconomic barriers—capital, labor, technological, and other market failures—which retard the entry of new people and products to the marketplace and result in ever higher unemployment rates.

Traditional policies have not provided solutions. There is another route to follow. We can integrate social and economic policies by expanding the opportunities to produce. The states are strategic actors for such integration and many are beginning to explore this new direction. In pursuing this course, they face several constraints:

the difficulty of acting independently of federal economic policy and the importance of international economic conditions that limit states' influence;

restrictive categorical and programmatic separations that inhibit the formation of an integrated policy;

a primary and precedent responsibility for exercising traditional police powers (including child protection, and ultimate responsibility for the mentally ill, as examples);

federal mandates and restrictions on programs funded with federal funds;

tight fiscal conditions;

shifting federal-state roles; and

a difficult and relatively unexplored mission.

Economic issues are an important subset of all issues involving women. This chapter recognizes the changing relationships of women and the economy. It points out the implications and possible options for the states concerning these trends. It explores the various initiatives to help targeted groups of women in the following major clusters:

working women, including both those privately and publicly employed as well as women business owners;

women students and those seeking employment and training; and women who are economically dependent on either public or private support.

It concludes by suggesting key directions that states might move in to better address the challenge of creating integrated policies and programs.

As has been recognized in other sections of this book, there has been since World War II two significant and countervailing trends in the United States economy that have had special importance for women. One has been the increase of female participation in the economy; the other has been the limited nature of occupational opportunities and financial rewards. We are also in a period of increase in the number of women who depend on their earnings for support but who are unable to derive a liveable income from their work or are unable to find work at all. The number of poor families headed by females has increased to over half the heads of households. Two out of three poor adults are women. According to this dramatic projection of the "feminization of poverty," if current rates were to increase, mothers and their children would compose almost 100 percent of the poverty population by the year 2000.

THE STATES' RESPONSE: INITIATIVES TO ASSIST WOMEN AND THE ECONOMY

The problem is clear: there is an amazing stability in the income disparity and associated occupational segregation experienced by women in the workplace. These trends have survived substantial changes in our economy and in occupational structures. Old solutions seem not to have touched these problems. New approaches, even as a structural transformation of work in America takes place, must be forthcoming if we are to prevent the continuation of these trends and rectify the inequities encountered by women in our society.

Addressing the challenge of integrating women into the economic mainstream requires the states to recognize and pay heed to their traditional roles and to assume new ones. Understandably, this can be difficult.

Although the roles of state government are changing, history has its claim. The program framework of the past fifty years along with its limitations is deeply engrained in governmental structures and policy-making capabilities. Program implementations and enforcement, of necessity, still require the great bulk of state attention and resources. States often have small policy staffs. There is still a tendency in state administrations to think categorically, according to federal grant program lines, instead of in terms of overall challenges and responses.

Federal mandates and prohibitions govern many aspects of most programs, particularly in the social service/income maintenance area, and these often shift so rapidly that they prevent state innovation even where states are inclined to move in that direction. Current preoccupation with funding levels—constrained from above and below—helps to obscure policy design issues. And, finally, there is a general tendency to view economic policy solely in macroeconomic and national terms. The rise of global competition further weights the question of how effective the states as economic policymakers can be. Funding limitations—imposed by the federal budget cuts, popular referenda, and recent recessions—cut both ways: they limit the capacity of the states to enact new programs but they also increase the necessity of finding ways to make existing monies have more impact. For example, due to local popular referenda that have swept the country, local property taxes have eroded as the primary base for financing public education in the country. The states have expanded their fiscal support as a result of this lost local tax base and simultaneously they have required that more "output accountability measures" be inserted into the education enterprise. Since 1980 and no doubt continuing on until the end of this decade, state-focused education reform initiatives will continue to be high on the list of gubernatorial and legislative priorities. Aside from the merits or demerits of any particular reform initiative, the pressure will continue for making better use of the dollars available. Fiscally there is little choice; in some states education is approaching 50 percent of the total state revenue expenditures.

Another example of this fiscal push results from funding limitations imposed by reductions in federal resources. Health care programs, particularly those with an individual entitlement status (Medicaid, Women Infants and Children [WIC] and child nutrition programs), have pushed states into altering (fighting) eligibility criteria on the one hand, while simultaneously experimenting with a variety of new market incentives to increase better pricing for health care services.

Public demands for government performance have increased to the point where the risk of business as usual is exceeded by the risk of experimentation. Increasing state economic development activity has resulted from the pressure of economic problems—unemployment, economic dislocation, poverty—and economic disparities in the regional impact of development. This increase in state activity has been aided by growing recognition of the importance of small businesses as job generators and the other small entities more easily touched by state than by federal policy.

Although the states have forged ahead in the past decade in the economic policy area, there is still a need for them to come to terms with women's economic issues as mainstream economic policy questions rather than relegating them to the context of social service concerns.

In this section, we will describe a range of current state responses designed to deal with women's and economic issues. These listings are suggestive. The emphasis here is on initiatives that have been designed to assist targeted groups of women through basic changes in the law and in organizational structures.

Initiatives for Privately and Publicly Employed Women

State governments are assisting women working in the private sector through a variety of mechanisms. Areas that are of concern or reflect new directions for state government include: a) childcare tax allowances; b) incentives for the creation of employer-sponsored day care; c) pensions; and d) pay equity legislation.

State Tax Allowance for Childcare. Even when women find suitable childcare, the cost of such services has been a barrier to employment, often cutting deeply into the income generated by women's employment. To offset this disincentive, tax allowances have been introduced to reduce the financial burden and enable more women to consider outside employment as an option. This approach has practical fiscal implications for states where the choice for women may be between receiving public assistance or maintaining employment.

The federal government initiated a special allowance for childcare expenses through a change in the federal income tax legislation in 1954. The specific provisions of this law have changed over time, but the allowance has consistently been available for employment-related childcare expenses. As of 1981, twenty-seven out of the forty-one states that have state income tax laws provided some type of broad-based income tax deduction or credit for employment-related childcare expenses. In eleven states, there is a state tax credit specified as a percentage of the federal tax credit for childcare. Five states specify a portion of allowable expenses that may be taken as a credit against state tax liability. Eleven states have an itemized deduction or adjustment for income for childcare expenses rather than a tax credit (Duncan, 1982).

There is continuing evolution in existing state laws. For example, one state recently changed its tax allowance procedure from a deduction to a tax credit, incorporating a sliding scale to determine levels of credit, and assuming some progressivity. This change may anticipate changes in other states, since advocates and analysts assess the tax credit system as likely to be progressive and beneficial to low- and moderate-income families.

Tax Incentives to Employers to Set Up Employee Day Care. Some states have created a "carrot" to encourage private sector employers to provide day care for their employees, either through the actual provision of day care at the worksite or by subsidizing the day care costs of their employees. One state has passed a tax credit for corporations that establish new worksite day care centers. Another recently passed a bill that gives employers a tax deduction for childcare provided by employees. State initiatives to promote employer-sponsored day care are not to be ignored, but their impact has limits. Site day care is generally thought to be most feasible at sites where over 100 workers are employed. This base would cover about half of the workers in the United States. Clearly more can be done using this base:

currently there are only about 600 worksite day care centers in the country, and half of these are located in hospital settings (Blank, 1983).

Pensions. Pension policies are an area of concern because of the high rate of women who experience poverty or near-poverty in their later years. Pension issues are important for two target groups of women: working women, both in the public and private sectors, and economically dependent women at two possible points in their lives— if their marriages dissolve and in their later years.

Twenty-one percent of working women are covered by an employer-sponsored pension plan. This lack of coverage is due to the limited number of women who attain continuing full-time employment and who are in a workplace that provides pension contributions as a part of fringe benefits. "Even when women do receive pensions, either through their own or through their spouses' entitlements, they get a lower dollar amount from both public and private pensions; the median private pension amount was $4,830 for men and $2,750 for women" (Women's Studies Program and Policy Center, 1981:11). The pension providers' reasoning, of course, is based on the greater longevity of women.

Some plans do not pay widow's benefits if the husband, who has the sole discretion, decides to turn down that option in order to receive a higher benefit level during his lifetime. Other plans pay no widow's benefits if the primary wage earner dies before he begins drawing the benefit.

While private pension plans are controlled to some degree by federal legislation through the Employee Retirement Income Security Act of 1974 (ERISA), amendments to ERISA, it can be argued, would not be an efficient or necessarily an appropriate strategy to deal directly with the spouse's rights.

At the state level, an indirect method has been devised to mitigate some of these problems by changing the divorce laws to include pension plan assets in the marital property considered for disbursement in divorce settlements.

Pay Equity in the Private Sector. Forty-one states have fair employment practice laws that broadly prohibit sex-based wage discrimination for all employers in the state. Fifteen states have equal pay acts that contain a comparable worth standard. In some states, new laws

305

or amendments to existing statutes are being considered as a way of strengthening this comparable worth language. The impact of these efforts, particularly regarding comparable worth, is yet to be determined, but the potential for structural transformation is great and no doubt will generate controversy and debate over the next decade.

Initiatives for Women State Employees

State governments control and shape employment practices for their employees. Some states are reviewing personnel policies with the goal of reducing the problems encountered by women working in state government and those who are seeking access to state government. In the 1960s and 1970s, personnel reform activities were initiated under the framework of affirmative action and equal employment opportunity. These have now been fairly well incorporated into the operational procedures within state governments.

The orientation of these activities at the state level is two-fold: 1) the reform of employment practices as they adversely affect female state employees; and 2) the creation of improved practices that employers in the private sector could replicate. In the latter instance, the "trickle out" theory, public sector practices eventually influencing the private sector practices, may be difficult to document but cannot be disregarded. Currently, state initiatives of special interest include: a) pay equity; b) alternative work structures; and c) day care.

Pay Equity. State governments as employers have become a focal point for the issue of pay equity, a concept that has the potential for bringing about major changes in compensation practices. The arguments supporting action are directed at two causes of wage inequity encountered by working women—the differential in pay between men and women in the same job (the equity issue) and occupational segregation (the comparable worth issue). While women who are paid less then men for the same work can seek redress under the twenty-year-old Equal Pay Act, women who believe they have been segregated into job classifications that are low-paying simply because they are "women's work" have much less clear-cut recourse. Proponents of comparable worth argue that many occupations traditionally dominated by women require equal measures of skill, effort, and responsibility as those dominated by men, and are of "equal worth" to the employer. The fact that these occupations tend to be compensated at a much lower level, they argue, is due to illegal discrimination. These arguments remain highly controversial, and the direction provided by federal courts is far from clear.

The pressure on state governments increased recently with the court decision in the case against the State of Washington brought by the American Federation of State County and Municipal Employees (AFSCME). The union charged that the state refused to correct pay inequities that were documented by job evaluation studies. The case was decided in two sections. In the first, the judge found violation of Title VII of the Civil Rights Act. Then in mid-December, the judge ruled that the State of Washington had ninety days to upgrade the salaries of its women employees. This decision did not set an amount for the financial remedy the women will receive in order to make up for the discrimination, but AFSCME had estimated a price tag of $100 million a year (*Education Daily,* 1983). The State of Washington has already announced plans to appeal the court findings and other states are watching with a careful eye because of the enormous financial ramifications this case may have for the states.

Fourteen states are currently conducting or have completed job evaluation and pay equity studies. Additionally, four states are committed to undertaking such studies (Grune, 1984). Eight states have completed studies of their civil service systems and several states have funded studies on the wage gap (Hartmann and Treiman, 1983:406). Two states have passed appropriation bills to begin upgrading depressed wages for female-dominated jobs and three states are investigating comparable worth complaints (Perlman, 1982:3).

Alternative Work Schedule Options. Women's advocates have urged alternatives to full-time employment in order to provide a greater range of opportunities for women to combine childcare responsibilities with employment. Many state governments have initiated some kind of alternative work schedule option through legislative action, executive orders, reforms of state personnel policies, or more informal changes in state agency practices.

Options include flex-time, compressed work weeks, permanent part-time employment, and job sharing. Flex-time gives full-time employees some choices in their starting and stopping times. Forty-two states have some form of flex-time. Implementation varies from being widespread throughout the state government, selectively available, or permitted on an informal basis at the discretion of the agency director. Compressed work weeks allow employees to spread their work hours over fewer but longer workdays. Thirty-two states have compressed work week programs in self-selected agencies. Permanent part-time work opportunities are available in at least thirty-five states. Permanent part-time employment means that employees can work substantially fewer hours or days per week but they are eligible for the same kinds of benefits as full-time employees. Job sharing enables more than one employee to divide the responsibilities and duties of one full-time position. Nineteen states currently employ some form of job sharing (Long and Post, 1981:99–102).

Child care. States are beginning to address the problems of affordability, licensing, quality, and the number of day care facilities for both private and public employees through a variety of means. While the figures for the extent of childcare state-supported programs are not available, these efforts have all been instituted on a pilot-project basis or are available only to a select group of workers. Several states offer programs for selected agencies. Two states are looking into the development of pilot day care programs for state employees. In addition, several states run information and referral services to help match children with the desired form of day care. It is not possible to determine if any state has provided day care to all government employees or has set a goal for the creation of such a program.

Initiatives for Women-Owned Businesses

States have initiated two types of programs to assist and promote women-owned businesses. These efforts parallel the already established and accepted methods of support for minority-owned businesses. One of the first state activities is to assign an organizational unit to provide technical support for women seeking to capitalize upon their entrepreneurial skills. Twenty states offer such assistance, ranging from compiling directories of women business owners to helping to arrange loan packages and offer advice on obtaining contracts. Another approach is using set-asides, an earmarking of a percentage of the total monies appropriated, through states' purchasing power. Four state highway departments have set-asides for women contractors. Set-asides for women and minorities in public work projects and state construction projects are available in two states. Five states allocate a percentage of contracts ranging from 1 percent to 15 percent to women-owned businesses. Additionally, one state provides a 4 percent tax credit to small or minority businesses (U.S. Small Business Administration, 1983).

Initiatives for Women Students

The state has the responsibility for shaping educational policy for the public school system. This activity is framed in conjunction with both federal law and programs as well as with local governmental units that exercise traditional management control over education.

Within the context of federal programs, the state education units are implementers of federal initiatives and enforcers of federal regulations. This role is most pronounced in public education at the elementary and secondary level. State/local relationships are often delicate, with the local agencies finding themselves in the position of defending local control, while the state, acting as the enforcer, at times has little choice but to "erode" local control.

Within these operational constraints, it is important to recognize the critical role schools play in preparing young women for involvement in the workplace. The potential for developing educational programs and counseling that will better prepare young women to make career choices that lie beyond traditional roles and segregated jobs is critical to the ultimate resolution of many of the disparities we have noted.

The federal government was the initiator of equal educational opportunities for women through passage of Title IX of the Education Amendments of 1972, which mandates sex equity in education. Since that time, thirty-two states have passed some kind of parallel sex equity law, either through passage of an ERA-type amendment to the state constitution, or through prohibition of discrimination by

309

sex in the state education system. As federal funding has diminished, states are assuming increased responsibility in this area. Sex equity programs include a range of activities: policies to ensure that stereotyped materials are not used in the classroom; equal opportunities in physical education and athletic programs; inservice training for teachers on sex equity; and hiring and promotion policies of school employees for underrepresented groups, such as women in school administrative positions (Council of Chief State School Officers, 1982).

Vocational training is a critical area for attention, since training has a significant impact on occupational opportunities and long-term market options. "In secondary school programs, nearly 70 percent of the girls are in programs leading to below-average-wage occupations and less than 10 percent are enrolled in programs leading to the highest paid jobs. . . . Jobs for which women and minorities are trained in vocational schools are still the lowest paid, the least skilled and the most restrictive of upward employment mobility" (Wider Opportunities for Women, 1983). Clearly more needs to be done to alter these patterns.

At the post-secondary level in the last decade, public institutions of higher education have set up a range of support servics, some particularly designed to assist women who have been out of the labor market for a long period who now wish to return to school. These services include: counseling, remedial education, childcare, and part-time enrollment options. The comunity college system has led in the expansion of these services. Due to the dispersed accountability structure within higher education systems, these initiatives have, of necessity, emerged as individual programs at the institutional level. It is difficult to discern if there are state-wide plans for all public higher education that sets as a priority meeting the needs of young women students and of women returning to school in any states.

Displaced Homemakers

One of the impacts on the changing labor market in the past three decades has been the increase in the number of women entering or reentering the workforce after some time in the home devoted to nurturing the baby boom generation (earlier sections described

310

the reasons for their labor market entry and reentry). For many of these women, the transition into the workplace is very difficult. Some lack the necessary training to obtain an adequate job and some do not have the job search skills needed to find a job in a tight market. Many face age discrimination, competing for jobs with women half their ages who have comparable work experience.

Exactly how many women are "displaced homemakers" is not known: there are a variety of causes creating such displacements, so precise statistical definitions of which individuals actually constitute this population remain elusive. However, we do know that today one out of three women who works is forty-five years of age or older and some portion of these women may have been displaced homemakers. It is projected that another 3.5 million women between the ages of forty-five and fifty-four will enter the job market in the next two decades.

There have been several state initiatives designed to assist women through the transition period into gainful employment. Many "displaced homemaker programs" have been created to provide the guidance and support services needed to help such women.

Twenty-six states have passed legislation to provide some program for displaced homemakers, though in some cases state appropriations for these programs have not accompanied enabling legislation. In many cases these programs emerged out of the Comprehensive Employment and Training Act (CETA) program, in which the category of "displaced homemaker" was one of the target constituencies. It has been reported that some of these programs stopped with the reduction and/or termination of the CETA funds. It is not clear what will happen to displaced homemaker programs with the implementation of the Job Training Partnership Act (JTPA) that replaces CETA; but indications are that when the program has been picked up by state funds, states have been reluctant to shift the program back to federal funding because of the uncertainty of continued federal support.

Initiatives for Women Dependent on Public Support

The policy-relevant distinctions between women dependent on private support and those dependent on public support may seem illusory, but they are not. Too often there are class and race distinctions. As one observer noted: "A black displaced homemaker is a welfare mother." In this chapter, the two target populations are separated solely because state responsibilities are substantially different for each group.

Unlike most other industrialized nations, a confusing array of individualized means-tested entitlement programs exist in the United States. The federal government, as a fiscal agent and regulator in all the programs described below, has required the states to have processes that assure equity and access for all eligible participants. It has, however, refused as yet to establish nationwide standardized benefit levels and eligibility criteria in all but the Supplemental Security Income, Food Stamps and Social Security Disability Insurance (SSDI) programs. While the percentages will vary slightly by program, it is important to remember that females and/or their dependents are the major recipients of entitlements under the Medicaid, Food Stamps, AFDC, Supplemental Security Income (SSI), Social Security Disability, Child Nutrition, Social Services Block Grant, and Child Welfare Service programs. In programs other than SSI, Food Stamps, and Disability Insurance, states to one degree or another are empowered to establish benefit levels, define services, and construct administrative mechanisms to deliver the services.

Food Stamps, AFDC, SSDI, and SSI/DI tie eligibility for at least some recipients of aid to some attachment to the labor force. A fifth, the Social Services Block Grant, allows funds to be used to assist in enhancing the employability of recipients (e.g., by the provision of day care services).

States have a major responsibility in the management and administration of these work search and work test requirements. Currently in AFDC, there are two federally driven mechanisms available to the states to provide job searches, training, or direct work for those dependent upon public support. These are the WIN and WIN Demonstration programs funded at 370 million dollars in 1983 and the Community Work Experience Program (CWEP), more commonly known as workfare.

During the 1970s, the Work Incentive (WIN) program was the main method used by welfare agencies in cooperation with state employment service agencies to assist AFDC recipients to obtain training and find employment. Under WIN or WIN Demonstrations, all "employable" AFDC recipients are required to register for work-related activities with the employment agency. WIN or WIN Demonstration programs typically can provide job search training and unpaid work (up to thirteen weeks in WIN states). Over the last twelve years, however, WIN has become little more than a work registration program. Basically, the recipient had only to provide proof of rather marginal job seeking activities to remain eligible.

In 1981, Congress authorized demonstration projects to permit states the option of having welfare agencies administer the program alone rather than jointly with the State Employment Security Agency (SESA). Fewer than half the states have WIN demonstration programs and some of the programs tend to be used to support their CWEPs.

While about half of the states are administering CWEP, implementation is usually limited to a few counties within a state. Only six states have statewide workfare programs and only four have more than two thousand AFDC recipients involved in CWEP. More importantly, the majority of the people working in CWEP are men who are eligible under the unemployed parent portion of the AFDC program or women with school-aged children who do not require day care. In the vast majority of states with CWEP projects, AFDC women who would need day care for their children are exempt from CWEP participation.

The Food Stamp program also permits states and localities to establish workfare programs for food stamp recipients. This program is operational in only a handful of counties across the country and usually limited to food stamp recipients who are not on AFDC or SSI (Sklar et al., 1983).

States report widespread acceptance of CWEP by welfare recipients; states also report that the program has not been implemented broadly because of cost considerations. Support services such as day care and transportation, as well as the additional costs of supervising CWEP participants and worksite sponsors, can be costly to states and localities (National Governors' Association, 1983b).

In addition to the programs discussed above, other programs financed through the Social Services Block Grant and the Job Training Partnership Act (JTPA) provide childcare, job training, and

313

other support services for individuals dependent upon public assistance. In fact, JTPA targets individuals receiving public assistance and has as one of its major objectives the reduction of welfare dependency among those who are served by the program.

Volumes have been written on the strengths and weaknesses of each of these programs. Reform initiatives of one sort or another are always present in the public policy arena at both the federal and state levels. A fundamental problem with the current programs that provide income support to low-income households is that the benefits provided still leave the welfare family in poverty. Only half the states have AFDC benefits above 50 percent of the poverty level for a three-person family, and in only three states do the combined benefits of AFDC and Food Stamps exceed the poverty level.

Some would argue that low welfare benefits are consistent with a policy that encourages the work ethic and that financial incentives should be offered to encourage labor force participation. Unfortunately, a consistent approach to incentives between and among the programs does not exist, resulting in a system that often impedes rather than promotes recipients' transition from public dependency to economic self-sufficiency.

First, an AFDC mother is no longer provided a special financial incentive to work beyond four months. After four months, a working parent's AFDC grant is reduced one dollar for every dollar earned, after deductions for a certain dollar amount for work expenses and childcare. If work-related and childcare expenses exceed the amounts permitted by current regulations, the AFDC parent is actually financially worse off from working in the fifth month of work.

Second, Medicaid eligibility, although not linked to active job seeking or training activities, is tied to such requirements through the AFDC program requirements for AFDC recipients receiving Medicaid. The earlier references to inadequate fringe benefit programs in the occupational clusters available to most women is typified in the Medicaid program. Women, especially those with children, are often reluctant to change their employment status if their Medicaid eligibility will be lost. In thirty states, there has been some attempt to address this issue. By expanding Medicaid eligibility to incorporate a so-called medically-needy-only cohort, it is pos-

314

sible for AFDC recipients and others to more realistically participate in job seeking and training efforts discussed below.

It is well recognized that both the Medicare and Medicaid systems
are in need of substantial reform. "During the two-year period from
1981 to 1983, Medicaid expenditures increased by 17 percent while
Medicare outlays increased 34.5 percent" (Bartlett et al., 1984:31).

For the states, it is clear that it is in their ultimate fiscal self-
interest to reduce the demands for "entitlement dollars." One of the
ways to help do so and also assist individuals dependent upon these
services is to design and administer work-related programs in such
a fashion that occupational segregation is not casually perpetuated,
and that, in particular, day care and health facilities are accessible. The ultimate goal, of course, for this target population is self-
sufficiency.

Additional Initiatives for Women Dependent on Private Support

Another area for state initiatives relates to child support collection. Many women who are divorced or separated assume the sole
or primary financial responsibility for the support for their children.
This can be a heavy burden, especially given the economic impact of
divorce on women: after one year of divorce, women's standard of
living decreases 73 percent, whereas the men's standard increases
42 percent. In divorce proceedings, child support was awarded in
only 59.1 percent of all cases where children were involved. Of these
awards, only 49 percent are honored fully; in 28 percent of the cases,
no support is ever received and in 23 percent, only partial payment
is made. Of those who do receive such payments, the average is
$1,800 per year (Children's Defense Fund, 1982:71).

The basis for family law has been the domain of the states, so child
support payment requirements vary. However, the trend is toward
strengthening the income-withholding and wage-garnishing laws.
Four states, all in the south, have no state laws governing income-
withholding options in cases of default of child support payments.
Eleven states have a strong form of childcare collection laws called
mandatory income assignment, which requires judges to fix pay-

315

ments for each child support order entered. Eight states have mandatory income-withholding that becomes operational once it has been proven that payments are in arrears. Twenty-eight states give the court the option to assign income-withholding. In 1982 ten states moved to amend their discretionary laws to make them mandatory or to increase the use of income-withholding (National Governors' Association, 1983a). There is current a discussion among the states to establish a voluntary interstate collection mechanism that would build upon the AFDC interstate model but would make income withhholding available across state lines for all entitled to child support.

The federal government since 1975 has supported a child support enforcement program because of its direct interest in increasing child support payments in order to reduce federal contributions to the Aid for Families with Dependent Children program. The program is in effect in all states.

Along complementary lines, states are moving to expand and tighten paternity laws and responsibilities. The growth in illegitimate births highlights the need for additional enforcement in this area. Between 1970 and 1979, illegitimate births increased from 10.7 percent to 17.1 percent of all births. Of the children on public assistance, 30 percent are born out of wedlock.

This series of initiatives unfortunately is just descriptive in nature. With limited exceptions, most notably rather dated evaluations of WIN and some current foundation/state supported evaluations of the WIN/CWEP programs where the findings are just emerging, nationally available evaluations of these initiatives are sparse. Clearly and unfortunately no evaluations exist based on a research design that approaches the issues from a wholistic women's need perspective first and then analyzes program intervention models to see if those needs are being met.

The federal government, and to some extent private foundations, have been the primary and logical supports for evaluation research. Unfortunately over the past decade, most of this evaluation research has focused on rather narrow program administrative issues and not on individual impact evaluations. Additionally since 1981 there has been a substantial reduction in any funds for research and evaluations throughout the federal government, so it is not surprising that in the mid-decades of the 80s such evaluations are scant overall.

STATE ACTION AGENDA TOWARD A MORE VITAL AND EQUITABLE ECONOMY

The evidence that economic issues are central to women's well-being is overwhelming and is being increasingly appreciated. Many states have accepted the responsibility for addressing at least some portion of the problem and are incubating significant initiatives toward that end.

What is less appreciated is that the economic issues of the most interest to women are also at the center of both the economic equity and efficiency challenges that states confront. To address these challenges and opportunities, states must not only replicate and build upon successful initiatives, but move toward a more comprehensive strategy that mobilizes the entire gamut of state program/policy areas and retargets it at economic issues.

The choices will not all be easy and the process may sometimes be contentious, but it cannot be ignored. The following are suggested steps for state action.

1. **States should ensure that education and training programs prepare citizens for a workforce characterized by equal participation and at the same time, recognize that the demand side of the labor market represents the key constraint to opportunity.**

Several states are attempting to help women seeking employment by running job training programs and displaced homemaker programs. These programs may be state-funded or covered under the Job Training Partnership Act (JTPA). West Virginia and Louisiana both run a job training program funded under JTPA. Louisiana is also operating a state-funded displaced homemakers program that includes counseling, employment skill development, and job placement. Colorado, which also runs a displaced homemaker program, has a unique funding system for this endeavor. Recently it passed a

317

new divorce assessment fee (the fee charged to process divorce proceedings) and a portion of these revenues are dedicated to the state
displaced homemaker program. New York runs a similar state-
funded program through its Department of Labor. It is a pilot program targeted toward women over thirty-five who are not currently
in the job market, although some men have participated in the program. It offers counseling, a job readiness training program, job
shadowing, and job placement services. Shadowing means following
an experienced worker around to learn the tasks within the job
description.

States are also actively involved in promoting sex equity in vocational education. Several states publish newsletters highlighting
equity programs or directories of nontraditional workers. The persons listed in the directories are usually available to talk with
parents, students, and community groups about their work. Additionally, states are attempting to educate students about the availability of nontraditional career opportunities. The Utah State Office
of Education cosponsors a prevocational career education project,
"Looking Out the Window." This project is designed to provide preschool through second-grade students with an opportunity to explore thirty-six different careers. Kentucky has developed another
program entitled "Try Non-Traditional." It includes pamphlets
describing available vocational education programs and a video-
documentary on women training for nontraditional careers. (Council of Chief State School Officers, 1982: 81–82.)

2. **States should continue their efforts to expand the number
of new jobs including assistance to indigenous new and
young enterprises.**

A number of states are providing technical assistance and financial
support for minority- and women-owned businesses. South Carolina,
Illinois, Massachusetts, Louisiana, Colorado, and Ohio help women
start and manage their enterprises. They offer a variety of services
including business counseling, one-on-one technical assistance, sem-
inars, publications, networking and information clearinghouse functions. Texas has sponsored a conference bringing together women-
owned businesses and large corporations in the state. Additionally,
Maine, North Dakota, and Pennsylvania have all sponsored semi-

nars to assist women business owners. Ohio, Michigan, and Montana have agencies to aid women in the development of loan packages and financial planning (U.S. Small Business Administration, 1983).

Massachusetts has a slightly different approach to aiding women business owners. While many states have units that are run and shaped by state agency personnel, Massachusetts recently formed the Women's Business Development Council, which is composed of women in business. This council is charged with looking at existing state activities designed to help women in the business sector and to develop recommendations for their improvement.

3. States should continue to become model employers of women.

Progress in pay equity, alternative job structures, childcare, and pension provisions are important. States do have great flexibility in these realms. States serve as model employers and have the ability to set precedents for other public and private employers to follow.

Minnesota is probably the most advanced of the states in terms of pay equity implementation. In 1982 the state civil service law was amended to require pay equity and in 1983 the legislature allocated $21.8 million to begin upgrading the salaries of undervalued female jobs (Hartmann and Treiman, 1983:406). The State of Washington has also enacted two comparable worth bills, one providing $1.5 million to begin upgrading the pay of female-dominated jobs and the other committing the state to achieve pay equity within ten years. Two other states, California and Hawaii, have committed themselves to pay equity as an official policy, though the final forms their policies will take is not yet clear (National Committee on Pay Equity, 1984). In the private sector, Pennsylvania and Illinois have pay equity bills currently in the hearing process in the state legislature, which would cover employees in both the private and public sector.

Many states employ some form of alternative work schedule options. Arizona, California, Hawaii, Illinois, Maryland, Massachusetts, Minnesota, Ohio, Oregon, Virginia, and Washington have all passed legislation permitting some form of these schedules (Long and Post, 1981:99–102).

319

Two states have taken positive steps to provide childcare for women who are training for employment. California and Maryland issued statewide policies that anyone participating in JTPA will receive childcare support if it's needed. Additionally, Ohio and Massachusetts are attempting to develop a pilot day care program for state employees.

4. **States, when carrying out their duties as legislative initiators, regulators, and administrators of programs targeted to the at-risk population, must attempt to design programs in a coherent, wholistic manner that promotes the ultimate goal of independent self-sufficiency for women.**

Coherent state policies are particularly needed when it comes to income maintenance and social service programs. States would be well served in reviewing what other states have done and developing a matrix of benefit levels and other provisions related to how Medicaid, the Work Incentive program, Food Stamps, and general assistance programs are administered within the state. States can use their own source materials to review their initiatives, as well as the following materials to see how they compare to other states.[1]

In taking these steps, the participation of women in the decision-making process must not be ignored. Most states have created at least one unit of government specifically to address women's issues. While many of these units did not originally focus on women's economic issues, many now do, and it is prudent to seek their active involvement in one or more of the proposed action steps.

One Final Observation

The state organizational unit that is most pervasive is the Commission on the Status of Women: approximately half of the states have them. The concept of the commission has evolved and has been incorporated into the standing structures of state government. Separate line agencies, or agencies and divisions within larger state departments, exist now in almost all states. Additionally, high-level interagency subcabinet task forces or interagency commissions exist in some instances and these may provide a useful administrative mechanism to assist in policy development and im-

320

plementation. This suggestion is based on the recognition that in order to be successful in almost any of the suggested action steps, the entire spectrum of the state government policy-making machinery will need to be involved.

Several states have women's commissions or some form of administrative structure that currently has the responsibility for running programs. The commission in West Virginia directly manages a job training partnership funded job training program for women. The North Carolina commission has $72,000 in block grant money to run state programs for sexual assault and domestic violence. It also ran the pilot program for displaced homemakers, although this program has since been spun off to the Department of Employment Security. In Louisiana, the Women's Advocacy Bureau has a million-dollar budget, of which $600,000 is federally funded. The bureau directly runs a wide range of federal- and state-supported programs or contracts them out. Current activities of the bureau include job training, funded under both JTPA and the Work Incentive Program (WIN), a family violence program, a displaced homemaker program, a program for women in prison, and a model teen-parent center.

States, when addressing economic issues, should give equity high priority and recognize that state programs and policies can affect these issues. Much remains to be done. In addressing women's economic issues we are beginning to address the twin issues of how to manage the economy in order to more effectively meet the needs of our people and how to ensure governmental programs are designed to reduce economic risks of individuals.

Notes

1. Suggested Sources: *Characteristics of general assistance,* U.S. Department of Health and Human Services, May 1983; *Work programs for workfare recipients—Issues and options,* Jeff Koshel, National Governors' Association, April 1984; *Harnessing state program expertise to contain health care costs: The potential of medicaid, health planning and employee health benefits,* National Governors' Association, February 1984; *1983 Update to the catalogue of state medicaid program changes,* National Governors' Association, March 1984; *Reducing excessive utilization of medicaid services: Re-*

cipient lock-in programs, National Governors' Association, February 1983; *State guide to medicaid cost containment,* National Governors' Association in conjunction with the Intergovernmental Health Policy Project, September 1981; *Implementing work programs for welfare recipients,* National Governors' Association, February 1984.

Reference List

Bartlett, Lawrence, Carol Schechter, Jack Weedham, John Luehrs, and Susan Hansen. 1984. Harnessing state expertise to contain health costs: The potential of employee health benefits, medicaid, and health planning programs. Washington, D.C.: National Governors' Association. February.

Blank, Helen. 1984. Children's Defense Fund. Interview with Barbara Bular 3 November. Washington D.C.

Council of Chief State School Officers. 1982. *Policies for the future: State policies, regulations, and resources related to the achievement of educational equity for females and males.* Washington, D.C.: Resource Center on Sex Equity Council of the Council of Chief State School Officers.

Children's Defense Fund. 1982. *Employed parents and their children: A data book.* Washington, D.C.: Children's Defense Fund.

Duncan, Harley T. 1982. The treatment of child care expenses in state income taxes. Washington, D.C.: National Governors' Association. May.

Education Daily. 1983. Judge orders Washington to boost the pay of women workers. 16(December):1.

Grune, Joy Anne. 1984. Director, National Committee on Pay Equity. 1984. Telephone interview with Barbara Beelar 2 April. Washington, D.C.

Hartmann, Heidi I., and Donald J. Treiman. 1983. Notes on the NAS of equal pay for jobs of equal value. *Public Personnel Management* 12 (Winter):406.

Long, Martin C., and Susan W. Post. 1981. *State alternative work schedule manual.* Washington D.C.: National Council for Alternative Work Patterns in cooperation with the National Governors' Association.

National Committee on Pay Equity. 1984. Who's working for working women? A survey of state and local government pay equity activities and initiatives. Washington, D.C. March.

National Governors' Association. 1983a. Information for governors: Child support enforcement. Washington, D.C.: National Governors' Association. September.

National Governors' Association. 1983b. Survey of state welfare administration. Washington, D.C.: National Governor's Association. December.

Perlman, Nancy D. 1982. Equal pay for work of comparable value. Testimony before the U.S. Congress, House of Representatives, Committee on Pay Equity. 16 September. 97th Cong. 2d sess.

Sklar, Morton H., Erica E. Tollett, John Lawlor, and Daryl Hollis. 1983. States cautious in adopting workfare; advocates report abuse. *Jobs Watch* 1–2 (February):18–24.

U.S. Small Business Administration. 1983. State and city services provided women-owned businesses. Washington, D.C.:

Wider Opportunities for Women. 1983. Changing technologies: Changing jobs for women? Washington, D.C.

Women's Studies Program and Policy Center. 1981. *Older women: The economics of aging.* Washington, D.C.: George Washington University and the Women's Research and Education Institute of the Congresswomen's Caucus.

List of Contributors

LESLIE B. ALEXANDER is currently an Associate Professor at the Graduate School of Social Work and Social Research at Bryn Mawr College. Her research interests include psychotherapy and clinical research, which have led to her participation in an ongoing study in the Department of Psychiatry at the University of Pennsylvania School of Medicine that is examining the factors affecting how patients choose their therapists. Further, she has just completed a follow-up study of 95 percent of the working mothers described in her and Sheila Bennett's chapter in this volume. She has also initiated a study with Lenard Kaye on the patterns and consequences of part-time work for a sample of men and women aged fifty-five and over.

MAXINE BACA ZINN is Professor of Sociology at the University of Michigan–Flint. She has published extensively on family and gender among racial ethnics. She is co-author (with Stanley Eitzen) of *Diversity in American Families* (Harper & Row, 1987), a textbook that demythologizes the family and shows how public issues shape the private lives of a population varied in class, race, and gender.

CAROLE W. BAKER, M.C.R.P., is Research Associate at the Center for Urban Policy Research at Rutgers University. She is co-author of the *Model Subdivision and Site Plan Ordinance* for the State of New Jersey. In 1982–83, she conducted research on patterns of development associated with the Washington, D.C., Metro subway system. The results were published in *American Demographics and Planning*. Her general interests are in forces affecting urban development and their implications for public policy.

BARBARA BARAN is a postgraduate research fellow at the Berkeley Roundtable on the International Economy, where she is co-directing a study on work reorganization for the Carnegie Forum on Education and the Economy. Her research has focused on the technological transformation of white-collar work, with particular emphasis on changes occurring in the structure of women's employment. She has a B.A. in history from the University of Wisconsin–Madison and an M.C.P. and Ph.D. in city and regional planning from the University of California at Berkeley.

BARBARA BEELAR is a professional researcher. Her work on women and economic public policy was invaluable to the article by Joan L. Wills, Martha Warren, and Robert Friedman.

LOURDES BENERÍA is Professor of City and Regional Planning and Women's Studies and Director of the Program on International Development and Women at Cornell University. Her published works include *Women and Development* (Praeger, 1982) and *The Crossroads of Class and Gender: Domestic Piece Work, Subcontracting, and Labor Markets in Mexico City* (University of Chicago Press, 1987).

SHEILA KISHLER BENNETT'S research has focused on women's employment across the life course and in historical perspective. She has addressed particularly the origins of post–World War II employment patterns and trends. A second area of continuing research is institutional climates and women's educational experiences. After receiving her doctorate in sociology, Bennett taught at Swarthmore and Bryn Mawr colleges, and is currently Associate Dean of the Emory University Graduate School of Arts and Sciences.

BARRY BLUESTONE is Frank L. Boyden Professor of Political Economy at the University of Massachusetts–Boston and Senior Associate at the McCormack Institute of Political Affairs. He is co-author (with Bennett Harrison) of *The Deindustrialization of America* (Basic Books, 1982) and is completing a sequel to this study to be published in 1988.

SARAH ELBERT is working on a long-term study of women and American family farms; her most recent research focuses on the development of home economics and rural extension services. *A Hunger for Home: Louisa May Alcott's Place in American Culture* (Rutgers University Press, 1987) evidences her longstanding interest in the contradictions between women's work and domestic life. Currently Visiting Professor at California Polytechnic State University, Elbert

326

is Associate Professor of History at the State University of New York at Binghamton.

ROBERT FRIEDMAN is founder and President of the Corporation for Enterprise Development, a Washington, D.C.-based economic development, research, technical assistance, and demonstration organization. For eight and a half years, Friedman and CfED have worked extensively with state governments, corporations, and community groups to design and implement innovative and effective development strategies. Friedman has published numerous articles in the field, and his book credits include *Expanding the Opportunity to Produce: Revitalizing the American Economy through New Enterprise Development* (co-editor, 1981); *Building the New Economy: States in the Lead* (contributor, 1986); and *The Safety Net Ladder: Transfer Payments and Economic Development* (author, 1987). Friedman is a graduate of Harvard College and Yale Law School.

HEIDI I. HARTMANN is currently Director of the Washington, D.C.-based Institute for Women's Policy Research. Beginning in January 1988, she will also join the faculty at Rutgers University as Professor of Sociology and Director of Women's Studies. During 1986–87 she held an American Statistical Association fellowship at the Census Bureau where she conducted research on women's poverty. For eight years previously she was a staff member of the National Research Council/National Academy of Sciences, where she contributed to many reports on women's employment issues, including the 1981 report on pay equity, *Women, Work, and Wages: Equal Pay for Jobs of Equal Value.* She also lectures and writes on feminist theory and the political economy of gender and serves as an editor of *Feminist Studies.* She has a B.A. from Swarthmore College and M.Ph. and Ph.D. degrees from Yale University, all in economics.

MARGOT B. KEMPERS received her doctorate in sociology from Brandeis University in 1986, and is currently Assistant Professor of Sociology at Fitchburg State College.

ALICE KESSLER-HARRIS is Professor of History at Hofstra University. Her books include *Women Have Always Worked: A Historical Overview* (Feminist Press, 1980) and *Out to Work: A History of Wage-*

Earning Women in America (Oxford University Press, 1982). She is currently working on issues of women's culture in the workplace.

SARAH KUHN received her Ph.D. from the Department of Urban Studies and Planning at M.I.T. in 1987. She is interested in labor and employment issues, and has also done work in economic development. Her research includes case studies of the computer and department store industries, and work on the employment of women in computer programming.

RUTH MILKMAN is Associate Professor of Sociology at Queens College and the Graduate Center of the City University of New York. She edited the volume *Women, Work, and Protest: A Century of U.S. Women's Labor History* (Routledge & Kegan Paul, 1986) and is the author of *Gender at Work: The Dynamics of Job Segregation by Sex during World War II* (University of Illinois Press, 1987), as well as numerous scholarly articles. Her current research concerns technological change and job security in the U.S. automobile industry in the 1980s. She is on the editorial boards of the journals *Feminist Studies* and *Politics & Society*.

DAVID C. O'CONNOR is an independent consultant on international economic development. He has worked for the United Nations Industrial Development Organization and the Government of Malaysia, and is currently advising the Philippine Government.

PAULA M. RAYMAN, Ph.D. is Research Director, the Stone Center, Wellesley College. She has taught at Tufts and Brandeis and has held two fellowships from the National Institute of Mental Health at Children's Hospital, Boston, and the Bunting Institute, Radcliffe College. Her published works include *Nonviolent Action and Social Change* (with Severyn T. Bruyn, Irvington Press, 1980); *The Kibbutz Community and Nation Building* (Princeton University Press, 1982); and *Out of Work: The Consequences of Unemployment in the Hartford Aircraft Industry* (with Barry Bluestone, Social Welfare Research Institute, 1982).

KAREN BRODKIN SACKS is Director of Women's Studies and Associate Professor of Anthropology at UCLA. Author of *Sisters and Wives: The Past and Future of Sexual Equality* (Greenwood Press, 1979) and co-editor (with Dorothy Remy) of *My Troubles Are Going to Have Troubles with Me: Everyday Trials and Triumphs of Women Workers* (Rutgers University Press, 1984), as well as many scholarly and popular articles, she is presently working on a book on feminist theory and a videotape on urban fishing.

ROSEMARY C. SARRI is Professor of Social Work and Faculty Associate in the Center for Political Studies, Institute for Social Research, University of Michigan. Her research interests include children and youth welfare systems, deviance and criminal justice, women and poverty, and the effects of social policy and social administration on the delivery of human services. She has served as advisor and consultant in social welfare and social work education at both national and international levels. She is the author of more than sixty books and articles on juvenile justice, female crime, women and poverty, the management of human services, school malperformance, child welfare, and social policy. Her most recent works include *The Impact of Federal Policy Change on AFDC Recipients and Their Families* (1984) and *The Entrapped Woman: Catch-22 Strategies in Deviance and Control* (1987).

GEORGE STERNLIEB is founder and Director of the Center for Urban Policy Research at Rutgers University. His publications include *Patterns of Development: Demographic Trends and Economic Reality* (1986) and *Post-Industrial America: Metropolitan Decline and Interregional Job Shifts* (1975). He is on the editorial boards of *American Demographics* and *Society* magazine, and serves as an advisor to the Census Bureau.

CATHARINE R. STIMPSON is Professor of English, Dean of the Graduate School, and Vice Provost for Graduate Education at Rutgers University. Now the editor of a book series for the University of Chicago Press, she was the founding editor of *Signs: A Journal of Women in Culture and Society* from 1974 to 1980. She was the first director of the Women's Center of Barnard College and of the Institute for Research on Women at Rutgers. Author of a novel, *Class Notes* (1979), and editor of six books, she has also published over one hundred monographs, essays, stories, and reviews in such places as *Transatlantic Review,* the *Nation,* the *New York Times Book Review, Critical Inquiry,* and *boundary 2.*

SUZANNE TEEGARDEN is Director of the Re-employment Assistance Program (REAP). REAP is a division of the Industrial Services Program of Massachusetts, which assists firms and employees in mature industries. Her work includes oversight of the development and implementation of employment and training programs and innovative job creation and retention programs for workers affected by plant closings and large-scale layoffs. These programs have included projects on nontraditional training for women and on the impact of technology on skills and employment. Teegarden holds a Master's degree from the University of California at Berkeley in urban and regional planning.

MARTHA WARREN received her B.A. in political science from the University of Kansas in 1984, and a J.D. from the University of Kansas School of Law in 1987. She is currently working as an associate attorney for the law firm of Shook, Hardy & Bacon in Kansas City, Missouri.

JOAN L. WILLS is currently the Director of the Office of Research and Development for the National Governors' Association. For five years she was the director of the association's employment and vocational training program. She has also served as the director of the Governor's Office of Manpower and Human Development in Illinois, and the director of the State Economic Opportunity Office in Ohio. Prior to her state experience, she worked in Columbus, Ohio, for the local Community Action Agency and United Appeal Planning Agency. Wills has also served as a presidential appointee to the National Commission on Employment and Unemployment Statistics, a member of the National Child Labor Committee, and a member of the American Council on Education, Commission for Educational Credit and Credentials. She completed her undergraduate work at Franklin College in Indiana and her graduate work at Ohio State University.

Index

accounting program (Rutgers graduating), 98

AFDC. *See* Aid to Families with Dependent Children (AFDC)

AFL-CIO, 112, 121, 124. *See also* unions

Agricultural Adjustment Act, 178

agriculture. *See* farming families

Aid to Families with Dependent Children (AFDC), 165; employment and, 277, 281, 290, 291; family crises and, 284–287; federal policy changes and, 271–276; federal programs and, 312–315; health of respondents and family and, 283–284; impact of changes in (coping behavior), 274–275, 289–291; income and, 280–283, 287; personal and social characteristics of study respondents and, 276–278; poverty and, 272, 292, 293, 294; study implications and discussion and, 291–294; study methodology and, 275–276; support network and, 287–288; welfare use and, 278–280, 287, 289–290

American Association for Labor, 72

American Federation of State County and Municipal Employees (AFSCME), 307

American Women's Association, 144, 148

Anderson, M., 273, 282

Angel, Ronald, 165

Angell, Robert C., 137

apparel workers, 164, 243

Applebaum, E., 17, 236

Asians in semiconductor industry: Asian workers in U.S. and, 247; global restructuring and women workers in, 262–265; incorporation of (into international market), 249–261; internationalization movement and, 243–244; investment patterns and, 261–262. *See also* microelectronics industry

automation. *See* office automation

automobile industry, 11–12, 22

autonomy, 46–49, 52–53, 57–58, 60, 78, 81, 135–136, 192–193

Bakke, E. W., 136

Bane, M. J., 278

Bell, C., 149

Belle, D., 275

Bendick, Mark, 5

Bergman, B., 45

Birnbaum, B., 13

Bishop, L., 168

blacks: childbearing and, 39; female-headed households and, 165–166; family patterns and cultural resistance or adaptation analysis and, 167–168; family structure and poverty and, 164–167; marriage and, 37, 40–41; non-nuclear family households and, 79; part-time work and, 228, 230; similarities between Chicanos and, 157–160; social science research and, 155, 156; underclass theory and, 160–161; unemployment research and, 145, 148; wage convergence (black women and black men) and, 103; wage increases since 1940s and, 23–26; wages of women and family structure and, 70. *See also* minorities

Bluestone, B., 20, 51, 59, 140, 144–145

boarders, 68, 142

Tilly, Louise, 168
Time (magazine), underclass theory and, 160
turnover (employee), 15; sex differences in, 113

underclass theory, 160–161
The Unemployed Man and His Family (Komarovsky), 137–138
The Unemployed Worker (Bakke), 136
unemployment, 35, 111; AFDC changes and, 275, 293; black, 145, 148, 164, 166; coping patterns of women and men and, 141–147; difference between women and men, 21–22; differentiation of experiences with, 147–150; effects of, 118; female, 99, 105; Great Depression and, 133, 134, 135–138, 141, 142–143, 144, 147, 150; male, 71, 113–114, 117, 118–119, 121, 141–142, 146–147; manufacturing, 5–7; research on, 135, 136–141, 147–150; social roles of women and, 135–141, 150; women (comparing 1930s to 1980s) and, 111, 112, 113–117
unions: "family wage" ideology (of 1930s) and, 121, 122; garment, 79–80; office automation and, 220; women in 1930s and 1980s and, 122–126; women joining, 76; women in labor movement and, 122–126, 127
Union Wage (women's group), 74
U.S. Civil Rights Commission, 247
U.S. Women's Bureau, 138–139, 147–148

Vietnam War, 74
vocational training, 310
Vogeler, I., 174

wages: black women and, 23–26; demographic analysis and, 44–45; distribution inequality in, 12–21, 22, 23; domestic ideology and, 72; equal pay for equal work movement and, 74; family structure prior to WWII and, 67–68; family structure since WWII and, 69; "family wage" ideology and, 120–122, 158–159; farm family, 193; husband and wife and ownership of, 70; a "living wage" and, 67; manufacturing, 8–9; married women and, 26–28; men and loss of, 50, 51; occupational recomposition and unemployment and, 115–116; part-time work and, 226; pay equity in private sector and, 305–306; pay equity for women state employees and, 306–307, 319; public discussion of differences in, 56; single women workers and, 106; unions and, 125; of women in labor market, 55, 102–105. *See also* income
Wandersee, W., 67
Waters, W. F., 194
welfare, 159; AFDC respondents (Michigan study) and, 278–280, 287, 290; state and women dependent on, 311–315
welfare state, 53
Wharton, A., 215
Wilkening, E. A., 181
Women Office Workers, 74
women's movement, "family wage" ideology and, 121–122
Women Workers Through the Depression (Pruett and Peters), 138
word processing, 205
Work Incentive (WIN) program, 312–313, 316, 320, 321
working conditions, 57
work schedule alternatives, 307–308, 319